P9-AOG-783

3 9098 01451912 7

FIC Freem
Freeman-Keel, Tom
The disappearing duke : the
improbable tale of an
eccentric English family
Kitchener Public Library
KPL-Main Fic

THE
DISAPPEARING
DUKE

Also by Tom Freeman-Keel

From Auschwitz to Alderney and Beyond

Also by Andrew Crofts

Maisie's Amazing Maids: A Novel
Freelance Writers' Handbook

Ghosted and co-authored by Andrew Crofts

Sold
A Promise to Nadia
Heroine of the Desert
The Kid
My Gorilla Journey
Through Gypsy Eyes
Hijack
The Tutankhamun Deception
The Princess and the Villain

THE
DISAPPEARING DUKE

The Improbable Tale of an Eccentric English Family

Tom Freeman-Keel and Andrew Crofts

CARROLL & GRAF PUBLISHERS
NEW YORK

THE DISAPPEARING DUKE

Carroll & Graf Publishers
An Imprint of Avalon Publishing Group Inc.
161 William St., 16th Floor
New York, NY 10038

Copyright © 2003 by Tom Freeman-Keel and Andrew Crofts

First Carroll & Graf edition 2003

All rights reserved. No part of this book may be reproduced in whole or in part without written permission from the publisher, except by reviewers who may quote brief excerpts in connection with a review in a newspaper, magazine, or electronic publication; nor may any part of this book be reproduced, stored in a retrieval system, or transmitted in any form or by any means electronic, mechanical, photocopying, recording, or other, without written permission from the publisher.

Library of Congress Cataloging-in-Publication Data is available.

ISBN: 0-7867-1045-4

Book Design by Paul Paddock

Printed in the United States of America
Distributed by Publishers Group West

CONTENTS

INTRODUCTION

This is a dramatization of a true story in which the truth is tantalizingly elusive, and the main character is a man steeped in layers of deliberately manufactured mystery. It's a work of historical detection, following a web of deception and intrigue, which continued for half a century and ended in a headline-grabbing court case. The events took place mainly in the nineteenth century, and so many of the facts are now impossible to ascertain for certain that we can only work from what evidence there is.

The story centers on one of the greatest and most eccentric British aristocratic families of the nineteenth century, the Cavendish-Bentincks, at a time when the British aristocracy were at the height of their wealth and power. It involves fratricide and disputed fortunes, secret underground passages and stately homes, mock burials and clandestine marriages, fraud and bribery, perjury and blackmail and corruption and the financing of a prime minister.

Whenever a great fortune is in dispute there are bound to be people who are willing to distort the truth in order to protect or further their own interests. During the period of the story one of the greatest private fortunes ever amassed was at stake, as well as one of the most senior aristocratic titles. So everyone had a reason to lie, and many who didn't deliberately lie indulged in gossip and rumor-mongering to such an extent that it was almost impossible to discern what was based on truth and what was the product of pure imagination and invention. There were also the political reputations of some of the highest people in the mighty Victorian Empire at stake, and the possible murder of one of those people, which threatened to topple the previously unassailable aristocratic establishment.

What is indisputable is that the major characters in this book existed and that this story sprang up around them and resulted in one of the longest and most sensational court cases in British history.

The court records show what was said by those who fought for what they believed was their birthright, but many of them were lying. The history books give us other clues and insights, but even they are strangely quiet about the life of the fifth duke of Portland, beyond accepting that he was one of the most eccentric and secretive men that ever lived.

We have taken all the evidence that we have been able to find, including birth, death, and marriage certificates, and we have constructed the following story of two families. It is the most extraordinary of tales.

Tom Freeman-Keel
Andrew Crofts

1

TROUBLE IN THE CEMETERY

T he grave diggers saw her coming but kept their eyes cast down on their shovels, hoping the one-woman hurricane just might be diverted off course before she reached them. But Mrs. Anna Maria Druce was not about to be diverted by anybody. Her eyes were entirely fixed on the bent backs of the men as they labored in their parallel graves in the earth. It was June 1898.

They knew who she was. Not because they'd read about her in the papers, although their bosses at the London Cemetery Company had most certainly been following Anna Maria's exploits with exceptional interest, but because they'd grown used to seeing her at the cemetery every day, accompanied by a man who looked as if he was a professional of some sort—an expert, a man who might be consulted on matters of some importance.

They were aware that over time her manner had become more and more agitated. With each visit she had exhibited more signs of being close to a complete breakdown. She seemed to be losing all grasp of what was likely to be true in the corporeal world and what might be some cloud of confusion buffeted uncontrollably by the storms of suspicion and doubt that appeared to darken her unhappy mind. The power of her personality, however, and the strength of her convictions meant that her arguments still carried an intimidating force, one that she exerted on anyone she chose to take issue with, particularly with manual laborers who were entirely unused to any sort of discussion or discourse with the likes of her.

The men preferred to keep to themselves, but they had overheard heated conversations between her and a number of officials. They knew her to be a woman of unpredictable temper. Ordinarily, one of the great pleasures of laboring in a graveyard was that, by and large, the general public left you alone with your work and your private thoughts. These were men who did not relish the prospect of being drawn into conversation with anyone, least of all a lady with trouble on her mind.

Anna Maria had spotted the workmen from some distance. She had been striding along the gravel path toward her usual destination when she noticed them laboring about fifty yards away. The man accompanying her was a mining engineer who had been making the daily pilgrimages to Highgate Cemetery with her for several weeks. Her sudden veering off the path onto the grass between the gravestones had taken him by surprise, but he knew better than to protest. Anna Maria Druce had become increasingly reluctant to take his counsel, or that of any of the other experts she had hired over the previous two years. He wasn't sure why she bothered to bring him along with her at all anymore. He had nothing new to tell her that hadn't been said before, but he believed she took some comfort from his professional and masculine presence among the shadows of the commemorative stones and the spirits of the departed. So, as long as she continued to settle the monthly accounts that he respectfully submitted to her for his time spent in her service, he was willing to continue the ritual of the visits.

Even on a sunny summer's day the cemetery oozed an air of

chilly threat. The dampness that more often than not filled the English air had done its worst to the stones and monuments that had stood there for years or decades, and some for centuries. Moss and lichen thrived, crawling across surfaces, clinging to anything that was no longer attended to regularly by bereaved relatives. Forgotten graves surrounded the few that were fresh enough to still be tended and dressed in flowers and other tributes, outnumbering them a thousand to one: a terrible warning of the great void, of the world's forgetfulness that each of us falls into eventually, a time when no one remembers anything about our lives or cares to find out. Dust to dust, ashes to ashes, nothing but weather-beaten stones to show that any man had ever passed this way before.

Some of the graves were of grandiose proportions, obviously built for the wealthy and influential of the past; but even wealth and influence were no protection against eventual extinction. Once a grand family mausoleum was full, or once the family no longer had the will or the money for its upkeep, it would fall into disrepair as quickly as any simple headstone. The noses and fingers would wear off the decorative cherubs until they became as smooth as beach pebbles; gargoyles would grow thinner and more fearsome in their ugliness, like the skeletons of the corpses they guarded.

It may have been the heat that caused the perspiration to break out on the grave diggers' foreheads, just as it made the dew steam on the mossy stones, or it may have been anxiety at the thought of the woman who looked as if she was about to physically attack them with her neatly rolled parasol. Her skirts were hitched up to avoid snagging on the occasional bramble that had yet to be cut back from the less well cared-for graves, revealing her step to be more than determined. It could even have been described as ominous. Certainly the expression on her face verged on the furious.

"Stop your digging immediately!" she shouted, while still a good twenty yards away, though closing in fast.

The men, in a last vain hope that she might be talking to someone else, even though there was no one else to be seen in any direction, didn't look up and kept to their steady pace of work, not even allowing their eyes to exchange a glance. Both were men who found communicating with others difficult. They received their orders first thing in the morning from the officials who oversaw the cemetery and then carried out the work in a companionable silence. Both of them had wives, neither of whom were anything like the approaching Mrs. Druce, and they never said much to them beyond grunts if they could help it. The prospect of even having to exchange the time of day with a lady of breeding and education was frightening enough; the possibility that she might actually wish to discuss some matter with them was almost too terrifying to contemplate.

"Grave robbers!" she bellowed when only a few strides away from them. "Nothing but common body snatchers, thieves of the night."

Neither of the workmen considered for a single moment pointing out that it was in fact a warm summer's day, not dark at all, and that they were merely doing the job assigned to them, which was to dig fresh graves in anticipation of the arrival of funeral corteges later in the day. They did, however, take the precaution of stopping their digging, since there was now no doubting that Anna Maria was talking to them and that to continue with their work would have made them appear insolent to someone who was, quite obviously, their social superior, and a lady.

Although they'd ceased their work they still kept their eyes firmly on the freshly dug ground beneath their feet, waiting in the holes they had been digging to be told what to do next.

Anna Maria towered above them and they could clearly hear her breathing from the exertion of hurrying across the cemetery, not so much a panting sound as a roaring of breath through flared nostrils. The mining engineer was also a little winded, his heavy breakfast lying uncomfortably beneath his waistcoat and causing him to perspire more than might be considered dignified. He waited for his employer to speak first, thinking it unwise to speak, until he had managed to get a clearer picture of what exactly was troubling her. He had seen this look on her face a good deal recently, and it did not bode well for anyone who might come within shouting distance of her in the near future. Her eyes had something of a wild stare to them, a look that he had at first believed to be no more than a sign of the strain that she had been under for the previous two years, but which he had come to realize was something more than mere tiredness or anxiety. Mrs. Druce, who, when she had first come to him had seemed the most reasonable and sensible of women, was giving the appearance of being on the verge of a panic so terrible it threatened to engulf her entirely. Not to put too fine a point on it, her behavior increasingly resembled the style of someone who had lost her mind. He certainly didn't believe that she had actually lost her mind, not as yet, but he didn't think she would respond well to reasonable argument. He therefore held his peace until his opinion was asked for.

"What are you doing?" she demanded of the men once she had recovered enough breath to speak with authority. When they didn't reply she continued. "Well may you be struck dumb with guilt. I know exactly what you are doing. You are preparing to steal the coffin from that vault over there." She gesticulated toward the grave that she had conjured a belief they were tunneling toward.

All three men looked in the direction of her wagging finger, a distance of at least a hundred yards, and said nothing. The tomb they were all looking at now was one of considerable substance. It stood proudly among its more modest neighbors, clearly proclaiming that it belonged to a family of importance. It had not yet started to fall into disrepair, suggesting that it was still in use, not yet full with forgotten bodies but awaiting new ones in the future. It was a crypt that seemed to be still in its prime, if such a description could ever be given to a final resting place.

One of the workmen wiped the beads of sweat from his forehead with a piece of rag while a fly buzzed irritatingly beneath the brim of Anna Maria's hat.

"Very well," she said, with all the considerable authority she could muster. "I can see I'm going to get no sense from either of you. One of you go to fetch your superiors here to speak in your defense."

Both men scrambled to get out of the graves and away from their tormentor.

"Just one of you!" she snapped. "The other one must stay here to ensure the return of his partner in crime. I don't want you both running off to hide in whatever den of thieves it is you come from. Tell them the duchess of Portland wishes to speak with them. That should shake them up."

The men exchanged glances for the first time and the elder of the two gave an almost imperceptible nod of agreement for the younger one to be the one who made his escape while he, the senior in years, surrendered himself to the custody of this formidable woman. The younger man dropped his shovel and loped away toward the building where the men who ran the cemetery sat behind their fine mahogany desks and ran their meticulous filing system.

The managers of the London Cemetery Company were startled to have one of their workmen bursting into the office in a state better suited to a less formal setting. His lank hair was stuck to his head with sweat and some of the dirt from the grave he had been digging fell from his boots as he stood on their polished floor. They all looked at him with raised eyebrows as he searched for the right words to describe the reason for his uninvited appearance in their midst.

"The lady wishes to speak with someone in authority," he said eventually, his eyes fixed on his feet, horribly aware of the trail of dirt he had brought in through the door.

"What lady?" the director of the company, who had been in the process of giving a reprimand to one of his juniors, asked impatiently.

"Says she's the duchess of Portland," the man muttered and a ripple of amusement went around the clerks in the office until the manager's eyes quelled them.

"Very well," he said, allowing no emotion to show in his voice. "Tell the lady we will be with her forthwith."

The man nodded and left the office without a backward glance, grateful to be away from his superiors, people who never seemed to miss an opportunity to remind him of his place at the bottom of the social pile. An office junior scurried to fetch a janitor to clean up the mess on the floor.

The director signaled to his senior manager to join him and they both donned their hats, making their way at a discreet pace in the wake of the hurrying grave digger.

"Will this woman never leave us in peace?" the director said as they made their way along the gravel path with all the dignity that their formal attire and top hats could bestow upon them.

"It seems she's determined to prove her case to the world," his manager suggested. "I don't think she'll rest until that's done."

"The sooner they commit the damn woman to an asylum, the better," the director grumbled under his breath. "She's a menace.

What on earth makes her think she will ever succeed in her ridiculous quest?"

"Not everyone believes she's deluded. Many of the newspapers have been writing in her defense," the manager ventured, but went no further as his director silenced him with a glare.

"What the newspapers care to print is no concern of ours," he said. "The Highgate Cemetery will be here many centuries after all the editors in London have disappeared, taking their meager reputations with them. We'll outlast them all, never forget that."

Anna Maria was waiting for them with sternly folded arms. The engineer gave them just the tiniest shrug of apology as they approached, at least so it seemed to the director, but it could have been wishful thinking.

"I've caught you red-handed this time, Mr. Director," she said, before he'd even had time to wish her a good morning. "You obviously weren't expecting to see me today, but I'm onto you and your tricks."

"We are always pleased to see you at the cemetery, Mrs. Druce," the director purred in his most funereal of tones.

"Is that why you called the police to take me away last week?" she asked, waving the point of her furled parasol dangerously close to his eyes. The director didn't flinch. "It did you no good. They took me to the station and their inspector wouldn't listen to a word they said. You're all making fools of yourselves. I have right on my side and the nation behind me. The people of Britain are not willing to have the wool pulled over their eyes any longer by the likes of you."

"What can we do for you this morning?" the director continued, his smile as fixed as if she hadn't spoken.

"You can tell these oafs to fill in this hole immediately," she said, gesticulating at the two men who were standing beside the graves, leaning on their shovels and looking more relaxed now that their employers were there to do the answering of the mad-woman's questions. "You are nothing but grave robbers, Mr. Director, and I will be reporting this to the authorities."

"I'm not entirely sure that I follow what you're saying, Mrs. Druce." The director bowed his head respectfully. "What makes you think we're robbing the graves that are supposedly in our care?"

"These trenches," she gestured toward the newly dug graves, "are the opening for a tunnel so that you can break into the vaults that hold the coffin purporting to contain the remains of my late father-in-law."

"Why would we want to do such a thing?" The director allowed no flicker of impatience to enter his voice or mar his expression of respect.

"Because you are part of the conspiracy," she screamed, her voice cutting through the warm, hushed air of the cemetery, making the director wince and the grave diggers shuffle uncom-fortably from one foot to another. "You're all determined to keep my son from his rightful inheritance, but I'll see you all damned to hell before I allow that to happen!"

"I wonder," the director's voice sounded eerily calm after the explosion of Anna Maria's temper, "if perhaps you're mistaken in this particular instance." He gestured toward the holes in the ground. "I'm confident that when you've had time to consider the situation you'll agree with me that it would be a considerable feat of engineering to reach the vault containing your father-in-law's remains from this particular point. We'd have to construct a tunnel of at least a hundred yards, which would mean excavating at least seventy feet down at this point. It would hardly be an oper-ation we could hope to achieve unnoticed, or with such a modest workforce. I would also point out that it would mean disturbing other graves in the process, something that we are not permitted to do."

"It's useless you trying to baffle me with science, Mr. Director," Anna Maria snapped. "I'm quite capable of making my own calculations. That's why I bring this gentleman with me on all my visits to your little fiefdom, because he will not allow me to be bamboozled."

All eyes turned onto the mining engineer who coughed in readiness to speak.

"I think, if you do consult your adviser," the director continued, as smooth as silk, "he"ll confirm what I'm saying to you. If we wanted to steal your father-in-law's coffin, there would be easier places to start from."

"Well?" Anna Maria arched an eyebrow at the engineer, with all the superiority of a woman who already believed herself to be a dowager duchess, regardless of what the legal profession might ultimately decide.

"I think the director may have a point," the engineer admitted, taking a step back as he spoke, as if expecting to receive a blow to the head for his impudence.

For two hours, as the sun climbed higher in the sky, the little group talked and argued and the men attempted to reason with Anna Maria as she paced around the cemetery, making measurements to prove her theory, ranting and raving at each of them in turn.

Eventually, with an air of reluctant exhaustion rather than any admission of defeat, she agreed to leave them to continue in their work, but only once they'd promised that the newly dug holes would be filled in by the time of her next visit. As the director knew there were two funerals expected that afternoon, which the holes were being prepared for, he was confident that complying with that particular condition would not be difficult.

2

AN UNCOMFORTABLE CHILDHOOD

The story that had brought Anna Maria to the forefront of the national stage, and led her to Highgate Cemetery that day, had its beginning many decades before, at the very pinnacle of British aristocratic society.

At the earlier end of the nineteenth century, in the summer of 1815 to be precise, one of the most privileged young boys on earth was preparing himself for manhood. To the eye of anyone who did not know his true birth date, Lord John Bentinck looked a great deal older than his years. Although he had yet to celebrate his fifteenth birthday he could, quite easily, have passed himself off as a clean-shaven young man in his twenties.

He had a maturity of spirit to match his looks and it was making him restless beyond his age. He could never have been described as a physically vigorous young man, although he rode with almost as much gusto as his brothers, but he possessed a mind that seldom allowed him to stay still for long. It darted from one idea to the next and gave him no peace or tranquillity. The slowness of home life was almost unbearable to him. He wanted to be doing something, changing something, learning something, and making a difference in the world. None of that was possible under the weight of his family and property.

While by no means unaware of his luck at being born at the very peak of the British aristocracy, Lord John couldn't wait to escape its suffocating grasp on his young life and to flee the many thousands of privately owned green acres that acted as his lushly wooded prison.

His childhood world, which he'd lived in for virtually every day of his short life, was Welbeck Abbey, a family home so enormous that it could, by someone ignorant of the niceties of architectural description, have been called a palace without accusations of exaggeration. It was a house that had started life in the twelfth century and had grown in the intervening centuries to reach a prodigousness of proportion unimaginable to anyone who had never actually stood in its grounds and gazed at its many mighty facades. To a stranger arriving at the gates it was an awesome spectacle, so grand it took the breath away and suggested to the imagination that it might be inhabited by a breed of men so much more gifted and powerful than ordinary mortals that they could hardly be considered to be of the same species. To young Lord John it was simply the place he was forced to spend his days and nights. To the many hundreds of people who worked in and around the house and its estates, it was a way of life, providing a degree of protection from the vagaries of the outside world. To be under the protection of a duke with unlimited wealth and political influence was a safe as well as prestigious place to be.

On that summer's afternoon in 1815 Welbeck Abbey was the domain of the fourth duke of Portland, Lord John's father and the author of the letter that Lord John was holding in his hand as he walked through a thin mist of rain across the lawns toward the riding school, trying to piece together the thoughts and emotions that jostled for space within his confused young head.

It was not unusual for him, or his three brothers and five sisters, to receive letters from their father. Although they all dwelt for the majority of their time within the same house, it was quite possible to live at Welbeck and not see one or another member of the family for weeks at a time, apart from the occasional formal meal-times, when they would all gather on the sounding of a number of gongs placed strategically around the corridors. When those meals did take place, with the family surrounded by footmen and other servants, and interspersed with distinguished guests, they never considered for a moment talking about anything personal or difficult. There were strict, if unwritten, rules about what would make suitable topics of conversation at the table. All the duke's children, apart from George, the third of his sons, preferred meals that they could take in the various apartments they inhabited, where they would not be called upon to make polite conversation to neighboring earls, visiting prime ministers, or members of the royal family who happened to be passing through the area.

It was also a great deal easier for the duke to sit down in the comfort of his own apartments and pen a letter, which could then be given to a servant to deliver, than to start searching the house and grounds for one or another of his offspring himself and then to have to talk to them face-to-face.

When he was not out hunting, shooting, or riding, the duke spent most of his time closeted in his own apartments, and so seldom came across his family unexpectedly. He certainly didn't ever want to embarrass either them or himself by speaking to them about personal, family, or financial matters; it was much easier to convey his thoughts in writing, so there would be no call to hear their replies, or to see the expressions on their faces. If, for some reason, one of the boys did meet him, because they were seated near him for a meal or a family gathering like Christmas, the conversation might revolve around sports or pol-itics but would never touch on anything as difficult or sensitive as the contents of the letter Lord John was holding so tightly in his hand that his fingers were starting to ache. The girls always made as much effort as their father not to find themselves in a position where he would be forced to make conversation with them, since neither side would have had the slightest idea how to interest the other.

A footman had delivered the letter to Lord John while he had been with his tutor in the library. He hadn't opened it until the lesson was over and his teacher had disappeared into another room, having left his young charge with a reading list for the rest of the afternoon. The arrival of any letter from his father always made Lord John's heart lurch with dread; he could never imagine that anything his father had to say to him was going to be good, with the possible exception of the decision to send him away to school. Lord John deeply regretted that he'd never been allowed to go away to school and escape the gloom of Welbeck for the company of young men his own age. Now, he rather feared he had grown too solitary and used to his own company to be able to cope with the boisterous world of the dormitory, but at least it would be something different, something to stimulate his mind. Some of the tutors he had had over the years had been nice enough people, and he was sure they'd taught him well in the subjects for which they'd been hired, at least well enough to equip him for the sort of life he was going to have to lead, but once lessons were over there was always a sense of pointlessness to the whole thing. Sometimes he would share lessons with one or another of his siblings and he would enjoy the feeling of being part of a class, but for many subjects they were all separated, since the duke believed they were less likely to be distracted from their studies that way.

At first reading the letter didn't seem to make sense to him. It was as if his mind refused to accept that the words on the page had any logical meaning. Then he realized that his hand was trembling, making the stiff paper rattle, and he knew that his father's message was touching some emotion inside him that would normally be under control, hidden from sight, impossible to reach. Deciding he needed fresh air before he read the letter again, and despite the dampness of the weather, Lord John made his way out across the terraces and lawns toward the riding school. He had no particular plan as to where he was heading, he just needed to do something while he waited for the shaking to calm itself and for his youthful self-control to return.

In the quietness of the grounds at Welbeck, hundreds of miles from the streets of the capital city, no boy as young as Lord John could have been expected to understand or feel the immense power of his family's position. Since he knew nothing of the outside world, he didn't know that life was any different for others. He had no idea what a struggle it was for the common man to earn enough money to put food on the family table. The house lay quietly at the heart of an enormous estate in a district known as the Dukeries, an area owned and presided over by a group of men like his father, who were the most senior in the land and among the most powerful who had ever walked on earth. The wealth of these few families was not simply huge; it was the foundation stone upon which the British Empire was being built. It was the rock upon which the British aristocracy had constructed their power base; it was the capital engine that drove the entire nation. Although Lord John had been taught in history about the greatness of the English ruling classes, he'd only taken the information in intellectually. He didn't have any idea what it meant in the real world, how his life differed from almost everyone else's.

Until six years before, the Portland dukedom had been ruled by Lord John's grandfather, the third duke who, as William Henry Cavendish-Bentinck, had died in harness as the country's prime minister. It was the old man's second term in the post and he'd accepted it with enormous reluctance, being frail and gouty and exhausted by a lifetime of service to his king and country.

He'd started in government as a member of the Whig Party, in opposition to William Pitt the Younger, but in 1794 had joined forces with that famous prime minister in a coalition created to meet the challenge of the French Revolution. In many people's eyes it was the coming together of these two men that was the foundation of the Tory Party, a force that would dominate British politics for the next two centuries. When Pitt died unexpectedly in 1806 the king requested the third duke to head the administration of Pittites, who were floundering hopelessly without their leader.

Lord John knew that people like his father and grandfather ruled the known world and provided him with his place in it, but he also knew that the inherited title and responsibility would largely fall upon the shoulders of his older brother, the marquess of Titchfield, who, as he approached nineteen, seemed to Lord John's young eyes to be a man already. His future, he knew, would have to be of his own making. He'd have enough wealth and privilege to live in comfort all his years without lifting a finger or taking on a single responsibility, should he so choose, but if he wanted more from himself, and from life, he would have to make his own plans.

Aware that the rain was beginning to drip uncomfortably from his hair down his face and the back of his neck, he pushed his way into the riding school, shaking his head like a gun dog emerging from a lake. His mind was so distracted that it was a few moments before he became aware of the thunder of hooves on the wooden floor. At the far end of the mighty school, his younger brother, George, was standing in the center of the room, training his new hunting horse on a lunging rein, under the watchful eye of two of the grooms. The horse circled around him as he snapped the whip at its heels and barked out orders, interspersed by praise and reprimands depending on how obedient the animal was. George was thirteen and a half years old but he too looked like a young man already. Taller than both the men watching over him, and more handsome than any other member of the Cavendish-Bentinck family, George had an air of confidence about him that Lord John had never been able to achieve. It was a confidence that had grown prosperous on the knowledge that although he was the third of the duke's sons, and not in line to inherit the title, he was still their father's favorite, the one who was most likely to bring fresh glory to the esteemed family name.

At family dinners he could actually voice opinions and his father would listen, nodding proudly. He'd even been known to contradict the duke in front of company. Whenever he did so his siblings would hold their breath, certain that a terrible wrath would issue from their father and sweep away any atmosphere of goodwill there might be in the room, but it never came. The duke would sometimes laugh and slap the table to indicate that his son had made a good point, or he'd respond to George's comment like an equal, as if the two of them were old friends sitting in a club room somewhere, rather than father and son. Lord John had worked hard to try to understand what it was that his brother did or said that so pleased their father, but he was never able to put his finger on it, let alone replicate it. George's comments never seemed particularly clever or amusing and he was sure that if they had issued from any other mouth his father would have responded with anger, or perhaps would have pretended not to hear them at all.

George's voice had already broken and he was able to talk above the crashing of the hooves, making himself heard without effort by the horse, whose ears were twitching irritably as it grudgingly agreed to follow the dictate of the powerful young man's voice and whip. It was a big animal, one of the biggest in the local hunt, but there was no doubt that George could control it.

Although Lord John knew that his brother was their father's favorite he bore him no grudges. Nor did he resent the fact that George excelled at all the sports that he did not. None of them were pastimes that interested him, so why would he mind being outshone by his younger brother? Sometimes he resented George's outbursts of temper, but the boy could easily win over anyone he offended, simply by beaming over them and slapping them firmly on the shoulders, making them feel foolish for ever taking his outbursts seriously. In his way George was more anxious to gain approval than his older brother. He worked hard at it and reaped the well-earned reward of popularity from all with whom he came into contact.

The horse, momentarily overcome with the boredom of going around in small circles at someone else's behest, bucked and kicked the air. The whip cracked down on its haunches amid an avalanche of swearwords, which had the grooms exchanging wry smiles. They'd known George since he was a baby. They were used to his ways. Like the duke, they were proud of him; they knew that one day, wherever they went in England, they would be able to boast about working with the young George Bentink at Welbeck and people would know who they were talking about. They also knew that he was turning into a man who would never tire of the company of horses, which meant their jobs were safe. Men who enjoy the company of horses nearly always enjoy a bond among themselves. It's like a miniature society that excludes all those who don't understand it.

None of them had noticed Lord John coming into the riding school, or, if they had, they made no sign toward him. He settled himself down in a corner of the hall, beneath the high ceiling that was painted with a sky scene and hung with mighty crystal chandeliers. He read the letter again, and again, until he felt certain that he was absolutely not mistaken in his understanding. It was not a long letter. Notes from his father were always directly to the point.

> *My Dear John,*
> *You're approaching an age when ideas of courtship may be entering your head, if they have not done so already. Something you must understand, as must your brothers, is that the normal life of married bliss cannot be for you. The strain of madness that ran in my mother's family is more than likely to appear in any offspring you might produce, bringing disgrace upon the family name and untold burdens upon yourself and whomsoever you may have decided to inflict your seed upon. Rest assured that as you grow older you will find many pleasant distractions in life, far more diverting and worthwhile than the production of mewling infants.*
> *Your Father.*

Lord John had always been aware of the "strain of madness" that had tortured his grandmother, but had taken it for granted. She had always seemed to those who liked her to be a lively, eccentric character, both witty and intelligent when on form, but terrifyingly morose when in the grips of melancholy. She was herself the daughter of the duke of Newcastle-under-Lyme and at the time she married the third duke of Portland his family name had been simply "Bentinck." The marriage not only brought another name to the family, allowing them to become the "Cavendish-Bentincks" from then on, it also brought the mighty Welbeck Abbey when she inherited it. Upon such fortuitous marriages great fortunes were continually increased.

Her depressions had just been a fact of life. Children accept the differences of their families without question, particularly if they have no others with which to compare. This was the first time it had occurred to him that this strain would have any effect on him. If it was true that he might be carrying the madness forward for future generations, then he could understand his father's concerns. "Fear Disgrace," the Bentinck family motto, had been engraved on all their consciousness from the very first days they could understand the meaning of the words. Lord John knew that as far as his father was concerned there could be no cause higher than preserving the family name and reputation. It would bring a terrible disgrace on them all should he and his brothers produce nothing but mad creatures.

While he could see the sense of the command not to bear children, it had never entered his head that he would have to live his life alone. What woman would be willing to marry him if it meant she was not allowed to become a mother? His elder brother, William, would have his dukedom and all its responsibilities with which to distract himself, and George would have his horses and his sports, and no doubt a glittering career in politics. But what would he have to pass the long lonely years between fifteen and the grave?

The very thought of it seemed to open up a void in his chest, a black hole of despair that threatened to engulf him. He wondered if this was the inherited madness taking its grip of his soul, and he stared with blank eyes as his brother broke the spirit of his new horse.

3

INCREASED EXPECTATIONS

Lord John and his two younger brothers stood together in the library, waiting for their father to come downstairs from their eldest brother's deathbed. The year was 1824. Lord John had become something of a stranger to his already loosely bound family in the previous years, but at that moment they all knew their fates would forever remain inextricably tied together. With the ending of his brother William's life, everything had changed for Lord John; his name, his title, his responsibilities, and his expectations.

The three boys knew it was all over, though the young marquess had passed on before they were officially told. They could hear their sisters crying in the next room, their sobs suppressed for fear of being heard by their father. No one wanted to annoy the duke in his moment of bereavement; no one wanted to risk causing an explosion during which things would be said that could never be retracted.

None of the men had taken any notice of the women, beyond pressing their hands sympathetically as they passed them by. This was one of those moments when the true nature of primogeniture made itself known. Each of the boys would always do all they could to protect their sisters from the potential unpleasantness of the outside world, but they did not include their sisters in any decisions that might be made on behalf of the family. That didn't mean the women were insignificant to the family's future. No doubt all of them would make good marriages and would, through their well-chosen husbands, form alliances with other great families and strengthen the Cavendish-Bentincks' grip on power and influence in the land. Still that didn't make them central to the matters of the moment. The male heir had died and everything would be changing among the men; the women did not have to be concerned with such affairs.

The doors at the end of the library swung open and the duke strode through. His face wore the same expression of concentration it did in the hunting field, a look of tightly reined-in fury and puzzlement at the ways of the world and the foolishness of all the people in it. He nodded to his assembled sons and walked past them to the window, staring out across the parkland toward the horizon, avoiding any further eye contact.

"What did the doctor say?" George asked.

"Doctors!" The duke spat the word out. "Pure bloody guesswork. Could have been his heart; could have been his lungs; could have been the first cuckoo of spring!"

The three younger men exchanged glances. None of them knew what to say. George, who would now be elevated to the title of Lord George, walked across and put a consoling hand on his father's shoulder. Neither of the other two would have dared to make such a gesture, but Lord George and his father understood each other.

Lord John, or the marquess of Titchfield as he would now be known, was well aware that his father wished George were the elder of them, the one who would inherit the dukedom and its colossal wealth when he passed away. It was knowledge he had to live with. He was used to it. The duke had preferred George over their deceased eldest brother as well, but not as much as he did over Lord John. It was obvious from every look he gave his second son that the fourth duke could see no redeeming features in the boy. If Lord John dropped dead then and there, he knew that in many ways it would be a relief to his father, because then Lord George would be in line to be the fifth duke of Portland and the fourth duke would know that the estate, the title, and the influence of the Cavendish-Bentinck dynasty were in good hands for at least one more generation. Knowing that your death would be a relief to your own father is a heavy burden for any child to carry. It was to escape constant reminders of his father's distaste for him that Lord John had decided to join the army seven years earlier.

It would take a while to get used to being known as the marquess of Titchfield, a title that had been his brother's since birth; it felt like sliding the boots off the dead man before he was even cold.

The new marquess was twenty-four years old and had never for a moment imagined that he would have to shoulder the burden that his father and grandfather had carried before him. To know that one day you will be a duke, with a private fortune so enormous it would be impossible to calculate even an approximate figure since it grew at an accelerating rate with every passing hour, was an awesome prospect for a young man who had come to imagine he might merely continue to make an undistinguished but respectable military career for himself. Military service had seemed like a safe retreat from the world of decisions and responsibility; you simply had to do what you were told. If he were told to move from one regiment to another, as often happened, he would simply obey. He didn't fool himself that he was a good soldier; it was unlikely that he would ever reach the rank of general, but he'd felt comfortable with the prospect of an institutionalized life, at least for the next few years. In a way it was like living out the school days he'd never experienced as a boy.

"You'll have to come out of the army, John," the duke said, without turning from the view.

"Will I?" John asked, as if the idea hadn't occurred to him.

"Can't imagine they'll miss you."

Lord George and their younger brother both looked away to avoid having to see the hurt in the new marquess's eyes.

"God knows how you'll cope with all this," the duke mused, almost to himself, looking out across the acres that stretched away from the house to the horizon. "At least you'll have George at your side to make sure you don't let the whole thing slide away. You'll have to do something else to prepare yourself, try to make some sort of impression on the nation before you inherit."

"Whatever you think, Father," Lord John muttered. He couldn't think of a single thing that he wanted to do to pre-pare himself for such an onerous role.

"We'll get you a seat in Parliament or something," the duke said, as if only half concentrating on the idea. "You need to spend more time down in London. Although God knows how you'll manage in that bear pit. They'll eat you alive. George should be the one we get a seat for."

"King's Lynn is in need of a decent member," Lord George suggested, as if he hadn't heard the last comment, and Lord John had the feeling the two of them were settling his future for him without a thought that he might have ideas or preferences of his own. Sadly, they were right; he had neither.

He thought he saw a flash of sympathy in George's eyes, but neither of them said anything.

"I'll make inquiries," the duke said.

"Very well," Lord John agreed. In fact the idea of spending

more time in London was not unappealing. He had been on short visits in the past, when his father had wanted him to be in attendance at some formal event, but had never had the opportunity to explore the city on his own terms. For a hundred years now the family had been building and running a luxury housing estate that stretched across Marylebone toward the other lordly slices of land that made up the center of the city. The growth of London had contributed colossally to the wealth of the family, rents on their hundreds of grand town houses escalating beyond anything their ancestors could have anticipated when they first bought up the green fields surrounding Westminster and sent in their builders and architects. For families who'd spent hundreds of years accruing wealth through the acquisition of rolling rural acres, the power of the fledgling city of London to generate money on their behalf had staggered them.

The streets and squares that bore their family names—from Welbeck Street to Portland Square, Great Portland Street to Cavendish Square—were exceptionally pleasant places to live, all within easy reach of the royal parks. Lord John, the new marquess of Titchfield, felt an urge to escape from the overbearing quietness of Welbeck Abbey, the sadness of his elder brother's passing, and the sports that obsessed his father and brother. He wanted to remove himself from the house where he'd always felt himself in the shadow of his younger sibling and do something with his own life. He wanted to be as far away as possible from the contempt of his father, which showed in the old man's face every time he looked at him. If he couldn't do it in the army anymore, then he would do it in London.

The election at King's Lynn was nothing more than a formality. There were only a couple of hundred people eligible to vote in the area and most of them were happy to humor one of the most powerful families in the known world. The marquess of Titchfield became a politician without any great wish to make a difference in the world. He would have been happy never to have gone near the palace of Westminster, and he certainly didn't wish to meet any of his constituents. He found the sycophancy and pomposity of the voting classes almost impossible to stomach. He longed for the straightforward company of the men he'd commanded in the army—men who had no ambition to control the lives of others, no wish to curry favor with him simply because he'd been born inside an historic house and bore an historic name. He admired men who had a skill or a craft and practiced it without pretension, whether they were gardeners, carpenters, or simple soldiers. He couldn't see the point of society as it existed, either in the town or in the country.

Lord George took seriously his father's suggestion that he should guide his elder brother through his new responsibilities. He would seek out his company whenever both of them were in London at the same time and continually chided him about his lack of political ambition. When he listened to his younger brother the marquess heard his father's voice: the voice of a man who knew the way the world should be and couldn't understand anyone who didn't share his vision. By that time Lord George was already working as a private secretary for the prime minister, George Canning, who was also their uncle, being married to their mother's sister. There was no doubt in anyone's mind that Lord George was going to enjoy a distinguished career, whatever might happen to his ineffectual older brother.

Just two years after taking up his seat in Parliament, John realized that the sham must end and that if he wasn't going to live a wholly miserable life, he must be true to himself. At the end of one long evening of being nagged in his own London house by his brother, after having filled the man with enough food and wine to silence any lesser mortal for hours, he spoke his mind.

"Father's right," he said. "You should be the politician in the family, George. I've no stomach for the fight. None of it seems worth a jot. Why don't I give you King's Lynn as a gift."

"What will you do?" Lord George enquired, apparently unsurprised to be handed a seat in Parliament as if it were a necktie he'd admired on a friend.

"I'll explore a little further afield," the marquess said, feeling it unnecessary to say any more.

"Making yourself free to do one of your disappearing acts?" Lord George inquired. "Escaping from your responsibilities again? When are you going to face up to life, John? When are you going to become a man?"

"Do you want the damned seat or not?" Lord John snapped back.

"I'll take it, if only because the people of King's Lynn deserve better than to be represented by a man who doesn't give a damn about anything except himself," Lord George said, pushing his seat back and finishing his port in one swallow, anxious to leave the company of a man for whom he had no respect left.

So, in 1826 the constituency of King's Lynn was passed from one brother to the other and the marquess of Titchfield was free of a responsibility that had been only the smallest of burdens on his time, but a heavy taxation on his patience.

Lord George took to going to the Houses of Parliament quite regularly in the evenings, using them, as Disraeli, the future prime minister, would later say, "rather as a club than a senate." More often than not he would pull a thick white overcoat on to cover the fact that he'd not troubled to change out of his scarlet hunting coat after a day in the field. No one took exception to such a cavalier attitude to representing the people in the House because, unlike his brother, he was careful to ensure that he represented his constituents' interests behind the scenes, pulling strings and oiling wheels in the gentlemen's clubs of London during the week and in stately country houses at weekends. Everyone knew that Lord George was a man of substance; the sort of man that the British public were used to being ruled by. The sort they were comfortable with, a grandee of the old school.

4

SWEET SIXTEEN

In a time when people were reliant on horses or their own feet for transport, small distances between communities became vast gulfs. The villages of England existed almost as tiny independent states, the villagers seldom seeing unfamiliar faces or playing host to travelers of any quality. Communities that had grown together over generations seemed rather impenetrable due to the difficulties of traveling. The Crickmer family lived in just such a community and had done so for as long as anyone could trace. They knew every other family within a ten-mile radius of their home and virtually no one outside that geographical circle.

To her parents, Elizabeth Crickmer was still a child, and although they had to accept that legally she was now a woman and perfectly capable of being wed, they did not think that the time was yet ripe. In many ways she was still a childish creature, just as they had brought her up to be, and they felt she needed more time to mature before she was ready to move out of the cozy family home and tackle life as a married woman.

They had nothing at all against Thomas Druce, except that they knew nothing about him. They certainly couldn't deny that he cut an impressive figure in the community. He had arrived in their village in 1816 as if from nowhere, although he was obviously not of traveling stock. He rode in astride a horse so fine that there had been little else talked about at the local inn for days, and the blacksmith had been bringing groups of locals to his stables to show them the mount when its young master was not around, assuring them that if they lived to be a hundred, none of them would ever get to see an animal this well bred again.

Most of the people who came wandering through the villages of Suffolk were tinkers or gypsies, men who made their livings sharpening knives, selling clothes pegs, or trading in horses. They were swarthy, their skins darkened and cracked from exposure to the elements and, though there might be tales of them stealing womenfolk in the night and carrying them away, no one had ever heard of them requesting the hand of a local girl in marriage.

Thomas Druce was very different. His complexion was pale and his clothes were obviously cut from the best cloth by skilled tailors. His delicate hands had been saved from wear and tear by the kid gloves that he wore when riding. They had never had to suffer the ravages of physical labor. His purse always seemed to be full and he did not appear to have any trade or profession. The Crickmers, who had taken in and discussed among themselves every one of these details, could not deny that he had a great deal of charm about him: a shy, sweet smile and a seriousness of mind that made him slightly intimidating despite his extreme youth. There was something about him that suggested he did not wish to be questioned about his past or his circumstances, something deeply private and secretive that made others skirt around him politely. He had about him an air of unpredictability. It wasn't that he acted like a madman, but his demeanor suggested that if he was provoked he would have no inhibitions regarding his reactions, and that made polite village people very nervous indeed.

The Crickmers themselves were immensely polite people and would never have dreamed of prying into the affairs of anyone who might prefer them not to, but this young man was making eyes at their child from the first day he arrived at the local inn and met her while taking a stroll around the village. She had been returning home from the greengrocer's where she had been buying fruit for her mother. It had been the fruit that had affected their introduction, by falling from her basket just as the young stranger was passing, allowing them to exchange smiles as he stooped to pick it up and making it quite reasonable that he would walk her back to her front gate. He had returned the next day with flowers that he had picked himself and a gallant concern as to whether Elizabeth was still as well as when he had left her the day before. The young man's obvious interest in their daughter meant that the Crickmers were going to have to overcome their natural reserve and ask some serious questions.

"You'll have to take him aside and enquire about his intentions," Mrs. Crickmer said to her husband as they sat in bed together one night, worrying, as parents do. "He can't be allowed to remain this man of mystery. It's too unsettling."

"He's just a pleasant lad who's taken a shine to our Lizzie," Mr. Crickmer replied, trying to convince himself as much as his wife. He'd been caught as unawares by this sudden intrusion into their lives as she had. It seemed like only yesterday they'd been worrying about the dangers of childhood like the whooping cough and measles, more concerned as to whether Elizabeth would be scratched by the kitten she insisted on clutching to her face to kiss and squeeze than in the possibility that she might make an unwise marriage.

"Then let him tell us as much," Mrs Crickmer persisted. "It's our duty to protect Lizzie from undesirable elements. We know nothing about this boy. He could be some criminal come from

London to prey on innocent country people, or a white slaver from the north coast of Africa."

"Now you're being far too fanciful, my dear," Mr. Crickmer admonished her, relieved to be able to feel confident that whatever the young man's plans might be, they were not to whisk their daughter away to a souk somewhere where the dignity of womenfolk was not respected.

"Perhaps I am," she agreed, "but it is quite likely that he's an adventurer of some kind, looking for a girl with a decent dowry. Elizabeth is far too young and unworldly to be able to judge for herself. He could fleece her of every penny she has and disappear back into the night as quickly as he has appeared. He may seem to be a gentleman but there are plenty of rogues who can do a passable imitation of one of those. For all we know he might have stolen that horse and his attire from some innocent man on the road, and is now passing himself off as someone he has murdered and left naked in a ditch somewhere." An edge of hysteria had taken a grip of her voice, making it quiver.

"Very well, my dear," he patted his wife's hand comfortingly. "I will deal with the matter."

Although he managed to sound confident to his wife, Crickmer was indeed anxious. He had not anticipated being confronted with this particular problem for some years yet. When it did come, he had always expected it to emanate from a young man in the village, or at least from one of the neighboring hamlets. He'd assumed he would be able to make all the appropriate enquiries into the boy's family background and prospects before giving his blessing to the union. Matters were made all the more worrying by the fact that the Crickmers had no money left. There had been money in the family once, and indeed Elizabeth herself had been well provided for by her grandmother. If, however, anything went wrong with her dowry, her parents would be in no position to support her or any family she might have. That made it doubly important that the Crickmers not make any mistakes when it came to choosing a husband for their beloved only daughter.

Mr. Crickmer need not have wasted the hours of sleeping time that he did, worrying about how he would phrase his questions to the rather forbidding young stranger, because the following day Thomas made his plans extremely clear. He arrived at the house unannounced, as he usually did, and asked Mr. Crickmer if he might have a few minutes of his time. Something in his voice did not make Mr. Crickmer think he was being offered an option. The two men went into Mr. Crickmer's study, a pleasant room with two comfortable armchairs and a view down the garden to the small stream where Elizabeth and her mother could be seen taking the afternoon air and making animated, if rather forced-looking, conversation. Both women were aware that something was afoot that would lead to changes in their well-ordered lives. "Thank you for seeing me, sir," Druce said as soon as they were seated and Mr Crickmer had succeeded in lighting his pipe. It was an action that he had thought might help to take the tension from the meeting, although it actually caused something of an awkward pause in the proceedings. "I think that you will have some idea of what I'm going to ask you."

"I can assure you, Mr. Druce, I have no idea at all," the older man replied.

"Since arriving in your village I have become increasingly fond of your daughter, Elizabeth."

"Very kind of you to say so," Crickmer said, puffing in a gallant attempt to keep the tobacco in the little clay bowl alight.

"And I would like to ask your permission to request her hand in marriage." Thomas spoke the words fast, as if anxious to get them out of the way so that they could move the conversation on to less personal ground.

"I'm sure Elizabeth would be most flattered to know what a strong impression she has made on you in such a short time." Crickmer measured his words carefully, determined to keep all traces of panic out of his voice beneath the steely gaze of his daughter's first suitor. "How long have you known each other? A week is it?"

"Ten days, sir. But I have to confess that I knew she was the woman I wanted to spend the rest of my life with the moment I laid eyes on her outside the greengrocer's." Thomas was working hard to keep the note of irritation from his voice at being forced to justify himself in this manner. All he required from the man was a quick yes and a handshake. He did not wish to be interrogated about his feelings, feelings that he was not entirely certain he understood himself.

"She's only sixteen, you know," Crickmer said, wanting to ask Thomas how old he was but not quite finding the courage for such impertinence. He doubted if the boy was more than twenty-one, maybe twenty-two at the most. "I think it would be wise for both of you if you were to spend a little more time getting to know one another before making such a momentous decision. You have a whole lifetime ahead of you. Don't rush into something so important. Take time to consider, I beg you."

"It would be time wasted," Thomas said, his voice changing and taking on an authority that Mr. Crickmer found offensive coming from one so much younger than himself. "My mind is quite made up and I'm confident Elizabeth would welcome my advances."

"She might well." Crickmer detected a slight tremor in his own voice as it rose in volume and he made a conscious effort to impersonate his normal air of calm. "But I repeat, she is only sixteen, little more than a child. She's ill-equipped by experience to make wise decisions about such important matters."

"I think you underestimate the maturity of your daughter, sir." Thomas's tone had changed again. To Crickmer's sensitive ear it sounded almost as if the young man was dismissing his protests as irrelevant, as if asking for his permission had merely been a formality anyway. "And I think you underestimate me."

"I don't know you, sir," Crickmer jumped to his feet, angry with Thomas for putting him in such an awkward situation and angry with himself for allowing it to happen. "And I cannot possibly allow my daughter to marry a man I know nothing whatsoever about. The idea is preposterous and your assumption that you can just stroll into our lives and take whatever you want is arrogant and insulting. If you are sincere in your intentions you will spend some time getting to know us and winning our daughter's heart in an appropriate manner. You must work to win us all over. Then, in maybe a year or two, we can consider having this conversation again and reaching a happier outcome for all of us."

Thomas appeared to be genuinely puzzled by the older man's outburst, as if it hadn't occurred to him for one moment that his approach would be unsuccessful. For a fleeting second Crickmer felt sympathy for the boy's predicament.

Thomas stood up, apparently at a loss for words at being so thwarted. He gave a curt bow and left the room. Crickmer sat down again with a grunt of irritation and stared out the window, apparently unaware that his pipe had gone out as he sucked angrily on the stem. Through the window he saw Thomas appear from around the side of the house and make his way down to Elizabeth and her mother. The three of them seemed to be laughing and talking as if they didn't have a care in the world and for a moment Crickmer wondered if he'd dreamed the whole thing. How could the boy be so rebuffed and apparently so unbothered a few minutes later, as if no other man's opinion was of any consequence to him? He was an unnerving young man.

Once he'd recovered his composure, and told himself that no harm had been done by the unsettling little encounter, Mr. Crickmer relit his pipe and made his way out into the garden to join his wife and the young couple, feeling rather proud of himself for the fatherly way in which he had protected his daughter from a possible mistake. As Crickmer sat himself down beside his wife on one of the wooden chairs that were set out in the shade of the willow tree, Thomas smiled at them both with the greatest of charm and asked their permission for him to walk across the bridge with Elizabeth for a little way. The Crickmers gave their permission with pleasure.

"Well." Mrs. Crickmer asked, the moment the young couple were out of earshot. "What did he want?"

"He wanted to ask for her hand in marriage," her husband replied.

"Oh, Lord love us!" Mrs. Crickmer fell back in her chair, fanning herself wildly with the book she was carrying. "We don't know anything about the man. Who are his family? Where do they come from? What's his financial position? Did you ask him all that? What did you say to him?"

"Calm yourself, my dear." Her husband patted her knee affectionately. "I've dealt with the situation. He's agreed not to ask her until we know more about him. Perhaps in a year or two." As he spoke the words, Crickmer couldn't help himself from wondering whether young Thomas had actually agreed to the demands or not. He had a strange feeling that he hadn't, but it was all now rather a blur in his memory. He decided not to confide any of his doubts to his wife. The uncomfortable rush of panic that had accompanied the interview was dying away now and he felt reluctant to do anything to rekindle it.

"I was asking your father for your hand in marriage," Thomas told Elizabeth as they walked, his eyes fixed on hers, seeming almost to bore through into her head in their intensity.

"What did he say?" she asked, barely able to breathe in her excitement, her legs wobbling beneath her skirts.

"He says you're too young and we must wait a year or two." Thomas watched closely to see what reaction his words would evoke, willing her to be as impatient as he was. He loved to look at her, to drink in her freshness and beauty, to imagine what it would be like to touch her and kiss her as a husband. The urge to put his arms around her was almost irresistible and he had to force himself to look away.

"I can't," she squeaked, her face a picture of horror. "I can't wait a day, never mind a whole year. We have to be married."

"Your father is probably worried that I won't be able to support you," he suggested. "After all, he knows nothing about me or my family."

"You don't have to support me," she said, suddenly excited again. "I have a trust fund. On the day I get married I receive fifteen thousand pounds, more than enough for us to live on. I'll tell him that it's what I want more than anything in the world. I'll make him change his mind. He can never refuse me anything."

"I assure you he will refuse you this. If we're going to be married we will have to elope."

"Elope?"

"Why should we be constricted by these stupid social conventions?" he asked, squeezing her hand and making the blood rush to her cheeks. "Our love for each other is something bigger and finer than that. Do you think Lord Byron would allow anyone to stand in his way once he had fallen in love? Where would the poetry be in waiting upon convention? We have to be able to tell our children that their mother and father were so in love they had to be married within days of meeting each other; that there simply was no choice."

Elizabeth's eyes sparkled at the very idea of being with a man who could compare their love to something the wicked and wonderful Lord Byron might dream up. This man had arrived in her life as a stranger and turned her from a little girl into a woman. He'd swept her off her feet and made her dreary life exciting. She wouldn't have dreamt of casting a moment's doubt on his bold, romantic plan. He was so obviously right in everything he said and did, while her parents were so obviously blinded by their own lack of vision.

"Be ready tonight," he said. "I'll bring a carriage at midnight and we'll be married tomorrow."

That night Elizabeth, a child who'd never for a moment thought about defying her parents, did not undress when she went to bed, merely pulling the covers up to her chin so that her mother would see nothing unusual when she came in to bid her good night. Mrs Crickmer couldn't help but smile at the sight of her girl, still so innocent to look at, still so safe in the family nest. She knew that soon she would be watching Elizabeth leave with a young man, and that man might very well turn out to be the enigmatic Mr. Thomas Druce, but not yet, not just yet.

At midnight Elizabeth rose from her bed and tiptoed downstairs to let herself out. She could hear the night breathing of her parents from their bedroom. There was no interruption to its steady rhythm as she left the house. The moon was bright and she could see the figure of her future husband in silhouette as he waited patiently by the gate, apparently not doubting for a moment that she would come to him. What doubts there had been, nagging at her as she had lain waiting for the minutes to pass, were now drowned out by the beating of her heart and the slight dizziness that made her head swim as he took her in his arms, kissed her, and led her down the road to the waiting coach and horses.

The coachman must have been instructed already as to where to go, because the two men exchanged no words as Thomas helped her into her seat and then sat beside her, pulling a rug over both their laps to keep out the chill. The moment they were settled the coachman laid his whip across the backs of the horses and the crash of the wheels shattered the stillness. No doubt the sound woke half the slumbering village, but it didn't matter to the young lovers because by then they were on their way. Thomas held his bride's hand tightly as the carriage rocked and rolled from side to side, plunging on through the shadows.

They arrived at the doors of the vicarage of St. James's Church in Bury St. Edmonds at dawn and Elizabeth was surprised to find that the vicar was expecting them. Somehow she'd imagined that it would take a few days before the arrangements could be made, but Thomas seemed to have thought of everything. When he'd said, "We"ll be married tomorrow," he'd meant it. For a second the doubts welled back up inside her and she wished she had her parents there to ask questions of her young groom and the smiling priest who was standing back to welcome them into his house. Thomas seemed so in control she felt there was nothing she could do but surrender herself to the chain of events as they unfolded.

They were taken through into the warm kitchen where the vicar's wife made them breakfast and fussed around them. Elizabeth noticed how both the older people seemed to defer to her husband-to-be and she felt proud to think that she was marrying a man of such strength of character and purpose. It was almost like being carried away in the night by Lord Byron himself. She didn't know that Thomas had promised the vicar enough gold sovereigns to build a new church tower if he agreed to perform this service without asking too many questions.

"Have you brought witnesses?" the vicar enquired and Elizabeth realized from the look on Thomas's face that there was one detail he had overlooked.

"Do we need them?" he asked. "Couldn't you and your wife witness the ceremony?"

"We need to find somebody. I could ask someone from the village," the vicar's voice suggested that he would prefer not to do that.

"I have some cousins just outside the village," Elizabeth piped up. "I think they would be happy to do me this service."

"Would you write them a letter," the vicar asked, "and I will have it sent over to them?"

"Yes, of course."

The vicar's wife brought a pen and paper while her husband went in search of a man who could be trusted with such an important message. Elizabeth allowed Thomas to dictate the words that would bring her cousins hurrying to their aid.

Once they'd eaten and the letter was written, the woman took Elizabeth to a bedroom and helped her to tidy herself. Elizabeth wished she had a wedding dress to change into and, away from Thomas's mesmerizing gaze, her doubts rose up once more. She felt suddenly tearful, but told herself it was simply tiredness after missing a night's sleep.For a moment she thought of confiding her worries to the older woman and asking for advice, but the vicar's wife seemed to sense that the girl was about to open her heart and averted her eyes, busying herself with removing some specks of mud from Elizabeth's shoes.

The Crickmer cousins came immediately upon receiving the letter. They were a young couple and while the woman seemed to be as excited by the romance of the whole thing as Elizabeth herself, the man appeared more reserved. He said he was worried about betraying his uncle and aunt, neither of whom had ever done him any wrong. Thomas opened his arms wide to the man and swept him along on a wave of charm. When he could see that young Mr. Crickmer was wavering, Thomas pressed a purse filled with coins into his hands to compensate him for the inconvenience he was being caused. Crickmer weighed the coins in his palm for a moment before slipping them into his pocket and nodding his agreement to proceed.

The wedding party made its way to the church in the late morning and by lunchtime they were married. Elizabeth cried as they walked back out into the sunshine, partly because it was all over and her life had changed irrevocably, and partly because she could not imagine for a moment what would happen to her next. The night before she had gone to bed in the little room that had been hers ever since she was born and now she could never go back there.

"Where are we going now, Husband?" she asked, blushing at her bold use of such an adult word as they climbed back into their carriage and bade the vicar and the cousins farewell.

"We're going back home to break the news to your family," he replied, as if it were the most natural thing in the world. Elizabeth felt a surge of relief at the thought of returning to the familiar world of the village, mixed with pride at coming back as a married woman and a terrible dread at having to face her mother and father, knowing she'd disobeyed them.

"Don't worry," Thomas said, kissing her lightly on the forehead. "I'll make everything fine."

He put his arm around her and she sensed that nothing would harm her now; that she was safe in the care of an extraordinary man.

Her parents were beside themselves with worry by the time the coach rolled back into the village. Elizabeth was surprised by the tightness with which her new husband squeezed her shoulders as they stood together in the hallway of the house as Mr. and Mrs. Crickmer let loose all the regrets and disappointments of their lives—an avalanche of recrimination and bitterness at having had their child stolen away from under their noses. During the tirade Elizabeth looked up through her tears at Thomas and was startled by the impassivity of his face. It was as if all the emotion and unhappiness swirling around her and her parents wasn't touching him, as if he was sitting watching a puppet show from some Olympian cloud. His aloofness comforted her and frightened her at the same time. Did it mean that he was wise and patient and knew that the storms would pass? Or did it mean he was cold and uncaring and impervious to the misery of others? Even for a child as intuitive as Elizabeth prided herself on being, it was a disturbing puzzle.

She had never seen her father so angry. It was as if someone had broken into his home and stolen everything he possessed. His normally placid, smiling face was contorted with fury as he shouted at them, his words making hardly any sense to her as she tried to hold her back straight and stop herself from fainting away. She leaned heavily on her husband. Her mother was shouting, too, and still Thomas seemed to be simply waiting until they'd exhausted themselves and ground to a halt. Eventually they fell silent and Thomas spoke for the first time since he'd announced that he and Elizabeth were married.

"We'll send someone to pick up Elizabeth's personal effects," he said. He then bowed politely and steered Elizabeth out of the house and into the coach.

They didn't travel far, only to the inn where Thomas already had a set of rooms, and there Elizabeth sunk into his arms, surrendering herself to the new master of her life.

Relations with her parents did not improve in the coming months. She and Thomas visited the family lawyers, who confirmed that now that she was married, she was entitled to use the money from her trust fund, a princely sum of £15,000. She happily signed over all responsibility for the money to Thomas. The lawyers didn't suggest that she should do otherwise; there was an air about Thomas that would not have encouraged small-town professionals to argue.

Once the money matters were settled the young couple bought themselves a comfortable home at the far end of the village from the Crickmers—not a great distance for anyone wishing to walk between the two establishments, but as good as a thousand miles for the distraught parents who felt they'd lost their daughter forever to some malevolent power.

The remainder of the village, however, was more willing to be charmed by the young stranger who'd moved into their midst and made himself available for the church committee and every other local activity that required the services of a good brain and an authoritative manner. People were impressed that such a young man should be able to exert so much natural authority when he was in charge of meetings in the church hall. If he called for silence he was immediately obeyed. No one questioned how such a young man could have acquired such a commanding air of self-confidence. He was particularly effective in his efforts at directing parish help toward the most needy, which established his reputation as a man of conscience.

When it was announced, two years later, in 1818, that he'd joined the army, it seemed to confirm that he was a man of considerable character. Although she was proud to think of her husband as a soldier, Elizabeth was appalled to think that she might have to cope with life in the village on her own when he was away on military business. She'd learned to depend on him for everything, just as she had depended on her parents before him. She had never learned to be an adult and now she was going to have to manage on her own for months on end while he was away on some foreign battlefield. She begged him to reconsider and stay at home. He brushed aside her protests with good humor. It was every man's duty, he told her, to serve their king and country in whatever way they could.

By the time their first son, Henry, was born, nine months after the marriage night, Elizabeth had discovered that the new father pacing anxiously up and down outside the bed chamber had lied to her. He was in fact the same age as herself, still only seventeen despite being a father and having become a pillar of the local community. Although she was shocked to discover that she had been swept away into wedlock by a mere boy of sixteen, she felt that this revelation made him all the more extraordinary. Neither of them, however, thought it would be wise to share the information with their neighbors. In fact, Thomas preferred not to share any personal details with anyone in the village. It wasn't that he was intentionally trying to create an enigma around himself, he told his wife, he just didn't see the necessity for intimacy with strangers. To others it made him seem all the more mysterious. His increasingly frequent absences on army business merely added to the mystery.

Elizabeth was surprised by how well she coped with her husband's absences once she had grown used to them. When he was at home he dominated the house in a manner that could sometimes be uncomfortable. It wasn't that she didn't love him, it was just that she had come to realize she could manage on her own when she had to, and that was a good feeling.

Henry was followed by Charles, another fine baby boy who added to Elizabeth's pleasure with the way her life was going. She still regretted the painful break with her parents, who seemed to want to have nothing whatsoever to do with their grandsons, her mother even going as far as crossing the street to avoid them if their paths accidentally crossed in the village, but her contentment with her husband, when he was there, and her children more than compensated for the abrupt ending of her childhood.

She often wondered about his family, still knowing nothing about his background or his childhood. Once or twice she even plucked up the courage to ask him about such things, but it was obvious from his manner that he didn't wish to share with her any of the secrets that lay locked inside his memory. She wondered sometimes if there was some great tragedy in his past that he was trying to forget. In the times that she spent alone, when he would don his uniform and travel away from home for several weeks or even months at a time, she would concoct all sorts of romantic visions, fed by the novels she avidly devoured to fill the long, quiet evening hours, of how his life might be when he was away from her.

Four years after the marriage ceremony, during one of his absences, Elizabeth realized she was pregnant again. She couldn't wait for Thomas to return to share the news with him. She knew he shared her dream that perhaps they would have a girl next, now that Henry and Charles had each other as playmates. She was disappointed when she received a letter in her husband's handwriting, knowing it was bound to mean he was going to be delayed for a few more days or weeks.

When she read the letter she let out a scream so piercing that the maid, who had been getting the children dressed in a nearby room, came running to see what had happened. The girl found her young mistress, white and shaking, looking as if she had seen a ghost and clutching the letter.

"My husband will not be returning." Elizabeth's voice cracked under the strain of holding back the tears.

"Is he dead, madam?" the maid asked, unable to think of any other reason why a soldier would fail to return home.

"No," Elizabeth replied. "He's not dead." The tears welled up in her eyes and the maid took the liberty of squeezing her young mistress's hand in an attempt to comfort her. "He's just not coming back to us. He suggests that we find ourselves a smaller house."

Six months later, in 1821, Elizabeth gave birth to Frances, the daughter she had been hoping for, and by that time her name was registered on the poor list of the county. All her parents' worst fears had come to be.

"The children should be with us," Mrs. Crickmer insisted, allowing herself to bang the dining-room table with her small fist in a most uncharacteristic manner. "She's little more than a child herself and she can't bring them up on her own." As long as Thomas Druce had been around to protect her grandchildren, Mrs. Crickmer had known that at least they were safe. Now that he was gone she wasn't so sure her daughter could cope with raising a family alone. She felt a sense of responsibility for the children, but not for the daughter who had betrayed her.

"Then we should invite her home with the children," her husband suggested.

"No." His wife was adamant. "I will not have her back in this house. It would not be in the children's interests anyway. Any day she might allow some other man to sweep her off her feet and carry her away into the night. They should come back without her and be free of her influence once and for all. You must talk to the lawyers."

"Are you sure your health is up to it?" Crickmer asked. "Three small children would mean a lot of work and we could not afford to have anyone to help you."

"I am quite strong enough to bring up my own grandchildren," she insisted. "Speak to the lawyers today, please."

Mr. Crickmer did as his wife asked, up to a point. Although he had more sympathy for Elizabeth than her mother did, he could see the sense in what his wife was saying. The house that Elizabeth had been moved to was not a suitable one for young children to be raised in, at least not young children of good breeding. At the same time he did not think that it was practical for the children to come to them. He and his wife were no longer young and there was little enough money to support the two of them in old age, let alone feed three more mouths. He approached the local parish council and asked that the children be taken into care. He explained that his daughter's judgment was faulty, that she had allowed a man to make off with her inheritance and leave her penniless, that the children would be safer in the care of the church.

When Elizabeth received the papers instructing her to give her children up, she went straight to Justice Chitty, a local dignitary who knew her and Thomas from their former lives as pillars of the village establishment. He could see that Elizabeth's heart would break if her children were taken from her, that she would have nothing left to live for. He took pity on her and ensured that the parish orders were quashed. Elizabeth's parents made no further attempts to help or hinder their daughter's progress through life. They both felt suddenly old and tired and there was barely enough money left to keep them for their last few years, let alone to provide for a young family. The children were going to have to manage as best they could.

5

A PROUD FATHER

Elizabeth managed as best she could to bring up her three children without assistance. Her parents, who appeared to have been driven more than a little mad at the loss of their daughter to an adventurer, never relented in their determination to have nothing more to do with her after failing to get the children taken into care. In the years after her husband disappeared life was not kind to Elizabeth, but she had refused to give up the struggle until her children were old enough to go out into the world and look after themselves.

Surviving with no money was hard work for any woman, particularly one who was always brought up to believe she wouldn't have to do anything more strenuous in her life than a little light sewing and perhaps some charity work. The pretty sixteen-year-old Thomas had married sank into a prematurely elderly middle age, worn down by the demands of the children and the strain of feeding and clothing both them and herself. She lost every scrap of the sparkle that had entranced him as a young man and made him want more than anything to hold her in his arms. In fact, it was unlikely that he would have recognized the woman within a few years of his departure. Her clothes were worn and shabby and what flesh there was still on her face dropped down to hang in folds from her chin, resting on her neck like an old woman's. Her teeth had blackened from poor diet and her eyes were rheumy from the hours spent leaning over smoky fires trying to warm her own chilled bones and produce something nourishing for the children to eat.

Sometimes, when she was able to get hold of paper and ink, she would write to her husband in care of the army, the last place where she knew he had been, sending the letters off into the ether with no idea if they would ever reach him. In the letters she tried not to paint too black a picture of the life that she and the children were living. She didn't want him to think that she was blaming him for her plight. Nor did she want to make the family's lot seem so terrible that he would never want to return. She didn't tell him that she couldn't afford to educate the boys, or that they were reliant on the charity of others for even the simplest of daily necessities.

Instead, she would give bright little reports about the progress of the children as they grew and news about the village and the church and the people he would have remembered from the years he lived among them. Sometimes, while she was actually composing the letters, she would convince herself that he'd see the error of his ways and would come back to them. She was sure that if she could just make the boys sound strong, intelligent, and brave, and make Fanny sound like the most enchanting girl in the world, he would be unable to resist coming back to take a look at them. She was sure that once he saw them, he would be unable to leave them again.

Later, during those optimistic evenings, when the coals of the fire had finally dwindled to nothing, reality would seep back through and she would wonder if Thomas was even alive still. Soldiers were killed all the time. If he fell on some foreign battlefield, would she ever learn of it? She doubted it. It was always with a heavy heart that she finally fell asleep, too exhausted to even bother to undress some nights.

She didn't talk about Thomas to the children at all. Occasionally they would ask about their father but they could see that the memories of how he had left them were too painful for her. Since they were all kind in their different ways, they didn't press her and the subject became a forbidden area for all of them. There were many other families in the village who had lost their fathers in the army or to accidents or disease. Women bringing up offspring alone were not unusual, although those without money were treated by the community as if they were invisible, an embarrassment and a burden on the consciences of those who had enough food on the table and a warm house to go home to.

Elizabeth wasn't completely without family support. Frances, the baby of the family, would go away for long periods to stay with some cousins of Elizabeth's in Yarmouth, a family called the Bentons. Although the cousins were not in a position to help Elizabeth financially, they were happy to take in Frances for several months of each year in order to give her mother a rest and to show the child a little more of the outside world.

Henry, the eldest son, was an intelligent boy who would have thrived if he had been allowed the privilege of an education. But poverty matures a mind in other ways, and being the eldest male of a family from the age of three gives a child a burdensome sense of responsibility. Henry took his family responsibilities very seriously, spending a great deal of time in silent thought. His mother always told him that he was like his father in that, by which she meant the thoughfulness rather than the taking of responsibility. When he was thirteen a picture of what he should do with his life came clearly into Henry's head. He went to his mother and told her his plans.

"I'm going to join the navy," he announced one evening in

1830, saying the words quickly as if to lessen the pain that he was sure the desertion would cause. He knew that his mother chose to believe it was the army that had taken her husband away from her. But joining the navy would mean even greater periods away from home and away from England. There were also the dangers inherent in the job. Henry knew that when he said good-bye there would be a strong chance he would never see his family again. He could think of no way to lessen this agony for his mother. Yet he could think of no other way that he might escape from the poverty and lowliness of his family's situation.

"Oh." Elizabeth couldn't stop herself from letting her sadness at the news show in her voice. "We'll miss you so much, Henry. You're our tower of strength."

"I have to do it, Mother," he said, determined not to be swayed by the tears that he could see welling up in her tired eyes. "I have to go out into the world to try to find something better. You'll still have Charles and Frances to help you, and I'll be able to bring money back whenever I'm ashore."

There was nothing Elizabeth could do to stop him. She had no better alternatives to offer. And in a way it lightened her load, giving her one less person to feel responsible for every morning when she awoke. She had faith in Henry and believed that once he was out in the world he would stand a good chance of making something of himself, within the limitations of his lack of education. In a way she envied him the chance of escaping from the life that she was trapped in and could see no way out of this side of the grave.

She cried when he left, one summer's day that year, starting out on the long journey to the sea on foot, still no more than a boy but with all the swagger of a young man. Frances, who was only ten, held her mother's hand tightly as she watched her brother go, dry-eyed and silent, while his twelve-year-old brother

Charles ran along beside him for the first two or three miles, begging to go, too.

"You have to stay and look after Mother and Fanny," Henry told him. "Your turn will come once Fanny is old enough."

"I'll join the navy, too," Charles promised him. "I'll come and look for you."

"You won't have to look for me," George laughed. "I'll always let you know where I am. I'm not going to disappear into thin air like our father."

But such promises are more easily spoken than carried out. Memories fade when they're replaced by new, more vivid experiences. The seafaring life suited Henry. He joined the revenue cruiser, the *Prince of Wales,* as a ship's boy, and enjoyed the camaraderie of his fellow men. The hardships and disciplines inflicted on serving men at the time seemed light to him compared to the tedium, cold, and hunger of the life of a pauper in the English countryside. He listened to the tales the older sailors had to tell, of distant lands and beautiful women, and dreamed colorful dreams in his hammock at night. During his waking hours he worked hard, eager to please his superiors. He was learning a trade, preparing himself for the life of a sailor, looking forward to traveling the world and enjoying any adventures that fate might send his way.

Three years after enlisting, in 1833, he was called to the captain's cabin. Nervous that he was in trouble for some misdemeanor he knew nothing about, he knocked on the sturdy wooden door and entered when he heard a barked command from the other side. He saluted in the manner that he had been taught and the captain looked up at him from the desk where he was sitting. He appeared to have been reading what seemed to be an official-looking letter.

"I've received a message, Druce," the captain said, waving the piece of paper at him. Henry hoped he wouldn't be expected to read it, reading being a skill he had yet to master. "You're to be sent ashore."

"Sent ashore?" Henry was stunned. Why would anyone bother to send the Captain a message about him? Who could possibly be in a position to know that he existed, let alone that he was running around on the *Prince of Wales*, scrubbing decks and polishing brass work? For a terrible moment he wondered if his mother was dead and he was going to have to go home to look after Frances with Charles.

"See for yourself." The captain passed the message across to Henry, who could just make out his own name, but nothing further. He stared at it for long enough to make it seem like he had taken in the contents and then passed it back, waiting to be told what to do next. He had now left it too long to admit that he couldn't read. He felt trapped in his own ignorance, helpless to understand what was happening to him. His mother had always promised to teach him to read and write, but whenever he'd asked her for a lesson she'd always been too busy or too tired. Eventually he'd stopped asking, not wanting to make her feel guilty.

"We'll be putting you ashore at Portsmouth in a week's time," the captain told him.

Henry didn't like to ask what he was supposed to do then. Admittedly, he did now have a little money, saved from his wages, but hardly enough to support himself on dry land for more than a few days. Was he being thrown out of the navy? The whole thing was a puzzle to him. If only he could have read the letter, it all might have been clearer to him.

A week later, as promised, the captain arranged for a boat to take him in to Portsmouth. The crew dropped him off and he climbed the steps up onto the dock with his life's possessions in a bag on his back. Once on shore, he watched his former colleagues rowing back toward the ship that had been his home for three years and would now be traveling on without him. With a heavy heart he turned round to face the town and saw a carriage waiting at the gates to the dock. The occupant, a well-to-do-looking man in a long coat and high hat, was making his way across the cobbles to meet him.

"Henry Druce?" the man enquired.

"Yes, sir," Henry said, pulling his hat off and touching his forelock respectfully.

"Good to meet you." The man extended a hand for him to shake. "I'm your father."

Henry could think of nothing to say. This imposing stranger was so far from being the sort of man he had imagined his mother to have been married to that he was struck speechless with a mixture of wonder, awe, and anger. He'd always pictured the father who had deserted them to be some sort of hopeless wanderer and vagrant, a charming gypsy or traveling player perhaps, someone who was simply unable to stay in one place long enough to bring up a family. The man before him was someone of substance, someone who could quite easily have supported a wife and children if he had chosen to.

All Henry knew about Thomas Druce was that he had been in the army, but Henry had come to realize that men sometimes become soldiers just to escape from their homes, just as when he had joined the navy. After a few years they give up the uniform and take to the road. For many years he'd dreamed of his father coming back, a lonely figure in uniform walking into the village, his kit on his shoulder, returning from some distant war. The scene had never become a reality and so he'd adjusted his dreams.

If this man had left his family it was because he chose to, not because he had to. This man had walked out on them with complete deliberation. But Henry couldn't possibly find the words to express any of the feelings that were going through him as he returned his father's firm handshake.

Thomas put a paternal arm around Henry's shoulders and steered him toward the carriage. "Come along. Let's find you some decent clothes."

As Henry sank into the well-upholstered seat of his father's carriage, he couldn't help but wonder at the gap between the world he suddenly found himself in and the world of his mother and siblings. Everything about Thomas was from a different class: his confidence, the cut of his clothes, the way in which he commanded the coachman to "drive on." Henry sat in silent, wide-eyed wonder as they rattled up from the docks to the more fashionable part of the town. His father adjusted the window curtains so that he couldn't be seen by passersby, but Henry was still able to see out through a crack that opened and closed with the roll of the carriage, looking down on the people on the street as they plodded about their business.

The carriage eventually drew up outside a tailor's shop and they alighted. Henry had never been through the doors of such a grand-looking establishment.

Inside, the shop was warm and cozy. Bolts of cloth were stacked up against the walls like nesting materials and the two tailors working at their old wooden workbenches looked as if they had never left the premises. Henry was still unable to find his tongue while the father he had just met told the men what he wanted. The tailors jumped up to do his bidding, recognizing a man of means and authority and eager to please in any way they could. If they were puzzled by the difference in the apparent circumstances of the two men before them, they were far too discreet to show it. They promised to work through the night and have two outfits ready for fittings the following day.

The two Druce men then repaired to a local inn where they ate a meal in silence before retiring to separate bedrooms. The following day, when he came downstairs for breakfast, Henry found his father already up and reading a newspaper.

"Look at that," Thomas grumbled, handing the paper to his son as he sat down. "I sometimes wonder what these politicians have between their ears."

Henry picked up the paper and stared at the story that he assumed his father was referring to. Thomas watched him for a moment and leaned forward, took the newspaper between finger and thumb, and turned it the right way. Henry didn't remove his eyes from the newsprint, which made no more sense to him that way up than the other, and his face burned with humiliation as his father waited patiently for him to abandon the pretense and hand the paper back. Neither of them said anything more throughout the meal. The clothes were finished late that afternoon and, after one more silent night together, they were able to leave the next day for London, with Henry dressed in his new finery.

From time to time Henry would attempt to instigate a conversation with his father, but all he ever received were monosyllabic replies and so he gave up trying. As they came closer to the center of London the boy was pleased by the silence since it gave him all the more opportunity to stare at the scenes around him: the bustling streets and the elegant houses, the roar of carriage wheels and horses' hooves mixing with the shouts of streets vendors, and the laughter emanating from bars and inns. He noticed that his father was careful to shield himself from prying eyes.

The carriage eventually came to a halt on Baker Street, in front of a mighty shop doorway, which proudly proclaimed itself to be the Baker Street Bazaar.

"Here we are," Thomas announced, climbing out of the carriage, stretching his stiff limbs and obviously expecting his son to follow. "This is the end of our journey."

"Good evening, Mr. Druce." A liveried doorman sprang out of the hallway behind the entrance, signaling for porters to join him and help with the unloading of cases from the carriage. Thomas acknowledged the man's greeting with more friendliness than he'd shown to his son throughout their three days together, and made his way inside. Henry fell into step behind him, assuming that this was what was expected. As they walked through the departments of the store at a deliberate pace, Henry was aware that all the staff looked up and greeted them or at least nodded their recognition. He felt that his father was annoyed and embarrassed to have to keep acknowledging their greetings although he was still unfailingly polite to each and every one of them.

Henry had never been inside a department store before and the grandeur of the place was overwhelming.

"Is this shop yours?" he asked when they finally reached the privacy of a sitting room and office on the topmost floor of the building.

"It is," Thomas replied, in a voice that suggested Henry should not get any ideas that he might be standing within his inheritance. "Don't be deceived by the size of the building. It's a hard business being a shopkeeper, with very small profit margins," Thomas continued, avoiding the boy's eyes and removing his coat and hat. "I have to carry the most enormous amount of stock in order to ensure that we can offer our customers whatever they want, and I have to meet the staff wage bills every week. It requires a great deal of capital to keep such a place going, and a great deal of work." Henry nodded his understanding and his father changed the subject. "You can stay here until we sort out some schooling for you."

"Schooling?" Henry was startled by this announcement from the blue.

"You need to read and write if you're going to amount to anything in this world," Thomas grunted. "We can have a bed brought in for you and meals will be served in the dining room down the hall."

Henry opened his mouth to protest and then closed it, realizing he had no alternative but to do as his father bade him, unless he wanted to walk out onto Baker Street with nothing but the new clothes on his back. Nothing in Thomas's tone suggested that he was open to any discussion of the subject. Henry also knew that his father was right; being able to read and write would be enormously helpful.

The following morning, as Henry was eating his breakfast alone in the heavily paneled private dining room, the food having been brought to him by one of the cooks, his father entered with a woman. She looked younger than Henry, but his father introduced her as "your aunt Annie May." Henry had no idea if that meant she was his father's sister or his mother's; something in the way the young girl looked at his father made Henry think that she might not be a blood relation at all and for a fleeting second he was able to imagine what his mother must have looked like when his father married her. This young woman was one of the prettiest creatures Henry had ever seen. She had shiny dark hair that she tied up loosely at the back of her head and eyelashes so long and thick they seemed to sweep her cheeks every time she lowered her eyes in modesty or embarrassment. He felt like shouting out a warning to her—"Stay away from my father, or he'll turn you into an old woman like my mother"—but he held his tongue. Thomas's eyes seemed to soften when he looked at the young woman and he seemed to smile whenever he spoke to her. Henry felt that he would very much like to spend more time in the company of the enchanting Annie May.

"Arrangements have been made for you to attend school,"

Thomas told him without any further preamble. "The carriage will be ready to take you there this afternoon. Annie May will spend the first part of the day with you in the store buying whatever you need."

With that Thomas turned on his heel and left the room, obviously feeling that his duties toward his eldest son had been dispensed with satisfactorily. Henry wondered if his mother had any idea that this was happening. He had mentioned her once to Thomas and received a gruff response that had not encouraged him to enquire any further. It seemed that his father thought his mother could live out her life in the cottage she had used to raise the children and that neither of them needed to worry about her any further.

Once Thomas had left them alone, Annie May gently took up the mantle of authority. Henry was not a great deal younger than she, but she could see that he was a great deal less comfortable than she was in the London department store. She took him from department to department, introducing him to the various managers and ensuring that they understood what the young Mr Druce needed. Whenever they were alone Henry would try to pluck up the courage to ask her what her relationship to his father might be, but there was never an opportunity for such an act of impertinence.

Later that day Henry departed for school, less than a week after meeting his father for the first time and discovering that he was a man of substance. He knew no more about Annie May than when he had first set eyes on her, except that he would never forget the sweet perfume that had emanated from her as they walked through the fine halls of his father's luxurious bazaar together. The boy's head was spinning.

A few weeks later, at the beginning of 1834, his sister, Frances, was staying with her mother's cousins the Bentons in Yarmouth.

A carriage arrived at the door of the house and a lawyer, accompanied by a woman of somewhat stern appearance, knocked at the door. Mrs. Benton, a kindly but harassed woman, answered it herself and was taken aback by the sight of two such austere-looking people calling on her.

"Is this the house where Miss Frances Druce is residing?" the man inquired, lifting his top hat politely.

"Frances is staying with us, yes," Mrs. Benton replied.

The lawyer passed her a letter, which she read through as thoroughly as she could under his steely gaze. The letter, signed by T. C. Druce, instructed that Frances, "his daughter" should be sent up to London where her father would be able to take care of her and prepare her for adult life.

"Mr. Druce sent you?" Mrs. Benton asked. She had always been told by Elizabeth that Thomas had failed in business and that was why he had been unable to stay and support his family. Anyone who could afford to send carriages all the way from London to Yarmouth and hire expensive-looking lawyers and chaperones did not, in Mrs. Benton's book, qualify as a failure in business. She wondered if there might be more to this whole story than her cousin had confided to her.

"You'd better come in," she told the grim couple on the doorstep, leading them through to the drawing room and going in search of Frances.

When the girl was summoned into the room, she looked more curious than frightened by the turn of events. Mrs. Benton explained to her that the carriage had come to collect her and take her to see her father in London. The young girl nodded her understanding and Mrs. Benton went with her to pack up her belongings, leaving the lawyer and the chaperone sipping tea together. Frances seemed slightly pale and tight-lipped at the sudden change in her fortunes, but did not protest. She was used to traveling back and forth between the Bentons and her mother, so the journey to London would just be another adventure; but the thought of finally meeting her father, a man who left before she was even born, made her shake inside.

On the trip she asked every question that came into her head and her traveling companions did their best to answer them informatively and discreetly. It was obvious, however, even to a thirteen-year-old girl of limited worldly experience, that there were enormous gaps in their own knowledge about her father and mother. The more she asked the more elusive and mysterious the truth about her own past seemed to grow.

The carriage took them to 71 Edgware Road, a short walk from Baker Street and the bazaar where her brother, unknown to her, had been staying a few weeks before. The door of the house was opened to them by a pleasant-faced woman in an apron who introduced herself as Mrs. Tremaine and escorted the wide-eyed girl to a sitting room at the back of the house, which overlooked a small walled garden.

"Frances Druce, sir," she announced, and a man stood up from the chair where he had been sitting reading.

"Come in, my dear," he said, studying her closely. "I'm your father."

Frances dropped her eyes to the floor and curtsied as he approached her. When she looked up again he was still staring.

"You're so like your mother when I first met her," Thomas said, his mind drifting back twenty years to when he had been a very different person, wanting very different things from life. "We were both very young," he added, as if that explained all the mysteries that were crowding into the young girl's head.

"This is Mrs. Tremaine," he said, pulling himself back to the present with an obvious effort. "She's your aunt. You'll live here with her. This is your new home."

"What about my mother?" Frances enquired.

"I'm sorry to have to tell you that your mother passed away while you were in Yarmouth," Thomas said. Frances's eyes dropped to the floor again, so she missed the exchange of glances between the two adults. They both knew that it was a lie, but had agreed that the girl would be better off if she did not have to feel guilty about leaving her mother behind.

"You don't need to worry about anything," Thomas continued. "I'll be looking after all your needs from now on. Mrs. Tremaine will help you to read and write and with any other skills that you will need in life. I have to leave you now. Let your aunt know if there is anything you require."

He walked briskly from the room and Frances heard the front door slamming behind him. Mrs. Tremaine didn't go with him. She stayed to put her arms around Frances and hold her tight as she cried for her departed mother and from the shock of her changed circumstances.

"Are you really my aunt?" she asked when her tears had finally run their course.

"No, child, but I will try to be whatever you need me to be."

Elizabeth knew nothing about what had been going on with her eldest and youngest children when there was a knock at the front door of her house. She assumed Henry was still at sea and Frances was with the Bentons. She shuffled slowly to answer it, her legs and back aching as they always did from bending over the stove or the washing or carrying firewood. When she opened the door she knew immediately that it was her husband standing in front of her, despite the fifteen years that had elapsed since she last saw him. He was no longer the romantic-looking boy she'd fallen in love with then, but he still had a magnetism about him. He hesitated before speaking, not sure if he was being greeted by his wife or by some elderly retainer. There was nothing about the creature he was looking down on that reminded him of the girl he'd carried away into the night all those years before, but something told him this was the same woman.

"Elizabeth?" he said, tentatively.

He squinted into the darkness of the room behind her. It was obviously the only one the house possessed, filled with smoke from the primitive cooker and foul with the smell of human bodies and old food.

"Yes," she replied, smiling shyly, showing him bad teeth and a face creased with lines. "Hello, Thomas."

"I've come to see Charles," Thomas said, making no attempt to step into the dark, damp-smelling room. "Is he here?"

"He's out back, cutting wood." Elizabeth gestured around the side of the house.

"Thank you." Thomas stepped gingerly through the brambles and weeds, able now to discern the sound of an ax splitting logs. The boy paused midswing when he saw the man appear. He looked incongruously tall to the boy in his top hat, towering over the low eaves of the house.

"Charles?" Thomas enquired, continuing without waiting for a reply. "I'm your father. I think it's time you received an education. Pack whatever you wish to bring with you."

As Charles gathered up his meager possessions, Elizabeth wondered why Thomas didn't ask about the other two children. "Henry is at sea," she volunteered. Thomas nodded curtly, but did not comment. "And Fanny is with the Bentons. She has grown into a beautiful girl. You would be proud of her." Thomas averted his eyes, willing the boy to move faster, and Elizabeth guessed that he already knew about them. She was too worn out with the drudgery of her life to have the energy to ask questions or even to speculate.

As soon as Charles was packed, Thomas steered him out to the carriage without looking back at the woman he had married. As the sound of the wheels faded, Elizabeth turned back into the empty house and closed the door. Despite her own terrible lone-liness, she was relieved to think that at least one of her children finally had a father looking after his interests. She would eventu-ally hear from the Bentons that Thomas had taken Frances under his wing. She only hoped that he would look after her well and ensure she made a wise marriage.

Thomas, for his part, felt that he had now done his duty by his children, preparing to launch them into their adult lives. He also believed he had finally closed the book on his unwise marriage to Elizabeth Crickmer.

6

A MAN OF MYSTERY

S ociety could hardly bear the exquisite agony of it all. Who was this Thomas Druce who'd appeared from nowhere and refused to have anything to do with them?

It wasn't that anyone in society wanted to admit that a mere shopkeeper was of any interest to them, however splendid his shop might be, but the rumors they heard, and passed on with embellishment, about Mr. Druce gave him all the allure of an outsider who appeared to have no interest in joining their exclusive club. He was as fascinating as he was frustrating.

The whisperers told stories of the fabulous sums of money that the Baker Street Bazaar made each year, while others pointed out that to own such a store in the first place required the most enormous amount of capital. How could a man who had previously been unknown to all of them have managed to accrue so much money without leaving any trace of his rise at all? It simply wasn't possible, unless he was merely a front man, acting on behalf of someone else. But if that was the case, who might that someone else be? Anyone who'd met Druce reported that he didn't seem to be anyone's man but his own. So who was he? Where had he come from? How had he made his money? What was he going to do next with his fortune? No one seemed to have any answers. It was all too intriguing to resist.

A number of hostesses had tried to lure the mysterious Mr. Druce to parties, despite the fact that it was rumored that he was living out of wedlock in Hendon with a beautiful girl young enough to be his daughter. But they had all been firmly rebuffed. Mr. Druce, everyone was told, was far too busy running his business to be able to indulge in a social life. Such an attitude made him even more an object of fascination since few people in society could understand why anyone who'd made a fortune wouldn't want to use it to better themselves socially. Apart from anything else, it made sound business sense for him to circulate among the rich and influential. How could he hope to attract the very best customers to his shop if he didn't mix with them, tempting them with his goods and offering them beneficial terms and extended credit? They weren't sure whether to feel slighted by this suggestion that working in a shop was somehow a nobler way to spend your time than socializing, or to be admiring of such a rigid work ethic.

They all went to the bazaar anyway, just to see it for themselves. Many of them reported back to friends that they had seen "that man Druce" and that he was actually standing at the door of his shop, "like a high street costermonger," greeting customers as they came and went. Nobody thought that was the way for a man of substance to behave, but he didn't seem concerned about what they thought.

Husbands who worked in banks were bullied into making enquiries into his financial background, but none of them could find any record of any money being loaned to Thomas at the time he emerged as the owner of the mighty store. Nor could they find any record of previous businesses in which he might have profited well enough to be able to set himself up so handsomely. It was agreed that he must have an income of over a quarter of a million pounds a year from the shop, but where was he spending it? He was never seen at the races. He never threw extravagant balls to impress the people who believed they mattered. He seemed determined to live as a simple shopkeeper.

"People in trade can be dreadfully mean," one duchess was heard to remark. "They're constantly afraid that they'll have to spend money if they enter society. So they prefer to stay home and count their coins."

Stories emanating from staff within the store claimed that so great was Thomas's urge for privacy about his movements that he was having special tunnels built for himself and his family, so they could get to and from the store without going out onto the street. There were rumors that Thomas's close friends were sometimes seen going into the shop, but then never emerged again. They must, the gossips decided, be spiriting themselves out to houses in the area through tunnels. Eyes then turned to a house in a fashionable area not far away, where fourteen-foot walls had been erected so that no one could see the comings and goings within. The house was owned by the Cavendish-Bentincks, the family of the fourth duke of Portland.

As with all gossip and rumor, there were always grains of truth mixed up with the fantasy and wishful thinking, but nobody could tell where exactly they lay in the soup of speculation about Thomas Druce that swirled around the salons of Mayfair and Belgravia.

Frances Druce knew nothing of the talk that circulated around fashionable London about her father, and fashionable London had absolutely no idea that she or her two brothers even existed. As far as Frances was concerned, her two brothers might just as well not have existed since she never got to see them again. She lived a quiet and respectable life with Mrs. Tremaine in the house on Edgware Road. She had learned to read and write and enjoyed her lessons. Mrs. Tremaine was fond of novels and had started her on easy romantic fiction. They were now reading the works of Benjamin Disraeli together. Disraeli was a young man soon to become a politician. At that time he was renowned in London for the fact that he was Jewish and for his flamboyance rather than for any great achievement on the public stage. He cut an exotic figure among the British aristocracy with his head of black curls, hooked nose, dark eyes, and pale complexion. He tended to dress in black velvet suits with ruffles and black silk stockings that caused many people not to take him seriously as the potential public figure he claimed he wanted to be. It was known that he was a man of inordinate ambition, but nobody yet had any idea just how far that ambition was going to be taking him. For the moment he was using novel writing both to earn enough money to stay in society and to increase his fame among the educated classes. He had already succeeded in running up catastrophic debts. His book *Vivian Grey* was considered to be largely autobiographical, revealing the author's vaunting social and political ambitions. When he wrote it in 1826, he was only twenty-one years old.

Frances wished she could have been allowed to develop such a peaceful, companionable relationship with her mother as she had with Mrs. Tremaine. In the afternoons they would take walks in Hyde Park, exercising the small dog that Thomas had given Frances on her first Christmas in the capital city.

Once or twice a week Thomas, who had developed a great fondness for his daughter, would call on them and take a cup of tea. The conversation was never relaxed, but he appeared to enjoy being there for an hour or two, until he would abruptly stand up and leave, as if unable to bear their company another moment.

When she had grown more used to his austere and authoritative manner, Frances ventured to ask her father a few questions. She missed both her brothers and wondered what had happened to them.

"Both the boys have gone away to school," he replied, without volunteering any more information.

"Is it possible to have the addresses of the schools so that I can write to them?" Frances asked, but Thomas pretended not to have heard and she didn't have the courage to repeat the question. She was an obedient girl and she assumed that whatever her father did would be in her best interests, even if she couldn't understand his reasoning. There were some things in life that were too difficult for an uneducated girl to grasp, she could see that. Her father seemed to be a man of the world. If he thought it wiser that she and her brothers should go their separate ways then he probably knew best.

In fact, Thomas's reasons for keeping his children apart were purely from self-interest. As long as they weren't talking to one another and comparing notes, they were less likely to make unreasonable demands on him. As long as he could keep them separate he could stay in control.

Although Mrs. Tremaine was a good companion to her, Frances found herself missing both her mother and the Bentons. She couldn't understand why Mrs. Benton never wrote to her or replied to the letters she sent. She would very much have liked to talk with someone who had known her mother, to remember her with someone else who was fond of her. As it was, it seemed like Elizabeth had never existed and that made Frances feel very sad. When she asked Mrs. Tremaine why she thought the Bentons did not respond to her letters, Mrs. Tremaine became curiously evasive. Frances assumed it was because the older woman was anxious to protect the feelings of her charge. She did not know that Mrs. Tremaine, in fact, had a guilty conscience since she, on her employer's instructions, was ensuring that none of Frances's letters to the Bentons ever reached a post box.

In another house, not far from Edgware Road, on July 4, 1846, Annie May gave birth to her first son, whom she and the baby's father, Thomas, christened Herbert. Since Elizabeth was not in fact dead, despite what Frances had been told, Thomas and Annie May were not married at the time of the birth. Consequently, Herbert's arrival could not be announced to the world. But Thomas would probably not have felt inclined to make such an announcement, even if his latest child had been born within wedlock. He never could see the point in furnishing the world with unnecessary private details. He and Annie May were both very happy with the cheery baby they'd been given. He saw no reason why anyone else should have any interest in the child whatsoever. Annie May, delighted to have been blessed with a healthy baby, was content to go along with whatever her partner thought was right. She was not a woman who needed to see her name flaunted in the newspapers. She had no wish to be admired or complimented by strangers. She was happy simply to be with her first son, and with Thomas when he was able to get away from the demands of his business. Thomas did not trouble to inform Frances that she had a new half brother.

These were times when rich and influential people could still guard their privacy. No newspaper reporter would ever dream of digging up a story about anyone respectable that was not voluntarily placed in the public domain, unless it reached the courts, in which case it would then be considered fair game. However much people might gossip about them in private, law-abiding citizens never had to fear that their privacy would be invaded by a newspaper without their permission. Even figures as scandalous as Lord Byron had been able to exercise control over what was and wasn't printed about them. Oscar Wilde, who would eventually fall victim to a rapacious press, would not even be born for another eight years.

Some men, of course, lived parts of their lives completely in the public domain. In 1846 Lord George Bentinck and Disraeli became front-page news almost from the day they joined forces. Disraeli had succeeded in getting himself elected into Parliament and, although no longer merely an impecunious novelist, was still making a splash on the London scene with his flamboyant clothes and outspoken views. His links with the robust, aristocratic figure of Lord George meant that many people who had previously dismissed Disraeli as a hopeless outsider had to think again. The Cavendish-Bentincks were powerful allies for anyone to have. It was beginning to look possible that the man might end up occupying a high office one day.

Disraeli and Lord George had succeeded in their aim of toppling Sir Robert Peel from his perch as prime minister, seeing him replaced by Lord John Russell in 1846. Lord George had agreed to remain leader of the Protectionists in the House of Commons and Disraeli was reported to accompany him to King's Lynn to address five hundred country squires at a dinner and another five hundred at a lunch the following day. Like Thomas Druce, Disraeli, it seemed to many of the newspaper-reading public, was another man who had arrived at the top of society, apparently having started from nowhere, but his ascent had been anything but invisible.

Lord George, now fully committed to the political struggle, was then reported to have sold his stud and to be planning to abandon the world of racing. Since he had a string of horses that were expected to win that season, the fashionable and racing worlds were stunned by such a move. No one, however, commented on the fact that his brother, the marquess of Titchfield and future fifth duke of Portland, was also involved in the sale. The marquess was not considered to be a newsworthy name: no one was likely to buy a single extra copy of any newspaper in order to read of anything he had done or not done.

Some individuals just seemed to be able to move through the world without exciting comment, whatever their pedigree or their actions. Lord John, the marquess of Titchfield, seemed to be leaving no ripples in his wake.

7

ENTER DISRAELI

Lord George's intention to link his interests with those of Disraeli had been as much of a shock to his family as to the general public.

"Disraeli?" Lord John said when Lord George told him to whom he had just written. "You mean the novelist?"

Lord John managed to convey, through his enunciation of the man's profession, a disdain so thoroughly mixed with incredulity that Lord George was unable to stop himself from laughing, despite his usual disdain for everything his brother did or said. Lord John bristled at the laugh, sensing mockery rather than humor.

They were dining together at the Carlton Club on a cold winter's night in 1834, as they did occasionally, when one or the other of them felt he needed to communicate in some way other than by letter. The clubs of London had grown to be a useful home away from home for people like the Cavendish-Bentinck brothers. They had grown out of the coffeehouses that had served as meeting places for men of substance in the previous century, and in their maturity they had achieved a grandeur and exclusivity that made them the true seats of power for the burgeoning British Empire. They were dominated by the ruling classes and aspired to by the increasingly wealthy middle classes.

Each one was characterized by its own professional class, and political interests. Gentlemen could rest assured that once within the splendid portals of their clubs they would only meet fellows of like mind on important issues, and they certainly wouldn't be troubled by the company of women.

Tory policy was now determined more at the Carlton than anywhere else, while the Whigs met at Brooks and the Radicals at the Reform. As well as the Carlton, Lord George was a member of the Coventry, which was almost exclusively for those of influence in the racing world and was where the rules governing the turf and the ring were determined. The clubs meant that men of influence could meet in private, without having to go to the trouble of entertaining in their own homes and involving the women who, it was generally believed, would inevitably trivialize matters with their silly gossiping and would cause annoyance and unnecessary argument. Neither Lord John nor Lord George had wives who could entertain for them anyway.

That evening they were discussing neutral subjects that both felt comfortable with, like politics. Neither man liked to venture into the dangerous territory of personal subjects; they had no experience in giving voice to their feelings. There was nothing in their emotional vocabularies between reasonable discourse and furious anger. That was how they had been brought up and it was unlikely they would ever change. Both could talk about horses, although Lord George was by far the greater authority, but neither liked to talk to the other about their family or their father, or to reminisce about their childhoods. Some things were best left in the past.

The marquess was well aware of the contempt that his younger brother held him in, believing him to be unsociable and idle, and he, in turn, had little patience with the bluster and boastfulness of Lord George's world. But both knew they had to keep up some form of contact; their fates were far too entwined by kin-ship and family trusts to ever be completely separate.

"Didn't this Disraeli man write to you some time ago about something, and you ignored him?" Lord John persisted, fasci-nated despite his dislike of his brother's mockery.

"Oh, good God," Lord George snorted, "that was over ten years ago, before Disraeli had got into the House. Lyndhurst had suggested he contact me with a view to helping him get in at King's Lynn. The man was a complete outsider. It was out of the question."

"And the position's altered now?" Lord John was genuinely intrigued by his brother's change of heart toward a man he'd been condemning as a nobody only a few months before. It was the sort of slippery moral behavior that made him despise the whole business of politics and made him glad he'd got himself out of it. For the life of him he couldn't understand how a gen-tleman could hold his head up in public if he didn't remain con-sistent in his views in private.

"It most certainly has." Lord George smiled broadly, well aware of his brother's opinions and caring not a jot for any of them. For him it was all a splendid game and he couldn't under-stand how anyone could fail to see the sport in it. "He's in the House and he's one of the cleverest speakers there."

"I was told his maiden speech practically had him booed out of the building," Lord John continued, unable to resist making mischief.

"You wouldn't know it was the same man now." Lord George refused to rise to the bait, remaining resolutely affable. "He'll be invaluable in helping us get our point of view across. Peel has to be stopped. If he gets these reforms through there'll be cheap crops pouring into the country from all over the world. English farmers won't have a hope in hell of surviving."

The Corn Laws had been a political issue in England since they had been introduced as a protective duty on imported corn in 1773. Robert Peel, the prime minister, had been trying to introduce a sliding scale of duty. Disraeli had been both for and against the Corn Laws at different times. Even though later, in 1843, it became widely feared in political circles that the shortage of food and lack of trade brought about by the laws was going to lead to nationwide riots, Disraeli and Bentinck did not want to see any repeal of the laws, since they benefited the English landowners.

Lord George had never felt comfortable about speaking in Parliament himself. It wasn't that he wasn't ambitious; it was simply that he wasn't comfortable standing up to speak with the opposition hissing and booing, jeering and stamping their feet. A childhood spent in the tranquillity of Welbeck Abbey was not a good training for life in a bear pit, as the fourth duke had suggested to the marquess, not even for a man as robust by nature as Lord George. As a result he'd remained for the most part silent in his first two decades in the House. His allegiances had shifted considerably during that time. When he entered he'd still been under the influence of his uncle, the prime minister, making him a sound "Canningite Tory." Once Canning died and Wellington took office in 1828, Lord George had moved toward the Whig side. The Whigs were the party that had traditionally supported the aristocracy and believed in limiting the powers of the monarchy, but they were coming around to supporting the new industrial classes and were gradually becoming the party of reform. It was like a treacherous game of chess and Lord George relished it.

In 1834 he'd moved into an opposition position, while gradually becoming an ardent supporter of Sir Robert Peel, then the new Tory prime minister. In the Peel's second term of office, Lord George realized what the prime minister's plans were for repealing the Corn Laws. He violently disagreed with the policy and immediately changed his allegiances. Throughout the years, however, he'd generally been in favor of Whig values such as tolerance and the right for everyone to have a vote. Not surprisingly, given his family's position, he believed wholeheartedly in the importance of a land-owning aristocracy.

Although he was well known in political circles, Lord George was even better known in racing circles. His stud was his greatest love and many of the horses his stables had bred or trained had become champions. Of the hundred or so horses he was training, forty were then running in public, making him by far the country's most important man in the sporting field. One of his fillies, named Crucifix, had won every important race on the calendar in 1840. He'd campaigned vigorously against corruption in racing circles, exposing a fraud in 1844 when a winning horse was found to be a year older than had been claimed.

There was barely a man in Parliament who wasn't also involved with the world of the Turf, which meant Lord George was something of a celebrity in his own right, regardless of his birthright. He now viewed Sir Robert Peel as little better than the crooks and fraudsters he'd rooted out of the racing world. He was as determined to bring down the prime minister as he had been to expose illegal practices in the derby, and once Lord George set his mind to a task there was nothing that could deflect him.

With all these achievements to his name, he found it hard to hide his contempt for his elder brother's apparent lack of any achievements at all. The marquess had left the army with no distinction whatsoever and had given up politics at the first opportunity. It utterly bewildered Lord George exactly how the man spent his days and nights. The fact that he now showed no interest in the matter of the Corn Laws made Lord George even more furious.

"I keep horses in three counties, John," he said, his eyes

narrowed with anger and his jaw clenched so tight the words could hardly make their way out. "They tell me that I shall save fifteen hundred a year by free trade. I don't care for that: what I cannot bear is being sold."

"Have you ever spoken to this man Disraeli?" Lord John inquired, seeing the danger signals and moving the subject back to more neutral territory.

His brother looked puzzled as to the relevance of the question. "Never had cause to," he grunted. "Doesn't mean I can't write to him."

"I thought you disapproved of his attacks on Peel."

"That was before I realized what Peel was up to. I was thinking of calling on the services of one of the legal members of Parliament, but I think Disraeli may fit the bill better. The trouble is, all the brightest men are on the other side. We need to have a genius on our side, someone who understands our needs better than we do ourselves. After all, we're little more than simple farmers. He's a professional debater."

"Why should he be interested in a man who snubbed him before?" Lord John asked, taking a sip at his port and watching his brother for any telltale signs that he might be about to lose his famous temper and cause a public scene.

"I can be as useful to him as he can be to me."

"In what way?"

"Oh, don't be so damned obtuse, John. You yourself just described him as 'the novelist'—most of the people we know wouldn't be that generous; they'd merely refer to him as 'the Jew.' They may admire his skills but they're hardly going to fall into line behind him. I doubt the man knows one end of a horse from another. The fact that I'm the grandson of one prime minister and the nephew of another does give me a certain advantage socially. He needs someone who can function in society."

His brother nodded his understanding. Whatever people might think of Lord George's temper or his language, no one could deny that he was a leader of men. Nothing Lord John had heard about Disraeli suggested that anyone would be willing to follow him into any battles. Together, however, the two of them just might be able to overthrow Peel. Lord John sent up a silent prayer of thanks that he'd bowed out of the murky world of politics when he had. He had other matters on his mind, one of which was beginning to fill his thoughts as his digestion took care of the fine meal and the port sent its warm fumes drifting through his head.

"We need to form a third party," Lord George was saying, "a Protectionist Party, consisting of all the people who can see through Peel and his plans. They want to call the new party 'Conservative.' I don't understand what they're getting at. It's just organized hypocrisy."

His voice continued in the background as his brother's thoughts drifted into the nearby theater, where Fanny Kemble was performing. He would rather have spent the evening listening to her from the back of the auditorium, as he did most of the nights that he found himself in London, but he'd been reluctant to turn down an invitation to supper with his brother. Both he and Lord George were aware of the mighty chasm there was between them in both taste and temperament. If either made the effort to build a bridge, now and again the other felt obliged to cooperate.

But now, bored as he was becoming with talk of politics and sport, Lord John was no longer able to maintain his concentration. There was one more thing he wanted to clear up with George before leaving. It was the main reason he'd agreed to the dinner that particular evening.

"The money from the syndicate," he said, interrupting Lord George's flow. "I'm told there's a reasonable sum now."

"Quite reasonable," Lord George nodded. He and his two brothers had formed a racing syndicate, exploiting their love of horses and George's considerable knowledge of the Turf. The profits had been pouring in but none of the three men had had any cause to call on them. "Do you want to take some of the money out?"

"I do, but I want it in a different name," Lord John said. "I have some investments in London I would like to keep separate from the family."

"Of course." Lord George nodded. He understood. Every gentleman liked to have some money of his own for which he didn't have to answer to family lawyers and relatives. "Just let me know the name and where you want it sent to and I'll make the arrangements."

"The lawyers will be in touch," Lord John said. Talking of money had made him embarrassed and he was now anxious to escape. "I'm going to have to make my way now," he said, consulting his watch. "Thank you for supper."

Lord George, who had a great deal more to say on the subject of Disraeli and Peel, looked as if he was about to respond with ill temper and then seemed to change his mind.

"Ah," he smiled, gesturing toward the watch that his brother was sliding back into his waistcoat pocket. "It's time to mount guard at the stage door, is it?"

"No idea what you're talking about," Lord John muttered, the color rising from his neck to his face.

"I heard the Kemble woman was back in London," George teased, "and newly divorced from the American. Planning to marry her yourself, are you?"

"She's an actress," John protested, irritated by his brother's vulgarity, while at the same time aware that the man couldn't hope to understand the situation with the Kemble family since he, Lord John, had never chosen to share the details of his passions with anyone else, leaving it to the gossips to create their own stories.

"I dare say it wouldn't be the first time a marquess has married below him," George laughed and watched as his brother left the dining room in some discomfort.

As John made his way toward the theater Lord George's words were spinning lazily in his head. The woman he'd wanted to marry was not Fanny Kemble, but her younger and altogether gentler sister, Adelaide. Like the rest of her family, Adelaide was a renowned performer—a vocalist who could bring up the hairs on the backs of her audience's necks, so pure were her notes. He'd pursued her as ardently as he knew how. He'd even asked her to marry him, willing to defy his father's edict that he should never marry. He would have been willing to risk producing any number of insane and demented children if it had meant he could spend his life with Adelaide at his side.

She'd rebuffed him so gently and sweetly that they'd been able to remain friends, even after she married a man called Edward Sartoris, but Lord John still felt the emptiness of his life without her. She'd explained to him that she thought he was the dearest of people and that she would always love him as a friend, but that the thought of one day being the duchess of Portland was far more than she could bear.

"Such a position would crush me within months," she admitted. "I would let you and your family down terribly."

Thinking about it made him angry with himself and with the position that he'd been born into. Was he going to spend his whole life in the half world of subterfuge and hypocrisy just because his father believed there was a strain of madness in their blood? Obviously his sisters had never received the same note about not marrying or reproducing, since all of them had gone on to do so, marrying into some of the other illustrious aristo-cratic families in the land. He'd never raised the subject with any of them, and never would; what gentleman could even consider broaching such a sensitive topic with ladies? Why should they be able to marry happily and create families for themselves while their brothers continued to remain lonely? Was it worth allowing the male line to die out just on the off chance that they might carry a seed of madness in them?

But it wasn't just Adelaide who held him entranced, it was the whole Kemble family, including the father, Charles, and both his daughters. Lord John had fallen under their spell the first time he saw Charles performing in Shakespeare. The idea of hiding behind a created character, of being able to strut upon the stage in front of a crowd without showing the slightest part of oneself entranced him. Charles Kemble was the preeminent exponent of his art and watching him practicing it took the young Lord John's breath away.

Being from the Cavendish-Bentinck family, it was only a matter of time before the young lord was able to meet the great actor in person at a dinner party, and it was there that he discovered the existence of Fanny and Adelaide. The powerful Fanny had bewitched him in the same way as her father, but it was the shy and modest Adelaide who had truly laid siege to his heart. It was the differences between the Kemble family and his own that really struck him. Although they were famous and feted by society, they'd taken on none of the onerous responsibilities of wealth, status, and power. Where the Cavendish-Bentincks were exhausted by the weight of their own privileges, the Kembles rev-eled in theirs. They'd achieved greatness through their own geniuses and they had no need to close themselves off emotion-ally from one another or from the rest of the world. While the noble Cavendish-Bentincks shut themselves away from the sight of their fellow men, the Kembles went out and searched for attention. They were warm and open and loving and Lord John felt intoxicated whenever he was in their company.

He'd sought them out wherever and whenever he could. When Fanny married an American called Pierce Butler in 1830 and left for the New World, he felt as if a part of him had been torn away. He renewed his efforts to woo Adelaide but it was to no avail and eight years later she, too, was married to another man.

He was lost in thought as he walked in through the stage door, giving a small wave to the doorman who was there to keep undesirables away, and who would never have dreamed of standing in the way of a man like the marquess of Titchfield, a gentleman from the top of one of the most distinguished families in the land.

Fanny, having divorced her American, was back in London and touring the city doing readings from Shakespeare. Lord John had already attended at least half a dozen of them and had been newly entranced each time. As he made his way to the star's dressing room he felt the familiar raising of his heart rate at the prospect of being in her company again.

"John, my dear." Fanny was already in the dressing room when he knocked on the door. She'd changed from her stage costume and had an open bottle of champagne on the table in front of her. "Come and join me."

Lord John sat down, somewhat uncomfortably, in the only other chair in the small room. Being in any of the Kembles' company was exciting but a little like being sober among drunks. She passed him a glass.

"I've spent the whole day with your Mister Danton, being done."

"I hope it didn't inconvenience you," John stuttered. Danton was a sculptor he'd hired to make busts of Charles, Fanny, and Adelaide. He felt embarrassed to have imposed upon their time so shamelessly, but was determined to preserve the great acting and performing dynasty in their prime. He also wanted to be sure he'd always have a likeness of Adelaide, since he could never have the real thing.

"Not at all, my dear. He's already finished father's likeness, he tells me. I can't wait to see it."

"You must all come to Welbeck for an unveiling," Lord John suggested, blushing at the thought of having Adelaide under the same roof as himself. "And Sartoris as well, of course," he hastened to add.

Fanny smiled at him with a sweet understanding. She was a woman of the world. She knew that her sister had broken the marquess's heart and she suspected it would now never fully mend.

8

A Death in the Family

In 1848, at the height of Disraeli and Lord George's political partnership, a horse called Surplice, from the stud that Lord George had just sold, won the derby. The day after the great race, Disraeli found his friend and ally in the library of the House of Commons. In front of him were laid out piles of books on international trade. Lord George was poring through them, squinting impatiently at the densely printed pages, tracking the price of sugar. He glanced up as Disraeli approached, looking tired and drawn.

"I heard about Surplice," Disraeli said, aware of how brokenhearted his friend must be.

"All my life," Lord George replied, "I've been trying to win that race, and for what have I sacrificed it?" He gestured at the columns of the books' gray print in despair.

"You've made a magnificent gesture by committing yourself to politics," Disraeli tried to console him. "What is the winning of a horse race compared to what we're undertaking?"

"You don't know what the derby is," Lord George moaned. "It's the blue ribbon of the Turf."

Disraeli decided it was not the moment to bring up the matter that was at the forefront of his own mind and left Lord George in peace. But a few days later he could leave it no longer. To get any further in the party he needed to become a landowner. He had to join the country gentry if he was going to represent a county. But buying a landed property took money, a lot of money, something that Disraeli did not have nearly enough of. All he had was debts.

Lord George had in the past suggested that he and his family would help out with a loan should a suitable property come up, but good country estates did not often come onto the open market. Normally country estates stayed in one family, passing down from generation to generation, until taxation or some expensive family vice forced a sale.

A few days before, an ideal property had been put up for sale at £25,000 and Disraeli felt he needed to move quickly if he was to secure it. Having no money of his own, he couldn't make any move without Lord George's help.

The house, which was small compared to the mighty Welbeck Abbey and other aristocratic seats, was called Hughenden Manor. It was a pretty house, white stuccoed with three floors and a garden surrounded by woodland. There was even a church on its 750 acres. Disraeli thought it would do very well and told Lord George so over lunch at the Carlton Club.

"I need to have a country seat," Disraeli explained unnecessarily. "This one would be more than adequate."

"Can you afford it?" Lord George asked with his usual bluntness.

"Not without assistance," Disraeli admitted, knowing that Lord George would immediately understand what he was asking for.

"I'll have to talk to the family," Lord George told his friend. "This is a hard time to raise cash for anyone, even us."

"I understand," Disraeli assured him, although he could see no reason whatsoever why the Cavendish-Bentincks couldn't come up with £25,000 almost overnight if they wanted to enough. He hated having to go cap in hand to the gentry, the very people who'd made him feel like an outsider in England for so many years. He had nothing but fondness for Lord George but he could just imagine what the rest of his family would say about the suggestion of funding a Jew's rise to the landed gentry. He was under no illusions as to how he, and all other Jews with ambition, was still viewed by the Establishment. He was aware that he would be seen as a "necessary evil" by the rest of the Cavendish-Bentincks because of his political abilities and it galled him that he had to go to them in order to get any farther. If there had been any alternative he would have taken it, but there was none.

Lord George, fully aware of how much his friend was relying on him, and how humiliating it must be for him, went back to Lord John and their younger brother, Lord Henry, with the suggestion that they should provide a loan for Mr. Disraeli, a man who looked as if he was set to have an even more glittering parliamentary career in the future than he had already enjoyed. He didn't think it would be worth talking to his father on the subject. The fourth duke was growing old and increasingly irritable with the younger generation. Even George, his favorite son, was becoming a mystery to him.

"We need the support of this man," Lord George pointed out to his brothers when they met at Welbeck. "There aren't many men of his caliber willing to speak in favor of our cause."

"Does he have no money of his own?" Lord John grumbled. He had no particular problem with Disraeli himself, but his growing distaste for the world of politics made him reluctant to back anyone, let alone someone as transparently ambitious and self-seeking as Disraeli. He was strongly inclined to withdraw himself even farther from public life in the future and the idea of bankrolling someone that flamboyant didn't seem a wise move for anyone wanting to lead a quiet life. There was also something upsetting about the way George simply assumed that he and Henry would agree with him. Lord John always found his younger brother's overbearing character annoying, and now that George had become a political leader he'd become even more domineering than he had been as a young man. He tended to treat other men in much the same way as he treated his hunting dogs, cussing them roundly when they failed to do his bidding. It puzzled Lord John as to how Lord George managed to remain so popular with the people and his fellow politicians when he was so frequently rude and bullying. But there was no denying that he was a well-loved figure among all the circles in which he moved in.

"He has enough money to keep himself and his wife in circulation socially," Lord George replied, attempting to be patient with Lord John's dithering. He found his older brother's negative attitude to life increasingly difficult to stomach. There were many times when he felt like taking him by the scruff of the neck and shaking him like an untrained puppy until he woke up and began behaving as if he was part of the real world. He dreaded to think what would happen to the man's character once their father was dead and the marquess had taken over the dukedom, if John survived that long, which George sometimes doubted since his health never seemed particularly good. "But he does not have enough to buy the house."

"What security can he offer?" Lord John enquired, more out of mischief than genuine concern for Disraeli's creditworthiness.

"I'll take full responsibility for repaying the loan should Mr. Disraeli default," Lord George snapped, knowing that upon the death of his father he would have an annual income of £30,000, even if his brother did inherit the title.

"Just give the man the money." Lord Henry tried to bring peace between his warring older siblings. "He deserves our support."

"I dare say he doesn't make much from his scribblings," Lord John agreed ill-naturedly. "It'll take some time to raise that much."

"Why not tell him we'll give him the money so that he can get on with negotiating for this house?" Lord Henry suggested, growing bored with his brothers and their barely concealed dislike for each other.

"Very well," Lord John nodded his agreement, not wishing to waste another second of his time thinking about the subject; the career of Benjamin Disraeli, a man destined to become one of Britain's most famous political figures, took a large leap forward.

A few months later all three of the Cavendish-Bentinck brothers were back at Welbeck together, each in their separate apartments, living almost separate lives. Lord George was spending most of his time out hunting on the estate, while Lord John wandered around the grounds in what appeared, to those who passed him, to be something of a daydream.

After a hard morning's riding in September 1848, Lord George returned to his apartment refreshed and invigorated as he always was after a gallop. He felt good about the world in general as his valet helped him out of his riding clothes and filled a hot bath for him. After Lord George had bathed and dressed, he set out in the early afternoon to walk the six miles to Thoresby Hall, the home of the earl of Manners, in response to an invitation to supper. The earl was a close friend and a fellow politician. There would be a great deal of political talk and discussion about the queen and her consort, as well as good food and wine. Lord George was looking forward to the evening and wanted to work up an appetite for what was bound to be a fine meal. It was not to be a particularly formal event so he told his coachman to pick him up at nine o'clock, by which time he was confident he would be ready to return to Welbeck, and his bed, after a hard day of exercise and a few glasses of good port.

The coachman duly set out at eight in the evening, just as the sky was beginning to darken with a hint of the approaching winter. He arrived at Lord Manners's house just before nine, as instructed, and made his way around to the servants' quarters, where he would wait until he was informed that his master was ready to leave for home, and where he hoped he might be furnished with a hot meal while he waited.

"Good evening, Mr. Cox," the cook, whom he knew well, greeted him as he walked into the kitchen. "You've taken your time. The dinner is pretty much ruined thanks to you and your master and I doubt if the earl's temper is too good."

"I was told to pick him up at nine," the coachman protested, puzzled by the woman's outburst. He noticed the butler coming into the room from upstairs.

"You mean you haven't brought Lord George with you?" the butler asked.

"I've come to collect him," the coachman replied. "He was making his own way here on foot."

"He hasn't arrived," the butler informed him. "Sit down there."

The coachman sat, gratefully accepting a bowl of soup from a suddenly solicitous cook, as the butler went back upstairs to report on the unexpected turn of events. A few minutes later he returned to tell the coachman that the earl would like to speak to him. The coachman wiped the last smears of the soup from his chin and followed the butler upstairs with his hat in his hand and his head full of confused thoughts. What had started out as a straightforward evening, with the prospect of an early night tucked up in bed, was turning into something altogether more uncomfortable.

Lord Manners, who had become extremely peevish at having

his dinner disrupted by a late guest, and missing the eagerly anticipated company of a friend, now appeared more worried than annoyed.

"Are you certain that Lord George set out on foot?" he asked, without any preamble.

"Quite certain, sir," the coachman replied. "He told me he would be walking here and I was to come for him at nine. He anticipated having an early supper with your lordship and then returning home to sleep in his own bed."

"It seems something must have befallen his lordship after he left home," the earl replied. "Take the coach back to Welbeck. I'll send a fleet messenger on ahead of you so they can start searching as quickly as possible."

By the time the coachman arrived back at Welbeck the earl's messenger had alerted the household and a search party was assembled outside the stables, their faces orange in the flickering light of their burning torches. The duke of Portland was walking among them, barking out orders. His bent, elderly frame was moving with agitated energy, almost as if he feared slowing down and allowing the thoughts that crowded the back of his mind to come through. It was obvious from his face that he dreaded what the search parties would discover. He was firing questions at everyone he came across, trying to discover which direction his son might have set out in. There seemed to be several conflicting stories.

"I saw him leaving with Lord John and two other men," he was told by one of the groundskeepers. "He took the path down past the river."

"What other two men?" the duke demanded.

"I couldn't recognize them, sir, not from that distance. I only recognized His Lordship and the marquess."

"Where is the marquess?" the duke barked, furious at the idea that Lord John wasn't as concerned as he was about his missing brother.

"We're looking for him, Your Grace," a voice from the dark called back. "He wasn't in his apartment. He might be at the stables."

"Did anyone here set out on the walk with Lord George?" the duke shouted, and there was a mumbled response in the negative. Everyone felt uneasy to see the duke so distraught. Even though he was close to eighty, he was still the bedrock that Welbeck rested upon. If he was shaken, they were all uncomfortable. Two of his daughters were standing close to him. One of them tried to take his arm and calm him down. He shook her off angrily and she stood back with her sister, waiting until she would be needed. The crowd of searchers divided into three groups and set off on the various routes between Welbeck and Thoresby that Lord George was likely to have taken. The duke wanted to lead one of the groups himself, but realized he would slow them down. The thought of having to wait around for news was almost unbearable. He watched as the flickering light of the torches divided up, grew small, and disappeared, leaving behind a terrible silence. The duke swore mightily, despite the fact that there were still women around him. They turned their heads away and pretended to have heard nothing.

A sound of running feet heralded the arrival of the marquess from the riding school.

"What's happened?" he asked.

"George was supposed to be walking over to have dinner with Manners," his father explained. "He never arrived. They say he set off with you and two other men."

"No." Lord John shook his head, apparently puzzled by the suggestion. "I've been out riding all afternoon. I've been in the riding school until now."

The duke looked down at his son's mud-splattered boots and jodhpurs and grunted his possible acceptance of the story.

"So, who would these other men have been? Does George have guests visiting?"

"I've no idea," Lord John said. "He doesn't confide these things in me."

To those around it sounded as if the marquess was being cross-examined, as if the duke believed his son knew more than he was letting on. They all kept their eyes averted, pretending to be straining their ears to hear shouts from one of the search parties.

The searchers worked in near silence, their flaming torches sending night birds and animals scattering as they poked into every nook and cranny in search of Lord George. No one called out his name. It was as if they didn't expect him to still be able to respond. The party that had followed the river path had only been walking for half an hour when their torches suddenly illuminated the body in the blackness, making the searchers break the silence with shouts of surprise and horror, calling their colleagues over to help. Lord George was draped across a gate, as if someone had hung him up to keep him off the wet ground. The men who had found the body lowered it down, while others held torches above their heads so they could see what they were doing. They carried his body back to the house.

The duke and Lord John heard them approaching before they saw the lights. The normally silent night air of the abbey was filled with confused and nervous shouts as the servants prepared for the return of Lord George and tried to work out the correct way of proceeding with the events. Everyone knew that Lord George had been the duke's favorite, and to be predeceased now by two of his sons was going to be a difficult burden for the old man to shoulder. All eyes were focused on his bent figure as he walked out toward the returning search party. Lord John stood back in the shadows, watching his father and waiting to see what would be required of him.

By the time the body reached them, both men had had time to compose themselves and swallow their emotions in the way they'd been brought up to do. Neither dared catch the eye of the other, for fear of the feelings they might unleash. Lord John knew that if he saw his father's eyes resting on him he would know the old man would be asking God why He'd chosen to take that son, the one who was so full of life and promise, the one who was bringing new fame and glory onto the family name; and why he'd left behind the one who didn't seem to be able to find any place for himself in the world, beyond that given to him by birth. Lord John knew that if he had seen that in his father's eyes he would have ended up hating his younger brother forever, even beyond the grave.

The body was carried into the house and laid out on a table at the duke's instructions. The old man stood beside his dead son for several minutes, apparently lost in thought, refusing all offers of a seat from his daughters and worried staff, who expected him to fall at any moment. He seemed to be swaying on his feet, almost as if he was in a trance. After a few minutes he came around with a start, as if snapping out of a deep sleep and realizing where he was for the first time. He issued instructions for the family doctor to be informed of the occurrence at first light and for the man to be asked to attend the abbey once he'd breakfasted. No one else, he told the surrounding servants, was to be spoken to on the subject, particularly any members of the press who might find their way onto the estate, until the full facts had been ascertained. He then retired to the privacy of his quarters so that no one would witness the true depths of his grief.

When the doctor finally arrived, he went to see the duke in private before being taken to where Lord George had been laid out. The duke, who was still in bed with an untouched breakfast tray lying beside him, had had time to recover his self-control and received the doctor with all the authority that his wealth and title allowed. The doctor asked respectfully what the duke's opinion of the situation was and the duke told him that it appeared to him his son had suffered some sort of heart attack. The doctor, a mild-mannered man who knew his place in the local pecking order, nodded wisely, agreeing that this was indeed the most likely fate to have befallen Lord George. Once the duke was sure that the doctor understood what was expected of him, he dismissed him and his valet helped him to dress.

The doctor was escorted to the chapel where Lord George was resting. He took a long, hard look at the corpse, shook his head in deep sorrow, and pronounced his verdict.

"His Lordship," he said, "has undoubtedly died of a spasm of the heart."

If he had noticed anything suspicious about the body, the doctor knew better than to draw anyone's attention to it. If the duke had wanted to know about signs of foul play he would have said something.

Those who overheard the prognosis nodded their heads in wise agreement. Everyone was always saying that Lord George worked far too hard, with all the traveling back and forth to London and the politicking until the early hours of the morning. He was well known for being unable to have a bite to eat on a day before speaking in the Houses of Parliament, which meant he often went nearly twenty-four hours without any nourishment. And, of course, there was the drinking. Everyone at Welbeck knew how much Lord George enjoyed his drink. What man, they asked one another, could hope to keep healthy under such physical pressures? He was a great man who had sacrificed his life to be of service to those less fortunate than himself.

The local registrar was more than happy to accept the doctor's pronouncement, and a statement was given to the press of the tragic death of Lord George, a man who might well have been a future prime minister had not his life been cut tragically short. The public mourned with all the respect that was due to a man of reputation. *The Times* reported, "An almost general mark of respect to the memory of the late lamented nobleman has been evinced among the shipping in the Docks and Pool by their colours being hoisted half mast high since his demise."

Disraeli and his wife, Mary Anne, were staying with the London-derrys, the society hosts, at their house, Wynward, when the news of Lord George's death reached him. Disraeli staggered visibly beneath the blow; his face turned to chalk and his eyes had something of the madman in their stare as he tried to see some sense in what he was hearing. Other guests caught him as his knees buckled beneath him, and they helped him to a chair. Water was brought and his necktie loosened. For a moment it looked as if he too was going to die, killed by the shock of losing his friend and greatest political ally.

A few hours later, when he'd recovered enough strength to be able to go for a short walk in the gardens with his wife, Mary Anne asked him what the death was going to mean to them.

"Does this mean we'll never see ourselves at Hughenden?" she asked. "Will the promise of money disappear with Lord George?"

"I don't know, my dear," Disraeli admitted, linking his arm with hers and squeezing comfortingly. "If it was up to Lord John I doubt if we would see another penny. The man seems to have no time for me at all. But he's an honorable man and he knows the money has been promised. He will probably honor the promise, if only out of respect for his deceased brother. Lord Henry is almost as good an ally to us as Lord George was, although not half the man when it comes to a fight. He may well be our champion at the final fence."

"If only we'd moved sooner and bought the house the moment the loan was confirmed."

"There are so many 'if onlys' in life, Mary Anne," Disraeli said, his mind racing as he tried to imagine how he would continue his climb to power without Lord George. He had never lacked the certainty that he could achieve anything, but he did not underestimate how important Lord George had been to him in his ascent, nor how fond he had grown of him in their years of working together.

A few days later Disraeli received a letter from Lord Henry Bentinck suggesting they meet. "I'm sure my brother's death has hit you hard," Lord Henry said. "He had no secrets from you."

Before their meeting at the Carlton Club, Disraeli was visibly nervous about what news the young nobleman would be bringing. He and his family had had plenty of time to reflect on their political situation at leisure. When Lord Henry arrived the two men exchanged only the barest of formalities before getting down to the business that was on both their minds.

"Dealing with the estate of my brother is proving complicated and costly," Lord Henry told him. "Titchfield (Lord John) and I have given a great deal of thought to you and your situation. We've a proposition to put to you. We haven't yet mentioned this to our father; we thought it better to speak to you first. Would you object if the duke paid off the twenty-five thousand pounds that you owe us, in return for receiving rents and becoming the mortgagee of your estate?"

"I could not agree to that." Disraeli attempted to stay calm at the suggestion. He did not intend to become a mere tenant to a duke. That would not be a position of strength for a man of ambition. "In fact, if you insist on such an arrangement I will sell off the estate, pay off the debt, and resign the county."

Lord Henry looked shocked. He hadn't expected such a

vehement response. He was somewhat in awe of Disraeli, just as he had been in awe of his own brother, and was anxious not to turn him against the family. Lord George had been more than just a brother to him, he had been his childhood hero, and Lord Henry did not want to do anything that Lord George would not have approved of, if he had still been alive.

"I'll be honest with you," Disraeli went on. "A career in politics would have no pleasure for me and would be of little use to you, unless I played the high game in public life; and I could not do that without being on a rock. It is impossible to play the great game unless your income is clear. I only require enough money for that; no more and no less. If you and your brother cannot help me then I will have to find someone else or give up hopes of high office. I am quite willing to pay your father a visit and explain the situation to him."

Lord Henry was horrified at the thought of alienating Disraeli and undermining Lord George's many years of work in the House of Commons for the want of a few thousand pounds. He was equally horrified by the thought of how Disraeli would be received if he turned up at Welbeck to see the duke.

"Please say nothing to my father at this stage," he begged. "I'll see what I can do."

They continued talking together for four hours, by the end of which time Disraeli felt confident that Lord Henry was as devoted to the fight as his deceased brother had been. It merely remained to be seen if he was able to convince the increasingly reclusive marquess of Titchfield of the validity of the cause.

"I wonder if you would do something for me," Disraeli said as their conversation was drawing to a close.

"Anything that is in my power," Lord Henry replied, anxious to provide any service he could to a man he was growing to admire more and more.

"It will seem like a sentimental request, coming from a man such as myself."

"I'm sure not," Lord Henry said, curious as to what he was about to hear.

"Your brother wrote me a final letter that I received just yesterday."

"Yes?"

"I wonder, might I prevail upon you to let me have the pen that he wrote it with as a keepsake."

"Of course. I'll speak to his manservant. I'm sure he'll know the pen."

"And might it be possible to have a lock of his hair as a keepsake?" Disraeli smiled disarmingly, aware that such sentimentality would mystify a man from a family like the Cavendish-Bentincks.

"I will speak to the undertaker," Lord Henry said, a little stiffly, wondering for the first time whether Mr. Disraeli really was cut out for high office.

Lord Henry then returned to Welbeck to see his brother, explaining Disraeli's reaction to their suggestion. Lord John remained silent and thoughtful throughout, making his younger brother fearful that he was going to throw up new complications. Lord Henry had no inclination to go and see his father over such a matter. The duke had become increasingly irascible and irrational since the death of their brother.

"I think that we should honor the spirit that this transaction was entered into by George," Lord John said eventually. "It will be awkward to raise the money just at the moment, but I think Disraeli is right; we should treat it as a political matter, not a business one, and we should not involve His Grace."

Lord Henry gave a sigh of relief. "I agree," he said. "And I'm willing to sell my stud in order to raise the cash quickly."

"Very well." Lord John nodded his agreement. He was anxious

for the meeting to be over. He was only willing to even consider backing Disraeli in order to honor his brother's commitments.

Despite his feelings, he'd been impressed by what he'd heard of Disraeli and by what Lord Henry had told him had been said during the course of their meeting. He felt sure it was in the family's interests to maintain the man's climb to power.

Toby Keene was by no means a revolutionary. He had no wish to overthrow the aristocracy. He wasn't even a muckraker in the sense that he enjoyed stirring up scandals. If anything, his curiosity was stimulated by his respect for the great families of England. As a writer who often sold his pieces to the newspapers, he felt certain that the death of Lord George Bentinck deserved more coverage in print than it had received. The man was a national hero, for heaven's sake, and yet the editors chose to give him no more than a few paragraphs of formal obituary after he'd been found propped up against a gate in the middle of nowhere, dead in his prime. It didn't seem respectful to simply announce that the man of such stature had died and was no more. There must be more to be written on the subject than that.

He decided, with no mischievous intentions, to make contact with the duke of Portland and offer to write a more fitting tribute in the way of a story about Lord George and his family.

To that end he sent several letters to the duke, both at Welbeck and at his London address, and received no response from His Grace at either abode. A little peeved by this lack of graciousness, but putting it down to absence of mind caused by an unsettling level of grief for the loss of a favored child, Toby allowed a decent time to elapse between the last of his letters and setting out to Welbeck to call on the duke in person. He felt certain that when His Grace realized that Toby's intentions were entirely aboveboard and honorable, he'd be happy to talk about his favorite son, and would no doubt introduce him to other members of the family, possibly even opening the family archives and allowing the writer access to some of their secrets. He had no doubt that, once he had the story, there would be any number of London editors who would be delighted to buy it from him.

He approached Welbeck on foot, believing this would be the best way to drink in the atmosphere of the estate in order to provide material for background color. It was only once the house had come into sight, while still a great distance away, that he began to feel misgivings about his mission. Everything about Welbeck Abbey seemed to have been designed and built especially to intimidate mere mortals who dared to approach its doors with anything approaching self-confidence. The sheer enormity of the place contrived to remind any who set eyes on it of their own insignificance, in size, mortality, and social stature. This place had stood for centuries and would still be there for many more centuries, long after Toby Keene and several generations of his descendants had vanished from the face of the earth. It also seemed, at that moment, likely that the Cavendish-Bentinck family, or their bloodline, would also still be there in centuries to come, as they had been for generations past.

Despite being something of a man of the world, at home in most situations, Toby couldn't deny that he felt intimidated as he approached the gigantic front door. He wondered if perhaps he should make his way to a side door, something of a more human scale that would not make him feel like a flea approaching the leg of a mammoth. He decided to persevere with a full-frontal attack, found a bell pull, and tugged on it. No doubt a ringing had been set off somewhere in the bowels of the house, but nothing disturbed the stillness and silence of the long, polished front door step. Just as he was about to turn and walk around to the side of the house in search of a more accessible entrance, he detected a rustle of activity within and the door swung open to reveal a footman.

"Is His Grace in?" Toby asked, the smile on his face withering beneath the heat of the footman's expressionless stare.

"Do you have an appointment?" the man enquired, in a voice that suggested he knew very well Toby had no such thing.

"I've written to His Grace a number of times," Toby said, trying to remain cheerful, although he could hear how weak his self-justification sounded. "It's about writing an appreciation of Lord George."

"His Grace does not see anyone without an appointment." The footman started to close the door.

"If you could just tell him I'm here," Toby said, hoping his words would stop the swing of the door.

"What name, sir?" the footman enquired, in a bored voice, as if he knew this was going to be a waste of his time.

"Toby Keene." Toby proffered an engraved visiting card, which the man took before grudgingly standing back a few inches to allow Toby to pass into the gigantic hall.

"Please wait here," he said and then left, at a sedate pace. Nothing happened for what seemed like hours as Toby stood, resisting the temptation to run out the door and back to London as fast as his legs would carry him. Eventually he heard the sound of slow footsteps approaching again and the same man returned to inform him that the duke was still not receiving visitors and that His Grace did not wish to make an appointment with Mr. Keene for the future, either.

Toby opened his mouth to protest but the front door had already been swung back and he could see he was meant to leave. The feelings of intimidation that he had experienced on his way to the house were now replaced by annoyance. He felt he had been snubbed and treated badly. He could quite understand why the duke might not have wanted to see him that day, but the lack of a response to his letters now rankled him. He walked out the door without saying another word and strode down the steps onto the long drive that would lead him back to the village. The farther he walked, the more angry and humiliated he felt.

He'd been walking through the grounds for only about ten minutes when he came across a man felling a tree. The man had stopped his work to take a break, his wife having brought him some bread and a flask of water. The woman had stayed to share the meal with her husband and both of them greeted the stranger in a friendly manner as he walked by. Having just suffered such a chilly rebuff at the house, Toby was particularly susceptible to their openness and warmth. They offered him some of their food, which he accepted with pleasure. As he sat with them under the shade of the trees that were still standing, he told them why he had come to Welbeck.

They stared at him in silence as they ate their simple meal.

"You don't want to go asking questions about the family," the man said eventually. "They don't like it."

Toby nodded as if he understood and tried a few more questions in the course of an apparently casual conversation, but the couple pretended not to hear him. After an hour or so he continued on his walk into Worksop and made his way to the Royal Lion, where he asked for a room. He didn't feel ready to abandon his story just yet. If he couldn't get anyone at Welbeck to talk to him, then he would build up a picture of Lord George from the local population. It might well be a more accurate depiction in the long run.

He stayed at the inn for four days, unable to find anyone willing to talk to him. He was on the verge of returning to London, defeated, when he found himself sitting next to a man who he was told worked on the estate. By that time the locals had grown used to the sight of him in the corner of the saloon and some of them were beginning to relax and talk to him as if he was one of them. He brought up the subject of Lord George's tragic end with the man, after supplying him with a large ale.

"I was one of them that carried Lord George's body back to the house," the man said. "He was in a sorry state. They said he died of a spasm to the heart, which perhaps he did, but it looked like he'd been in a fight as well. He was covered in bruises. No one mentioned that in the newspapers."

"You think he might have been attacked?" Toby felt his heart miss a beat. He hadn't expected anything like this.

"People say he was seen with Lord John and a couple of other men just before he died," the man said.

"Lord John?" Toby asked.

"The marquess of Titchfield; Lord George's elder brother. The one who inherits everything when the old man goes. The one who'll become the fifth duke."

"So, Lord John would have seen whatever happened to his brother?"

"Possibly. No one knows."

"There's no love lost between those two," another man chipped in, emboldened by the knowledge that Toby was buying drinks. "Everyone knows that."

"You mean it could have been a fight between the two of them that caused Lord George's death?" Toby couldn't believe what he was hearing. The men were warming to their subject.

"There are those who say the two of them are in love with the same woman," the first man confided, lowering his voice as if fearful of spies. "A woman called Annie May."

"Who's she?" Toby asked.

"I wouldn't know," he replied. "I'm just telling you what

people are saying. There have been all sorts of arguments in that house over the years—arguments about money, arguments about politics."

"But no one's going to write anything like that in any of the newspapers," the second man said, with a world-weary chuckle.

"Perhaps they should," Toby said, and a look of alarm passed between the two workers.

"Nah," the first man said after a moment's reflection. "No one's going to go against the duke of Portland, are they?"

"If this death was an act of violence, then the story should be told," Toby said, beginning to sense that he was becoming part of something bigger than he had imagined, that he might have a story here that would gain him a place in the history books.

The two men looked at him as if he was a simpleton and went back to drinking in silence.

Two days later Toby was sitting in the office of the editor of the *Morning Post*. He could see that he had the man's full attention. One of the reasons anyone would decide to work on a newspaper, even in the days when every story had to be respectful of the ruling classes, was the undying allure of the good story. This one had everything: two of the richest and most powerful brothers in England fighting over a mystery woman and one of the brothers, a potential future prime minister, dying as a result of an unlucky blow. The murder, if such it was, was then hushed up by the father of the two brothers, a man of unimaginable wealth and influence.

"Mr. Keene," the editor said eventually, once Toby had reached the end of his story. "There is nothing I would like better than to print your story. It would make my newspaper the talk of every salon and inn in the country. It would also bring every lawyer in the world knocking on my door. About a hundred years ago there was a man called John Wilkes who wrote an article criticizing

Parliament and was taken away to the Tower of London. I have no wish to follow his example."

"If I was to bring enough evidence to defeat any lawyers who might come calling, would you be interested then?"

"No, Mr. Keene, I would not. If you could prove to me beyond a shadow of a doubt that the marquess of Titchfield killed his brother, I should advise you to keep the information to yourself."

Every other editor he spoke to told Toby the same thing. The story he had was evidently unprintable.

9

THE DUKE IS DEAD, LONG LIVE THE DUKE

The fourth duke of Portland's funeral in 1854 was a major social event. Anyone who was anyone was there, and all of them noticed the fifth duke wasn't present to pay his respects to his father. The man who'd been known as the marquess of Titchfield for a quarter of a century was already established in the minds of those who knew of his existence as an eccentric and a recluse, but no one expected him to miss his own father's funeral.

Those who noticed his absence were torn between disappointment at not finally being able to set eyes on the mysterious Lord John, who had now inherited one of the largest private fortunes in the world, and delight at this evidence of hidden family scandals and deep-rooted feuds. Many had heard the whispered rumors that surrounded the death of Lord George, and the stories added to the frisson of excitement that surrounded the whole affair of the funeral attendance.

The fourth duke had finally expired in his bed at Welbeck, having ventured out of the house less and less often in his final years. After the death of Lord George, six years earlier, he seemed to lose all interest in everything, even his dogs and horses. If any of his children inquired whether he would like them to visit him in his apartments, he sent back word that he did not feel up to visits that day. Only his closest servants were allowed to attend to him in the final months of his life.

As his father's funeral procession rolled solemnly through the streets of Marylebone, the part of London owned by the family, the fifth duke was striding distractedly around the house and grounds at Welbeck Abbey, the epicenter of his inheritance. The family vault in London, into which the old man's body would be placed beside that of his beloved son George, was a surprisingly small building in a street that now seemed dingy and narrow compared to the many fine residential streets and squares that the family had built around it more recently.

After the funeral no one could find out what the new duke's plans might be. There was uncertainty in all the houses and estates that he now owned. Would he be selling up the inheritance or any parts of it? Would he be giving some of it to surviving brother and sisters? The many hundreds of people who relied on the Portland estates for their income tried in vain to discover what might lie in the future. As the months passed and nothing happened their fears began to subside. It seemed that the fifth duke was not going to change anything. The traditional rhythm of their lives returned to the steady speed it had held for generations. The new fifth duke spent most of his time at Welbeck, apparently lost in thoughts that no one dared question.

He cut a surprising figure in his top hat and long coat as he strode from one end of the estate to the other. Workers who raised their hats or nodded, or even called out greetings to him, sometimes received curt nods in return, but more often they were ignored, passed by as if they were invisible. Now and then he would alight on someone whose advice he required about some matter and he would be so charming and friendly to them, however lowly their status, that they might have thought they were his closest friends. He seemed not to recognize any of the class barriers that surrounded every echelon of British society at that time, binding it up as tightly as rope around bales of hay; if some people interested him he would talk to them, if they didn't he would ignore them. Minor local dignitaries like the doctor and the rector held no interest for him at all, and so he pretended they didn't exist, leaving them flailing in a swamp of uncertainty and inadequate etiquette.

As he settled into his newly acquired kingdom, his mouthpiece became his valet, a man called William Lewis, who he used to convey all his requests and commands to the outside world. Lewis was happy to take on the task, realizing that it gave him almost unlimited power within Welbeck.

"Have it known around the vicinity," the duke told Lewis one morning, as the man was soaping his master's back in the bathtub, "that when I am out and about on the estate I do not wish to be recognized or greeted by anyone. Should anyone come across me, they are to pass by me with no sign of having seen me at all, as if I were merely a tree in the surrounding landscape. Make it known that anyone who disobeys this order will not have a future at Welbeck."

Lewis sent the message out and it was greeted with a mixture of hilarity and resigned shrugs. They all knew that this duke was going to be very different from those before, but he'd already spoken to enough people on the estate for the word to have spread that he was a good man who looked after the needs of all those who worked for him. For that they were willing to put up with any amount of eccentricity. If the man wished to be ignored and to move around the world ungreeted, who were they to say he was wrong?

From that moment on he was able to walk anywhere he chose across the thousands of acres surrounding the house and he was left alone with his thoughts, untroubled by any obligation to be polite to those he passed, or even to give them a second's consideration if he didn't wish to.

And what thoughts he had turning over in his mind; what plans and dreams and fantasies, what wild schemes to create something that no one had ever done before, at least no one in his position.

Welbeck was a joy for him because of its vast size, which allowed him to disappear into its honeycombs of rooms and corridors. No one could be sure where he was, or even if he was there at all. He could lock himself in his private rooms, communicating with the outside world via Lewis, or he could wander down to the kitchens or the stables or any other part of the house and even Lewis wouldn't be able to keep track of where he was. Of course staff members would notice him passing, but as long as they were under orders not to signify that they had seen him, he could move past them like a ghost, feeling invisible and hidden, even though he was still as corporeal as they. The household staff were not a problem anyway. They'd all been working in the house for years and their discretion could be relied upon. They lived in their own little world, a society in a bubble, separated from the outside world by the fact that they lived and worked within the confines of the house and seldom had cause to discuss with outsiders anything they saw. In many cases they'd grown so used to the ways of the Portland family that they would see nothing remarkable in anything the duke did anyway. No, they were definitely not the problem.

The problem was going to come from the outside. If he wished to maintain his privacy and move around the world as and when he wanted, away from prying eyes, then he needed to find ways of getting on and off the estate without anyone seeing him. First, he ordered new carriages. They were to be sealed with curtains so that anyone seeing them pass would have no idea if they carried the duke, were going to fetch him, were carrying a messenger for him, or perhaps were nothing more than a ruse to confuse onlookers, traveling around the countryside empty. Like the deceiving hands of a conjurer these machinations would confuse his audience about his real movements.

The duke had the carriages made as small and lightweight as possible, so they could be lifted on and off a private train, which would wait for him at Worksop station and could carry him to London without the curtains ever having to be drawn back, maintaining the illusion and guarding his privacy. By the time the carriage was unloaded in London no one would know from where it had come or to whom it belonged. It was by no means a foolproof plan, but it made him feel less exposed and more able to conduct his life as he wanted. He also needed the carriages to be small because he had another plan for how he might be able to make them appear and disappear as and when he wanted.

To make it easier to load the carriages onto the train he collected six black ponies to pull them and hired young boys the size of jockeys to be his coachmen. By miniaturizing his entourage, he made the sight all the more extraordinary for anyone who witnessed it. He was not a small man and only just fit inside the tiny coaches, but he felt secure traveling in their darkened wombs. Sometimes, when rolling through the neighboring villages, he would pull back the curtains so he could talk to the children he saw playing outside. They would crowd around happily to answer his questions or to run messages for him; none of them seemed to share the adults' wariness of the great, mad aristocrat. If they prevailed upon him enough he would climb out of his carriage to organize games for them; for instance, he would set up races and work out the head starts that the older children should allow for the younger ones. If he didn't have time to stop the carriage, he would toss handfuls of silver coins out to the children as he passed, leaving them scrabbling after them in the dust.

If he saw a woman or an old man struggling with a heavy load, he would never fail to stop and give them a lift to their destination, even if it took him out of his way. The lack of space meant that they were almost sitting on their master's lap, but he appeared unconcerned by the intimacy. With these small and spontaneous acts of humanity and kindness he built a reputation in the area, and a great affection for him grew as the stories circulated.

But the carriage and the train were only an interim measure while he hatched a master plan for guarding his privacy still further. Messages started to be sent out from Welbeck, via the faithful Lewis, summoning the finest architects and engineers then working in the burgeoning Victorian Empire that would dominate the world for the second half of the nineteenth century. Many of them were then working on the mighty construction project for the London Underground system, which was then one of the marvels of the modern world. Armies of men were burrowing beneath the houses of one of the world's greatest cities to create a network of tunnels that would carry the people around the city with unprecedented speed, taking them away from the streets above with their congested cobbles and piles of horse manure.

At the same time the engineers who had planned and constructed the great Victorian sewage systems, which had so successfully relieved the stench of the River Thames, were turning their minds to ever greater and more ambitious concepts. The modern world was taking shape, albeit slowly, and the visionaries of the time were beside themselves with excitement at what would soon be possible. The duke read of all these developments and visited many of them. They fired his imagination and made him hungry to harness the power of modern technology and make it the servant of his own imagination. He wanted to create a private world for himself every bit as magical and hidden as what was going on beneath London.

No one who received a summons from a title as lofty as the fifth duke of Portland's would for a moment consider refusing to respond. The experts came from every corner of England to listen to what he had to say. They followed him around the estate, many of them having to run to keep up with his enthusiastic strides, as he pointed to distant horizons, stretched his arms in exaggerated descriptions, and outlined to them his plans, which were growing from month to month to rival the work of the Egyptian pharaohs. He would then take them back to the house and pore over sketches and diagrams that he had drawn in attempts to show the world his visions.

The fifth duke of Portland was starting to envisage an underground palace almost as mighty as the existing house, a subterranean mirror image of the mighty structure that towered above ground, with underground passages stretching out to the corners of the estate like the tentacles of an octopus, allowing him to travel to the outside world without anyone on the estate knowing he had even left the house. The more he talked and the more he listened to the experts, the bigger and bolder his plans became. The statistics and the costs were growing with every projection; but what was the point of presiding over a mighty fortune if you didn't use it to create work for the people who depended upon you? And if they were going to work, should they not put their efforts into an undertaking that would make them proud? Something about which they would be able to spin tales that would amaze their children and their grandchildren?

It was going to be magnificent. The succession of great architects who came to the house led to speculation in the local press.

The speculation grew and eventually it was reported as fact that the fifth duke intended to pull down the great Welbeck Abbey and replace it with a new mansion on a more elevated and healthier site. The park around the house, which was then around eight miles in circumference, was, they reported breathlessly, going to be "enlarged and improved."

In fact the duke had absolutely no such intention, but it bothered him not a jot what the chattering classes might be saying. He was beginning to develop a vision of the future that would stun everyone who eventually saw it, a building that would become probably the most costly in the country at the time.

He wanted to set the existing house in grounds planned along the most modern principles of landscape gardening, but he was hampered by the fact that some years before, his father, believing there would one day be a shortage of oak, had planted trees wherever he could, with little thought to the obstructed views and vistas that might be the outcome of their profuse growth. One of the fifth duke's first jobs was going to be to clear the excess woods and lay out some of the most perfect kitchen gardens in the kingdom. He set to the task with a gusto that left his army of gardeners breathless.

10

GOING UNDERGROUND

The book had lain beside the duke's bed for several years, ever since it was published in 1852. Every so often he would pick it up, flick idly through the pages, sigh deeply and put it down again, telling himself he would one day spend the time reading the whole thing, if only out of respect for his deceased brother. The author was Benjamin Disraeli, a man the duke still found himself thinking of as a novelist, even though Disraeli had by then served as chancellor of the exchequer, a job second only in importance to that of the prime minister and giving him control of the entire British economy, and Leader of the House. The subject of the book was Lord George. It was a biography and had been a labor of love for the distinguished author and statesman; as well as an exorcism of his grief. The duke thought it a trifle vulgar to commit such private emotions to print, and was not comfortable with the idea of his brother's life being sold at bookshops.

He still found it hard to think for any length of time about Lord George; he preferred to block out of his mind the mixed feelings that the memories evoked and rather to concentrate on other, more creative matters. There were too many things about Lord George's life and death that made the duke uneasy about himself and about his place in the world. Finally, in 1857, five years after the book was published, the duke, while confined to bed with an uncomfortable head cold, managed to steel himself to reading it. He turned the pages quickly, giving the odd snort of disbelief and the occasional sigh of despair. The fact that he wasn't mentioned once in the whole text brought a mixture of indignation and relief. When he reached the final sentence, in which the author described his book as "the portraiture of an English Worthy," the duke snapped it shut and hurled it across the room, making Lewis, his valet, jump.

"Get it out of my sight," the duke commanded, and Lewis abandoned the work he was doing in his master's wardrobe, scooped up the book, and left the room.

The duke sank back into the pillow and blew his nose violently, as if trying to cleanse himself of the whole distasteful experience. The sycophantic tone of the writing had made him feel even more ill. How could any man who wrote such drivel be able to hold high office? To think that George and Henry had talked him into lending the wretched man £25,000 to bolster his wretched career. How much he would have preferred to use that money to pay honest workers for their toils around Welbeck. How many families could be fed for a year with such a sum? Honest, hard-working people who had put in years perfecting a trade or a craft. Why should the money be squandered on allowing a self-serving politician to pose as a gentleman?

The duke decided, then and there, that he would demand the money back. He was well aware that neither of his brothers had intended to call in the loan, that it was meant as a gift, but he loathed the idea of a politician living off the fat of the land in such a way. Let the man go out and earn his own keep. The duke had always thought of himself as a Peelite and had only been persuaded to play a part in Peel's downfall by his brother's force of personality. Now, he decided, was the time to shrug off George's influence once and for all. He rang for Lewis to come back and sent him off with a hastily scrawled letter.

When the letter arrived at its destination, Disraeli was momentarily aghast. Financial problems seemed to have dogged him all his life and now, just as he'd thought he was safely settled and able to lead the life of a gentleman without worry, the damned duke of Portland who, according to every report Disraeli had heard, was going quite mad, had pulled the rug out from under his feet. He notified Lord Henry of what was going on and the duke's younger brother hurried to see him, assuring him he would do everything to make sure that Disraeli did not lose Hughenden.

"It would be as well for you to get out of the clutches of my brother," Lord Henry warned him. "I do not think he can be trusted with regard to Hughenden."

Disraeli looked surprised to hear a brother talking in such a way, particularly one from a family he held in such reverence. He had expected Lord Henry to find any number of excuses for the duke's behavior.

Lord Henry could see his surprise and shrugged. "I'm disappointed in the duke," he admitted. "I have been mistaken in my man. We must get clear of our obligation to him as quickly as possible. We certainly don't want to be negotiating with him. I don't think he would take a reasonable position in those circumstances."

Disraeli had no choice but to allow Lord Henry to do as he saw fit, but he took the precaution of researching other possible avenues of financial backing. The more he heard about the Bentinck family, the more he realized they were not to be relied upon. They seemed to take up causes with enormous fervor and then lose interest just as quickly. He'd heard tales of how Lord Henry, who was now even more fanatical about hunting than Lord George had been, spent every daylight hour that he was at Welbeck out with the hounds.

He'd also heard that the duke was making the most extraordinary plans for some sort of underground city beneath the estate. To rely on such people to the exclusion of all others would have been deeply unwise.

The local population around Welbeck were becoming accustomed to the duke and his unusual ways. The plans that he and his architects were drawing up had started to come to fruition and the estate and neighboring villages were teeming with workmen imported to supplement the local population. At the height of the construction works there were thought to be fifteen hundred people digging and building around the house and grounds. The tunnels from the house to the gates were high enough and wide enough for two full-sized carriages to pass one another, let alone the duke's miniaturized versions, and were the wonder of all who saw them; but they were no longer the high-point of the scheme. There were now vast subterranean rooms being planned, including a chapel that would later be changed to a ballroom, which would be the largest unsupported structure in the world.

"What does he want a ballroom like that for?" some of the older household staff would mutter to one another. "He never invites anyone to the house. He never throws any parties."

In truth, the duke simply wanted to build the room for the joy of the undertaking. He claimed it would be somewhere that young bachelors could make as much noise as they liked without disturbing other people in the house. Yet there were already plenty of rooms above ground that could fulfill that requirement. The room was big enough to comfortably house every bachelor within a hundred miles, none of whom had been invited to stay while the fifth duke was in residence.

But the practicality of the project was not relevant, either to the duke or to the hordes of men working for him. The point was simply the achievement of something extraordinary, a construction that would amaze all who saw it and heard about it. In that they succeeded without question.

The underground plans were not the only constructions under way on the Welbeck estate at the time. The duke was also building a new servants' wing to the house, new kennels for the hounds, new cottages for workers, and a new dairy, as well as the finest of all possible riding schools and a track to gallop the horses. Although he rode less and less often himself, the duke had retained his great fondness for horses, like his father and brothers. Dozens of the most beautiful animals in England were stabled around Welbeck and could be seen on any bright sunny morning, walking in long lines, two abreast with their grooms as they were moved to fresh pastures. The horses were treated with the same respect as the tenants; none of the grooms were allowed to use whips. There were lodges being built at every corner of the estate, as well as new walls around the gardens.

"The reason for putting these structures underground," the duke explained to Lord Henry when his brother asked what the point of the whole process was, "is to avoid desecrating the views of the existing house."

He would then walk away quickly before his brother could respond. While he was anxious to impress his peers with the magnificence of his dreams, he did not feel robust enough to face their possible criticism or ridicule.

The duke was at his most comfortable with the men who toiled on his projects, particularly since it was now well known that he did not wish to be greeted or deferred to by anyone unless he actually spoke to them. He would spend his days walking among them, talking about the work and about themselves, finding out what they needed and wanted and then providing it for them. His reputation as an employer and benefactor was second to none. He made sure his full-time employees had the best accommodations it was possible to construct and that they wanted for nothing. Visiting workers stayed in caravans, the Irish forming a camp for themselves, which was known as Sligo by the locals. (The navvies from the surrounding area and the Irish visitors were prone to get into fights if they were allowed to mix.)

To provide the workforce with a distraction from their labors on his behalf, the duke constructed a massive roller-skating rink, close to the boathouse, something that a hundred years later would be big enough to serve as a small airfield, and he insisted that all his servants and workers be given time to use it, whether they asked to or not. Roller-skating was a new craze at the time, imported from America. The duke was always attracted to anything new and different. He also provided boats for the use of staff. He sometimes stood in the shrubberies issuing orders on the best way to row as the self-conscious staff attempted to relax.

Household staff were instructed to take piano lessons, so they could entertain the duke in the evenings, when he finally grew tired of his own company and emerged from his private rooms in search of distraction.

The outdoor workers were catered for in mess rooms that sprang up around the estate, but the numbers were so enormous that they had to be fed in shifts. At the hours when the bulk of the force came to work or finished for the day, the small country roads across the estate and into the villages became clogged with lines of men talking and laughing, their tools over their shoulders. Sometimes the roads were so clogged with bodies that the men would spill out across the grass, climbing over the fences as they made their way home. The duke could see them from the windows of Welbeck when he was staring out, planning where to plant new trees and remove existing ones. He could also see the muddy tracks they left across the perfect green acres and issued strict instructions, via Lewis, that the practice of cutting across the grass was to stop forthwith.

The older or weaker men had donkeys supplied to them by the duke, and they plodded slowly about their business atop the beasts, often with long bundles of grass that they'd picked during their meal breaks and were taking home to feed their mounts. When the men were working, their donkeys would graze on the grasslands around the main laundry, continually braying in the hope of attracting someone with more interesting food.

Being all day among working-class people, the duke saw no need to slavishly follow fashion when he was at Welbeck. He did not care how the most popular tailors were dressing people in London; he had a style of his own with which he was perfectly comfortable and saw no reason to change. He was almost never seen outside the house without a hat of unusual height upon his head, which served to make him even more conspicuous among the army of men in their singlets and caps. He would also wear long thick coats whatever the weather. The colder it became, the more layers of coats and cloaks he would pull on, allowing them to flap and wave in the wind and adding to the drama and eccentricity of his appearance. He always wore old-fashioned shirts with high collars and double frills, some of them slightly stiffened with starch, much as he had since he was a young man, in a way he was most particular about, and sometimes a wrapped scarf around his neck.

When putting out clothes for Lewis to take down to the laundry staff, he would pin instructions to the various items, informing them exactly how he wanted them to be washed and starched.

In society the eccentricity of his dress was often remarked upon and sniggered over. He had actually appeared at a race meeting in the height of summer one year wearing a full-length fur coat, causing considerable amazement and mirth among the fashionable classes. It had been one of his last appearances in public; he felt he could no longer be bothered with their foolish vanities and idle ways. He had become deeply abstemious in his own habits, never eating more than two meals a day, and then only eating chicken. He would have a bird a day slaughtered when he was in residence at Welbeck, eating half for his luncheon and half in the evening.

Being among the workingmen, he saw that there were practical advantages to some of the things they did. Because of the acres of mud that the excavations threw up all over the grounds, particularly during the expansion of the lakes and the construction of the reservoir, the men would tie up their trouser legs to keep them out of the dirt. The duke copied the style and found it to be so satisfactory that he had his tailor sew straps below the knees of all his trousers so he could tie them up as a matter of course every time he left the house to walk around the grounds. He would wear boots with cork soles to help keep himself out of the mud, and always had on three pairs of socks, silk ones next to the skin with thicker ones outside.

The rain at Welbeck was a constant source of annoyance to him. It would teem down on the poor men as they trudged through the mud, trying to keep the torrents of water from filling up the trenches and holes as soon as they were dug. The duke became an avid admirer of the umbrella. Not only would he carry one with him at all times, summer and winter, just in case it should start to rain, but he would order huge quantities of them, which he would pass out to the laborers during storms.

Every labor-saving device that was invented would find its way onto the Welbeck estate. The duke ordered one of the first traction engines, which was used for heavy work like uprooting trees and bringing in the hay. He purchased steam plows, too; the primitive engines would often become defeated by the mud and would have to be rescued by horses, but these setbacks never dimmed the duke's enthusiasm for the new and experimental.

While the men labored on the construction, the women would work on the landscape, planting and watering the trees, which the men were later instructed to dig up and move, sometimes transferring whole woodlands from one part of the estate to another. The duke would recruit gangs of children to help him collect chestnuts, both for planting and eating, and for feeding to the herds of deer that roamed the parks. Many of the deer had become so used to His Grace, who frequently fed them biscuits and buns during his walks, that they would come up to him like dogs, begging for table scraps.

He would walk with the children through the woods as they filled their baskets. They would be less aware of the edict not to talk to their lord and master, but His Grace never seemed to mind, happy to answer their simple questions as he worked with them.

One morning a young boy from the estate, named Albert, was standing watching the construction work being undertaken on the roof of the new riding school when he was startled to be called by name from some distance. He looked around and saw that the duke was standing by the house and beckoning him over. The boy did as he was told.

"I need your help, Albert," the duke told him. "We're going to have a bonfire."

With no further words His Grace turned and strode into the house, Albert trotting at his heel. They made their way down corridors and up staircases, until Albert began to wonder if he would ever find his way out again. Eventually the duke led him into a room that had all its shutters tightly bolted. As the boy's eyes slowly accustomed to the darkness, he could make out the shapes of paintings, stacks of them on all sides.

"We're going to clear the room and burn this lot," the duke informed him, taking off his coat and rolling up his sleeves.

All day long they labored together, carrying the pictures out into the sunlight. Occasionally, the duke decided he liked a frame and he would produce a knife from his pocket and slice the canvas out, tossing it onto a pile with the others and carefully stacking the frame that was to be spared from the flames.

By midafternoon the room was empty and the pile was so high that they had to hurl the pictures toward the sky to make them land on the top of the heap. Albert stared in amazement at the portraits and landscapes, dog pictures and horse pictures, and scenes from lands he had never heard of as they lay where they had been thrown. The duke was bright-eyed and flushed from the exercise and with the exhilaration of the effort.

"Come on," the duke said. "There're more in the stables." And he set off again at a brisk pace, with Albert scurrying behind.

The light had almost faded by the time they'd finished heaping the old pictures up, and the duke handed Albert a burning torch with all the ceremony of an Olympic athlete.

"Light the pyre, Albert," he commanded, and the boy thrust the torch into the base of the pile. The parched old oil canvases sucked the flames up greedily and sparks rose thirty or forty feet into the night sky, making the boy laugh and clap his hands with pleasure.

"Excellent, Albert," the duke said, slapping his coconspirator on the shoulder as they stood admiring their handiwork. "We should do this more often. There is a great deal of rubbish that needs to be burned in this place!"

The duke occupied a single set of rooms in the house, but it still required a permanent household staff of twenty or more to maintain the place, running the kitchens and the laundry. Servants who bumped into His Grace as they went about their business were instructed to ignore him, just as those outside the house were instructed. Most of the women would freeze with their eyes fixed to the floor, or dive through the nearest doorways if they saw him coming down a corridor toward them.

At times, however, he would develop an interest inside the house and would be as amiable to them as he was to the workmen outside. He had a plan for building a railway system between the dining room and the kitchens, to help the staff to move food back and forth with speed, since serving cold food was always a problem in the grand houses of the time. The trams were designed to carry a complete course for ten people on each journey, even though the duke never entertained anyone to a meal. There was also the question of the elevators to be installed between the ground floor and the network of grottoes that were springing up among the foundations of the house, linking the above-ground interiors to the burgeoning underground rooms and carriageways to the outside world.

Lord Henry, if he was in residence, would occupy his own set of rooms, but the two brothers seldom met. If they needed to communicate they would send letters via their valets, just as their father had done before them.

If the duke did not appear at his excavations for a while, no one on the outside of the house had any way of knowing whether he was merely staying in his rooms, struck down perhaps by some infection or virus, or whether he had been spirited away to London in his closed carriage, along the first of the tunnels to be completed. His absences could sometimes stretch into weeks but life at Welbeck continued uninterrupted whether he was there or not.

When he was in London he was equally hard to find, secreting himself in his town abode, Harcourt House, at 19 Cavendish

Square, at the heart of the family's London estate. The house was surrounded with walls far too high for anyone to be able to ascertain whether or not the duke was in residence, and a porter's lodge guarded the gates from any curious intruders. The duke's invisibility added to his mystery and many myths sprang up around the eccentric nobleman. London cab drivers used to take their passengers on detours past the house and tell them about a glass coffin that was kept on the roof, waiting for the duke's body, and any number of other fairy tales that created enough of a sense of wonder in their passengers to elicit a generous tip.

The story of the glass coffin grew until it was widely believed that a dead body was being kept at the house. In the end the rumors became so strong that a sanitary official paid a formal visit to investigate whether there might be a health hazard, but could find no such body in evidence. The rumors continued to proliferate about why the mysterious fifth duke was so seldom sighted in public and what he might be getting up to in private.

One rumor that never quite seemed to be dispelled was the one that suggested there was a tunnel running from behind the walls of Harcourt House to the Baker Street Bazaar a few blocks away, the emporium belonging to Thomas Druce, a man almost as mysterious as the fifth duke himself.

11

A PAUPER'S GRAVE

enry Druce, Thomas and Elizabeth's eldest son, had had nothing else to do with his father since 1837, when he finished at the school to which he had been sent. It wasn't that he particularly hated the man for the way he'd left him, his mother, and his siblings all those years ago; actually, he didn't give the matter that much thought. He had no memory of Thomas ever being around as a father for him when he was a child, and he had no idea what had happened to make his father leave when he did. He certainly didn't feel that he would ever be able to ask Thomas why he'd deserted them so completely for all those years, and why he'd allowed Elizabeth and his children to sink into poverty when he himself was obviously a man of considerable means. Henry didn't return to the Baker Street Bazaar after graduating because it didn't seem that he and his father had anything in common anymore and he was anxious to get back to the independent life that he had already launched himself on before his father had made contact.

Thomas Druce was a difficult man for most people to communicate with, particularly a young man trying to be respectful to a distant and unfamiliar father figure. There were so many areas that they couldn't talk about. Neither of them had the courage to discuss Elizabeth or the other children. So it was as if the family didn't exist. Henry didn't like to ask any personal questions about the Baker Street Bazaar or about Annie May, who seemed to be living with his father as a wife. (Annie May didn't give birth to Herbert until 1846.) Thomas simply wasn't the sort of man who encouraged personal conversation of any sort. On his part, Thomas couldn't think of a single thing to say to the young man who just happened to be his firstborn son, unless it was to give instructions of some sort. So neither made any effort to develop the relationship.

Henry had no idea what had happened to his brother or his sister since their father had spirited them away. He'd raised the subject once but had received a noncommittal reply that left him with the impression that they too were being looked after and that it was therefore none of his business where they were or what they were doing. Henry left matters there, feeling that if he pressed his father for details he would merely ignite a wrath that would come between them forever.

The school that Thomas had chosen for Henry was a good one and, despite being older than most of the other boys there, he did well. The fact that he was from a very different background and could neither read nor write was compensated for in the eyes of his peers by the tales he could tell about life at sea and by the glamour of early adulthood, which clung to him, in stark contrast to their cosseted, childish lives. One or two of the boys tried to make fun of his lack of education, but none of them was any match for a young man who'd learned how to defend himself during three years at sea.

They would ask him continually to tell and retell his stories and, as he did, he realized how much he missed life aboard the *Prince of Wales*. He couldn't imagine a lifetime of confinement to the land and to the rainy shores of England, and he determined, once he'd finished the education that his father had bought for him, to return to the navy, this time old enough and sufficiently qualified to gain a rank as a junior officer. He wanted to see for himself the world he was hearing about in his geography and history lessons.

Once Henry finished school, now aged twenty, he paid his mother a visit. Finding Elizabeth hunched in a chair in the corner of her one-room shack, he was shocked by how ancient she had grown in the seven years since he had left, even though she was, in fact, still only thirty-seven years old. He was surprised to find that both Charles and Frances had disappeared from her life without any sort of contact, even though he had done the same thing himself. Elizabeth told him that Thomas was taking care of them. Not knowing that Frances had been told that her mother was dead, he was angry by his sister's apparent negligence toward Elizabeth. While young men were expected to go out into the world to seek their fortunes, young women were not supposed to abandon their mothers without so much as a letter or a visit.

Henry spent several days chopping wood and mending some of the leaks in the roof before setting off once more to sea. He didn't bother to see his father to say good-bye, or even to write him a letter. It troubled him that his mother had no idea where his brother and sister were, but he assured her, when she asked him, that their father would be sure to have looked after their best interests, as he had Henry's. It also troubled him to see his mother in such a lonely, impoverished state, and he swore to himself that he would make sure he sent money back to her regularly, aware that he hadn't done so in the past, despite his good intentions. The idea of escaping to sea, leaving his divided and troubled family behind, became increasingly attractive and, once he'd actually procured himself a posting and set out to see the world, he found himself thinking less and less about his home country and his childhood. There was so much planning to do for the future, so many places to visit and so many experiences that he would have. Within months he found that he needed all the money he earned to support himself. The picture of his mother in the one-room shack grew more faded in his mind. Occasionally his conscience would trouble him as he lay in his hammock on some distant sea and he told himself he would put things right the moment they docked at their next port of call. But it somehow became harder and harder to do so.

Elizabeth bore no grudges against any of her children. In fact, she was relieved they'd escaped from the life she was trapped in. She worried sometimes about Frances, knowing how vulnerable young girls could be to the idle promises of men, but then she remembered that Fanny was in the care of her father, and she told herself that fathers always took care to protect their daughters and that returned her peace of mind to her. She chose to forget how helpless her own father had been in the face of Thomas's determination and her own foolishness.

Her health grew worse with each winter, the damp air of the cottage clogging her lungs and making her joints ache. She spent much of her time huddled beside the fire, wrapped in as many shawls as she could find, rocking gently back and forth and humming to herself. It was as if nature were dulling the pain of her disappointment with life by dimming her mind.

In 1851 Henry arrived at Portsmouth after being away for several years and decided that he must pay his mother a visit and take her some money. He traveled up by train and coach, looking forward to seeing the excitement on the old woman's face as he came in through the door. He intended to stay for a few weeks in order to do all the chores that she needed. He was disappointed to find the little house locked up and silent. Peering in through the grubby windows he could just make out the shape of his mother's furniture and belongings inside, but there was no sign of life. Water had managed to infiltrate the roof in several places and everything was covered in a mixture of dust and mold. Wondering if perhaps she'd been taken ill and removed to a hospital, he made his way to the vicarage and knocked on the door.

The vicar himself answered and, being new to the area, didn't recognize Henry. Henry asked about Elizabeth Druce and whether he knew anything about her whereabouts.

"And who might you be?" the vicar enquired, suspiciously.

"Henry Druce, her eldest son."

The other man's eyebrows arched in surprise. It had never occurred to him that the sad old woman he'd buried in a pauper's grave a few months before had had any family left at all. People in the village had whispered about a scandalous marriage that had broken up some thirty-four years earlier, leaving "Old Mrs. Druce" to go quietly mad on her own. Someone had said they thought there were children from the marriage but assumed they had died.

The vicar, obviously deciding that Henry was not much of a son if he hadn't even known that his mother was dying, pointed him toward the graveyard where Elizabeth lay unmarked and unmourned.

Henry made his way around the church and found the patch that he thought the vicar was referring to. Exhausted from his long journey, he sank down on a nearby gravestone, dropping his kitbag beside him. The wind was cold and a light drizzle made the air wet. It started to soak through his clothes but he barely noticed, used to the feel of wet clothes against his skin.

He must have sat for an hour, remembering his childhood and his mother, yet all the pictures in his memory seemed to be gray and dark. The overwhelming sensations that came back to him were those of cold and hunger. He realized that he hated England and all it stood for. He hated the fact that his mother had been made to live as an outcast and that his father had a rich and comfortable life in London. He hated the miserable climate, and the grinding poverty that most of the people had to live in. He'd seen enough of the world to know that there were better places. There were places where the sun shone all the time, where everyone had a fair chance of success and where everyone was judged by his or her own efforts. He decided that he would leave the navy and he would leave England. He would find passage to Australia, where they were crying out for able men to build the new country, leaving all the misery and pain of his childhood behind him for good. Once he'd reached the decision, he knew he wouldn't change his mind. There was nothing for him in England anymore.

News of Elizabeth's death had arrived in the post at Thomas Druce's home. He read the formal notification over breakfast but said nothing to Annie May until he was clear in his mind what he wanted to do. He went to work at the bazaar as usual and that evening he called in Annie May to see him once Herbert, now five years old, had been settled by the nanny and everything in the house was quiet.

"It seems I'm now free to marry," he said, with an embarrassed cough, aware that the words lacked the dignity that a man of his age and wealth should be able to call upon at all times. "I was wondering if we might consider a wedding in about a month's time."

Annie May smiled sweetly, a pretty blush coming to her cheeks as she lowered her eyes and nodded her agreement to the plan. Although she had no more wish to become a member of society than Thomas did, she was pleased to think that Herbert's parents would be married. She had enjoyed bringing up the baby and liked the idea of having more. If Thomas was willing to marry her, then perhaps he would be willing for her to have more children. It wasn't a subject she would ever have wanted to bring up in conversation, knowing that Thomas would find the voicing of such intimate feelings embarrassing, but she chose to feel optimistic about his opinions of her.

"I don't think we want to make a big fuss," Thomas went on. "We don't want to draw attention to the state of affairs. It would not be fair to Herbert to alert people to the fact that he had been born out of wedlock." He gave another embarrassed cough and Annie May allowed her eyes to fall to the floor again with due modesty.

"Windsor is a pleasant enough little place," Thomas continued. "I think that we should arrange for a ceremony down there."

"That would be very nice, Thomas," Annie May said, her heart bouncing in her chest with excitement.

Not many people needed to know about the wedding, since not many people were interested in the marital affairs of a shopkeeper who never appeared in society. Those who knew Annie May always referred to her as Mrs. Druce anyway. No one in London had been aware of Elizabeth's existence or of the three grown children that Thomas had fathered with her; they were, for all intents and purposes, invisible to the outside world.

Mrs. Tremaine, Frances's caretaker, was one of the few people who knew anything about the first Druce family. Over the years of working for Thomas she'd been entrusted with a number of different jobs that had required her to understand the situation. She was not a judgmental woman and was quite happy to accept people as they were. She'd been delighted to be asked to take care of Frances when she was brought to London, and had watched with approval as Thomas had formed an affection for his daughter. She felt that Frances, now thirty years old, had become her friend and so it was with no malice in her mind at all that she let slip the fact, while the two of them sat sewing together in peaceful companionship one evening, that Thomas and Annie May were planning to get married.

"You mean my father and Annie May aren't married?" Frances asked in surprise.

"Good Lord no, child. They had to wait until your poor mother had passed away."

The silence that fell in the room made Mrs. Tremaine look up from her sewing and in that instant she realized what she had said. Frances's face had lost all its color. She was staring hard at her friend as her mind tried to take in what was being said.

"Do you mean to tell me that my mother has only just died?" she asked. Mrs. Tremaine opened her mouth in order to speak but no words came out, so Frances continued. "Is it not true that she died seventeen years ago, as my father told me?"

Mrs. Tremaine's mouth was still hanging open when Frances, realizing from the reaction that she had been lied to and deceived, ran from the room. Mrs. Tremaine heard the younger woman's footsteps on the stairs and then the bang of her bedroom door slamming shut. Frances lay on her bed, dry-eyed and horrified, imagining how deserted and betrayed her mother must have felt by a daughter who left without a word and never returned. For seventeen years she could have been visiting her mother and bringing her comfort, but all that time she had no idea she was alive. It was a long time before she was even able to cry about it.

The following day, when her father stopped by for tea in the afternoon, she waited until Mrs. Tremaine had left the room and asked him, very politely, if it was true that her mother had only just died. Thomas coughed and spluttered for a while and gave a long explanation about how he had deemed it better for her to believe her mother had died and not to have to worry about her while she was growing up.

Frances thanked him politely for his consideration for her feelings, but assured him he was entirely wrong and that she did not believe she would ever be able to forgive him for having separated her from Elizabeth so deliberately and coldheartedly. Thomas, irritated by her tone and puzzled by her lack of understanding about what had been a difficult decision for him, left the house early that afternoon and did not return for many weeks. He still remained convinced that believing her mother to have been dead was in his daughter's best interests, and dismissed her outburst as hysterics brought on by the discovery. He assumed the mood would pass in time and Frances would see the sense in what he had done.

12

THE DEATH OF MR. DRUCE

Herbert Druce, the illegitimate son of Thomas and Annie May, was eighteen years old when he was told in 1864 that his father was dying. It came as a surprise to the boy. He hadn't even realized that his father was sick. Thomas had always been of delicate health, but most gentlemen who had managed to live past their sixtieth birthdays were in a similar condition. Herbert was used to hearing that his father was feeling a little under the weather; it had not prepared him for the news that soon he would be the proud inheritor of the mighty Baker Street Bazaar and the fortune that it generated.

The British public had taken to the novel idea of a department store. Growing prosperity among the middle classes from the dramatic changes wrought by the industrial revolution had led to a rising demand for household goods, everything from kitchen implements to curtain material, from furniture and rugs to porcelain and fashion. The idea of being able to buy everything under one roof, without having to walk in the dust and dirt of the streets, made the idea of shopping even more attractive. Although Thomas would deny it if anyone asked him, the Bazaar had become immensely profitable.

For a month before Thomas's death there was a great deal of

activity around the house in Hendon. Nurse Bayly, who had been with them for many years, changed her role in the family from being a children's nurse to being a medical nurse for Thomas. She was a warmhearted and efficient woman, and had been a loyal servant to the family. She was happy, now that the children were growing up, to have found a new role in which she could be useful to them.

A hospital nurse was also recruited to assist her in the task of easing Thomas's passage from the world. Doctors came and went from the house and people talked in hushed voices, but nobody thought to confide in Herbert exactly what might be going on. His father seemed to spend most of his time in bed or locked in consultations with his medical advisers. It was a worrying and puzzling time for Herbert and the younger brother and sister who had been born after his parents married.

His mother was, as usual, stoic. Still in her mid-thirties, Annie May was a quiet and dignified woman who accepted her husband's word as law and expected her children to do the same. Following her marriage to Herbert's father she had given birth to a second son, Walter Thomas, who was still, at twelve years of age, too young to take on the responsibilities of business as his father neared death. Walter had been followed a couple of years later by a girl who they'd named Alice.

Herbert, who was already working in the store, learning the routines and skills required to be a successful retail trader, watched in silent amazement as his father, who appeared to be no closer to death than he had been a month or a year earlier, made preparations for his own funeral. A coffin-maker was called to the store and orders were placed. Lead was procured and a number of his father's friends came to the store for meetings behind heavy wooden doors, which Herbert was not allowed to attend.

There were many things in his father's past and present dealings that Herbert did not know about, and many questions that he would never have dared to be impertinent enough to ask. His mother never spoke of personal things to the children, either. They dealt in the polite business of the present and of tangible events, not discussing feelings or speculating about the past or future. Thomas came and went in their lives, a remote authority figure who led a life outside the bazaar that Herbert could only imagine. Thomas was occasionally there for meals, or he would be seen standing at the door of the store, in his top hat and overcoat, nodding politely to customers as they came and went, an aloof, almost royal figure greeting his subjects. Sometimes he would disappear from his family's lives for weeks on end, but no explanation would ever be forthcoming and he would return as if no time had elapsed since he last saw them.

Herbert was entirely unaware that his father had been married before, nor did he know that his parents had been unmarried when he was born. As far as he was concerned, he, Walter, and their younger sister were the only offspring of his parents. He felt no urge to find out any more; that was all he needed to know. Herbert did not wish to complicate his life; he was entirely contented with the way it appeared to be.

Annie May was greatly relieved by her son's lack of curiosity. She was not a dishonest woman by nature and would have found it difficult to tell him a direct lie had he asked her about his father's past life or the reasons why they did not marry until so late. At the same time she was painfully aware that her husband would have disapproved of any gossip about personal matters. As far as he was concerned he was a man of business who'd made an unfortunate first marriage that never needed to be alluded to, particularly now that the poor woman was dead and buried. If there was anything more complicated than this about the life of Mr. Thomas Druce, the second Mrs. Druce did not wish to dwell on it, even less did she wish to discuss it with anyone, especially her eldest son. She felt she was extremely lucky to have married a man of such eminence and wealth, a good provider for her children. She was herself from a modest background, although she believed that she behaved with a gentleness of demeanor that made up for her humble beginnings. She was always anxious to be the sort of wife that she felt Thomas wanted, even in the days before they were legally married. She did not wish to do anything to endanger the cordiality of her relationship with her husband.

Thomas died in the most businesslike of manners. To Herbert it seemed more like a legal event than an emotional and personal loss. His mother controlled her feelings of grief to the most remarkable degree, and Herbert assumed it could only mean that her faith was so strong that she expected to be reunited with her husband in the next world and did not therefore have to grieve too heavily in this one. Not wishing to behave inappropriately, Herbert took his lead from Annie May and reined in any possible emotions. Everyone who saw him at that time marveled at how mature and restrained he was—such an appropriate heir to the Baker Street Bazaar, despite his tender years. The store, everyone agreed, was going to be in safe hands with Herbert.

Anxious to get the whole event over and done with as quickly as possible, Herbert complied with his mother's request not to call in a doctor to sign the death certificate. One of his father's friends waved Herbert aside disdainfully when he asked if it were not required by law, and Herbert decided he would leave such matters to older and wiser heads than his own. Such pettifogging bureaucracy, it seemed, was not for the likes of the Druce family.

There were meetings with lawyers and accountants, funeral directors, and the managers of the shop. There were properties to be disposed of and debts to be paid, so there wasn't much time left for introspection or sadness. The reading of the wills confirmed that eighteen-year-old Herbert had inherited the business while twelve-year-old Walter had been left the princely sum of £18,601. Walter and his ten-year-old sister, Alice, did not attend the funeral, although Walter was told about it later. Annie May and Herbert told them it would be too harrowing an experience at their age to see their father incarcerated in a tomb.

Within a few weeks life for Annie May, Herbert, Walter, and Alice had regained a steady rhythm and they barely noticed the absence of the former master of the house. There had been so many times when he'd been away anyway, this felt little different. Herbert made sure that his mother and brother and sister were decently cared for financially, leaving himself free to concentrate on the running of the shop. There seemed to be no reason, as far as Herbert could see, why the family could not now melt into the respectable middle class, gradually expunging all hints of the eccentricity that his father had seemed to deliberately foster at times. Herbert had his eyes fixed firmly on the here and now. Even after his father's death he felt no compulsion to delve into the past, so he never questioned his mother about his father or about their relationship. He allowed a dignified silence to fall between them, in which Annie May was entirely happy to be complicit.

Henry Druce, the first son that Thomas had sired with Elizabeth, knew nothing of his father's death. In the heat and dust of Australia, the austere world of the wealthy London shopkeeper and the damp, sad end of his mother in the pauper's grave seemed almost like a dream to Henry. His daily struggle was now very different than his mother's had been. There was none of the social prejudice that had seen her disgraced and robbed of her right to even keep her own children. There was none of the helpless surrender to a class system that treated her as if she was nothing but an embarrassment to society. Australia was a land for pioneers and fearless souls. If you were in need of shelter, you didn't rely on the charity of the local churchmen; you cut down some trees and you built a hut for yourself. If you were hungry you didn't wait until some kind neighbor brought you soup, you snared some game and cooked it on an open fire. It was a hard life, but no harder than the existence of sailors aboard the ships that had brought him this far. There was a freedom that was worth any amount of sacrifice, and the promise of any sort of future that you wanted to build for yourself and your family.

On landing on the north coast of Australia in 1852, Henry had used the last of his savings to buy himself a horse and rode from settlement to settlement, sometimes going several days without seeing another soul. When he came upon a saloon he'd ask about the possibility of work. Everyone seemed to be doing the same, but it was only a few weeks before he found himself a ranch where they were hiring sheepshearers. If working the ropes in the navy had been hard, shearing sheep fast enough to make a good living was a thousand times worse. By the end of the first day his hands were bleeding and every muscle in his body was screaming with pain. But there was no chance that he would give up. To start with he needed to stay until payday, but, more important he couldn't be seen to fail by the other shearers. There was an air of competition so sharp you could almost smell it over the sweat. Henry had a long way to go before he could hope to beat the records held by the men he was working among for numbers of sheep stripped of their coats in a day. The men who did this job for several months every year were hard as iron and pleased to show off their prowess in front of a newcomer, especially when that newcomer had caught the eye of the only attractive woman on the whole homestead.

Rachel Hollamby was a striking woman. She was working in the laundry room of the big house and she'd noticed the young

English seaman the first day he arrived. Henry had noticed her, too. If there was one thing he'd spotted in the weeks he'd spent searching for work, it was how the men greatly outnumbered the women. He was as eager to impress Rachel as he was to impress the men he was working, eating, and sleeping among.

It wasn't hard for such an imposing young man to catch a girl's attention. All the men flirted with her at meal times but it was his eye she caught, exchanging shy smiles of encouragement. One evening, after the other men had become too drunk to notice anything that was going on, he found her folding sheets that had been out on a washing line. He offered to help and they started a modest conversation as they worked. She told him all about her family, who had come down to Australia together nearly twenty years before, and didn't press him when he was vague in his answers about his own background.

Each day he fought harder against the pain in his muscles and his numbers began to go up. There was no hope that he would be able to catch up to the most experienced men in one season, but by the end of his first week of work he was able to keep up with most of the average performers and even beat one or two of the older ones. All day he looked forward to the hour or two he would be spending with Rachel once all the work was finished and the heat of the sun had finally faded.

"Why do you all fight so hard to be best?" Rachel asked one evening as she studied his callous hands on the porch of the laundry room.

"I want to succeed," Henry replied simply. "I want to be a good Australian."

Rachel smiled, partly in amusement and partly because she recognized the sentiment as something similar to the desires of her own heart.

"Australia is going to be a great country," she said after a while.

"I know." He put his arm around her shoulder and gave her a squeeze. "I know it will be."

Despite the fact that the shearing season would soon be over and Henry would have to move on to find new work, they could both sense that they would be together again, that they were destined to spend their lives as a couple. That knowledge brought them both a tranquillity that allowed them the energy to continue with the day-to-day struggles of their existence.

For two years Henry led the wandering life, finding work wherever he could, saving money whenever it was possible, coming back to the ranch where Rachel worked in order to tell her his adventures and renew his promise that one day they would settle down together.

"I've heard about gold being found in the mountains," he told her on one visit. "There are men going out there by the hundred with no more than a shovel and a sieve. I'm going to go, too."

"Most of those men spend whatever they find on drinking and gambling and women," Rachel teased him. "None of them come back rich."

"None of them have you to come back to," he said, kissing her fondly. "Don't worry. I'll be saving every penny I can make."

Rachel was impatient, but aware that she could do nothing to bring her future to her more quickly. Exactly two years after he first set eyes on her, Henry returned once more and asked her to marry him, showing her that he now had enough money for them to be able to build a small house somewhere, where they could start a family and he could set himself up properly in the gold mining business.

"It's a good business, Rachel," he assured her, "for anyone who works steadily and uses his brain."

She accepted his proposal immediately. They married and set off together to find somewhere where they would want to settle.

A year later Rachel gave birth to their first son, Charles. Two years later they had a second boy, George Hollamby, named in memory of Rachel's father, who had died the previous year. The day that George Hollamby was born, Henry hit his first big strike. It wouldn't make them millionaires, but it meant that the family could live in comfort and security. By the time he was holding the tiny baby in his arms he was so brimming with happiness and optimism that he couldn't stop talking. Rachel was lying on a bed on the porch, half dozing and half listening, as Henry babbled excitedly about the future that he now felt was assured for them and their two sons. Under that warm, distant moon, with a new baby in his arms, there was no reason why Henry should care what was happening to the man who claimed he was his father but who'd deserted his mother while Henry was still a child. He knew nothing about Herbert or Walter, his half brothers, or Alice, his half sister, or the moderate fortune that was being shared out between them now that their father's coffin had been laid to rest in a tomb in Highgate Cemetery.

13

DR. HARMER AND THE MADHOUSE

Just for a moment let us digress from the twin stories of the Druces and the Cavendish-Bentincks, although, as readers will soon see, we may not be straying as far as it first seems. We need to witness a scene in an English madhouse.

Dr. Harmer stood in the corner of the room, watched by his keeper, Mr. Williams. He was not like any other lunatic that Williams had ever come across in his long career as a warder. There was an aura about him, a charisma that suggested that before this man had lost his mind, he had been a person of considerable consequence. Williams had been told that Harmer was a homoeopathic doctor but he seemed, in Williams's humble opinion, more like an aristocrat.

Dr. Harmer had struck what Williams would later describe to a reporter as "an attitude." The stance was made doubly dramatic by his attire, which was highly formal and always crowned by a high top hat, making it seem as if he was much taller than he really was. In fact, Dr. Harmer was quite short and heavyset with a graying beard. He had the contemptuous manner of one who believed he'd been born to a high station, far higher than those around him who seemed, quite inappropriately as far as he was concerned, to be in control of his life.

As Williams followed him with the calm, quiet eyes of a man who is quite used to the eccentric, Dr. Harmer began to shout, pointing at the floor and stamping his feet.

"Down there," he bellowed in a voice that could have carried across several fields against a strong wind. "It's down there, down, down." His face was contorted into ugly expressions as he wrestled with whatever demons were trying to come through to him.

Williams was no newcomer to the world of lunatics. He'd attended them at Bethnal Green Asylum and Northumberland House in Finsbury Park before coming into the employ of Dr. Forbes Winslow in Maidenhead. But in none of the other establishments had he come into contact with such a man as Dr. Harmer. If they allowed him out into the grounds he would dance around like a performing bear, throwing stones and having to be restrained for fear that he would injure some innocent passerby.

His only visitor was his wife, an unusually pretty woman in a place so full of ugliness, who would bring him a supply of cigars that he chain-smoked frantically through his hours of wakefulness. His sleep was as troubled as his wakefulness and Williams, who slept in the same room as he, would often be woken by the doctor's fearful shouts of warning that his bed was going to sink into a black hole.

When Williams had the temerity one day to ask Dr. Forbes Winslow about his mysterious charge, the doctor became extremely evasive.

"It is of no importance to you, Mr. Williams," he said, "where the patient comes from or what his medical history might be. All you need to know is that he's here as a voluntary patient, a man who has surrendered himself to us in the hope that he will find some sanctuary and peace of mind for himself within our care. That is our sole responsibility. We do not wish to expose him but to help him to fight the demons that trouble him."

In 1870, the same year that Dr. Harmer was struggling with his demons with the help of Dr. Forbes Winslow, Lord Henry Bentinck, the youngest of the four brothers of the Cavendish-Bentinck family, died at a respectable sixty-six years of age. The reporting of the death of the younger brother of the reclusive fifth duke of Portland was respectful and brief. He was not a man who had endeared himself to many beyond his own intimates. Unmarried to the end, like his brothers, he was probably missed as much by his horses and his hounds as by any living person.

Of the four brothers now only one remained, the man who had started life as Lord John, become the marquess of Titchfield on the death of his elder brother and the fifth duke upon the death of his father. He had survived both his younger brothers, Lord George and Lord Henry, and would survive for another nine years, tunneling and building around Welbeck until the end, eager to keep his life private and hidden from the outside world.

14

A Revelation

The final passing of the fifth duke of Portland in 1879, fifteen years after the death of Thomas Druce, had a considerable effect on the population of Welbeck Abbey and its surrounding villages. Seldom in history had any area enjoyed a patron so generous in the distribution of his wealth. The money might, in some people's eyes, have been channeled into some of the strangest and most useless of follies, but it created work for thousands of men and women and left a monument that they could forever point to as being the fruit of their own labors. It was an achievement that many men criticized as foolhardy but few could match for sheer grandeur and imagination. As well as the great construction of the underground passages and staterooms, he had also built model housing for all the workers on the estate; no one could say that they had suffered so that he could indulge his whims. Anyone from the estate or the workforce who came to him with a problem or a request knew they would receive a fair hearing and a generous response. If a widow couldn't pay her rent, it would be waived; if a child needed medical care, it would be provided.

Many would say that it's easy to be generous when you have all the wealth in the world at your disposal, but often those who have access to such wealth guard it jealously, preferring to see it growing in the bank rather than distributed to those who most need it.

A small army of bereaved servants, all shrouded in black, made their way to a local chapel to give thanks for the duke's life with all the sadness that befitted the passing of a man who had been kind to them and enriched their lives in his own, unusual ways. There were genuine tears shed for someone who had been a huge part of their lives and was now gone.

His death made less impact on genteel society, either in London or in the country. Few could remember the last time the elderly duke had made an appearance among his aristocratic peers. His passing was largely of interest to the gossiping classes because it immediately raised the question of who would succeed him, given that neither he nor any of his three brothers had produced any legitimate heirs during their lifetimes. No one knew why that might be, preferring to put it down as one of those tragedies that occasionally strikes individual families. There were some who said it was God's way of bringing in new blood and strengthening a breeding stock that had grown weak.

The answer to the question of who would inherit was soon known. The title and a great deal of the fortune, the world was told, would pass to a twenty-two-year-old cousin who was then serving in the Coldstream Guards. The announcement caused consternation at Welbeck since no one knew if this man would want to live in the house or even keep it going at all. Would he understand that for many of the people who lived and worked on the estate it was their ancestral home as much as his? He was an unknown force, and that made everyone uncomfortable.

Some of the properties in Scotland and London would pass to the fifth duke's sister, Lucy, who had married into the Howard de Waldens, a family already nearly as wealthy as the Cavendish-Bentincks.

Disraeli, who had never managed to patch up his relationship with the fifth Duke after the calling in of the loan for the purchase of Hughenden, saw an opportunity to reestablish his formally cordial relations with the family.

By that time many things had changed in Disraeli's life and he was serving his second term as prime minister. The first time he had been in power for only ten months before his greatest rival, the Liberal, William Gladstone, managed to unseat him. He had returned to power again in 1874, two years after the death of his wife, and succeeded in forging a relationship with Queen Victoria that made him arguably one of the two most powerful people in the world, Her Majesty being the other. In 1876 he had made her the empress of India and she had made him the earl of Beaconsfield in return.

"Who are his parents?" Disraeli asked Monty Corry, his faithful secretary, when he heard the identity of the sixth duke. Corry had become indispensable to Disraeli since the death of his wife, managing every aspect of his domestic life, down to the most tedious of details. He was a witty, amusing, and handsome man who moved easily in country house society. He was known for his propensity to seduce beautiful women, a trait that greatly endeared him to his master.

"His parents are both deceased, Prime Minister," Corry informed him. "But there is a stepmother of whom he is extremely fond."

Disraeli swung away and stared out the window, lost in thought, and Corry believed he had been dismissed. As he made his way to the door Disraeli stopped him in his tracks.

"Send a messenger to find out if the queen will receive me this afternoon," he instructed, without turning from the window.

A few hours later he and Queen Victoria were seated together in the corner of a reception room in Buckingham Palace, taking tea beneath the watchful eyes of her footmen. Disraeli was trying to make it sound as if he was making casual conversation.

"The new duke of Portland is an extremely young man," he said, sipping at his tea.

"So I've heard," the queen replied.

"I think it would greatly strengthen Your Majesty's present government to please the family with some trinket."

"Do you think so, Prime Minister?" She raised an eyebrow. "The man already has one of the noblest titles in the land. What else could we do for him? He's only a young soldier, after all. He has no distinguished war record that we could reward. He has rendered no particular service to his monarch beyond serving in my army."

"I believe his stepmother is a fine woman," Disraeli said.

The queen sipped in silence for a moment.

"I have heard nothing bad said about the woman," she agreed eventually. "But then I don't always hear the tittle-tattle from that class of people."

"Quite," Disraeli said. He waited a moment for the queen to continue, but she said nothing. He cleared his throat and prepared to be a little more frank. "Since I have no secrets from Your Majesty," he said, "I have to declare that I have some interest in pleasing the family."

"Do you indeed, Mr. Prime Minister?" The queen allowed herself the hint of a smile. "Then we shall have to give serious thought to the whole question of what to do about them."

A few weeks later the young duke found himself on a train with Monty Corry, making the journey to High Wycombe station, in order to take dinner with the aging prime minister and international legend. The young man was still in a state of shock at having visited Welbeck and discovered the desolation that his predecessor had left in his last years. In the will he was to receive most of the country estates and the fifth duke's considerable wealth in shares, stocks, and bank accounts. The will instructed him to use the money in England to buy more land in England and Wales, and to purchase more land in Scotland with the Scottish assets. He was also determined to return the Welbeck estate to its former glories, but the task was a daunting one. While he had always been aware that he was next in line for the title, the sixth duke had never been invited to Welbeck by his predecessor. Nor had the fifth duke ever spoken to him about the responsibilities that would be falling on his shoulders. A short career in the army, so far, was all the experience he had had of life. But he had every intention of bearing his new title with every ounce of honor he could muster.

Despite his youth and inexperience, however, the sixth duke was well aware of the complexities of Disraeli's past relationships with his family, and sufficiently aware of his own lack of experience to know that he was an innocent entering the lair of a wily old spider. He understood that without his family's backing Disraeli would never have been able to reach high office. He also understood that it was largely due to Disraeli that Britain ruled the largest empire the world had ever known. It was because Disraeli had secretly negotiated with Baron Rothschild to purchase the Suez Canal from Egypt, under the noses of the French, that the British had an eastern trade route from which to expand their empire. To be invited to spend the evening with a man of such historical significance was awe-inspiring for the young duke.

Corry, who had managed to strike up something approaching a friendship with the young duke at a number of different country house weekends, attempted to put him at ease as the train rumbled out of London and a heavy fog descended on the surrounding countryside, but the duke remained distracted by his own thoughts. He was an intense and likeable young man who, Corry imagined, was going to take his new responsibilities seriously. It was fortunate that the fifth duke had lived as long as he had, Corry mused, or the whole Portland estate would have descended onto the shoulders of a schoolboy instead of a callow soldier. It didn't seem to Corry that the sixth duke was anything close to being ready to take on his onerous responsibilities, but then he wondered if there had been a single member of the previous generation of the Portland dynasty who had been any better equipped. At least this duke had seen something of the outside world before he disappeared into Welbeck.

By the time they reached High Wycombe the fog was so thick it was hard to make out the shape of the horse and carriage that had been sent to meet them and convey them to Hughenden in time for dinner. The cold had penetrated through to the young duke's bones as the carriage rattled blindly along the roads, the horses trotting from memory and habit. He pulled his coat tightly around himself and allowed Corry to spread a rug across his knees with a nod of thanks.

Disraeli was waiting for them beside a fire in his drawing room and the young duke was startled by how bent and fragile the old man seemed to be as he welcomed them. The duke wondered how such an apparently frail old man was still managing to hold on to the reins of power. The prime minister seemed so lost in his own thoughts that he could hardly think of a word to say to the young man he'd invited to dinner. At moments, once they had gone through to the dining room, it seemed as if he'd entirely forgotten he had company. Corry did his best to put their guest at ease, but it was impossible even for a man as experienced as he was in dispelling awkwardness to disguise the fact that there were only two of them talking in the room.

The servants padded silently around the edges of the table,

pouring wine and removing and replacing plates, while the prime minister ate in silence and gave no indication that he didn't believe himself to be alone. Once they'd served the dessert the staff backed respectfully from the room and closed the doors behind them, no doubt as relieved to be out of the gloomy atmosphere as the young duke and Corry would have been. There was a scraping noise as the prime minister pushed his chair back and rose to his feet.

"My Lord Duke," he said, in a voice that would still have carried easily to the backbenches in Parliament, and gave a low, somewhat creaky bow. "It is the greatest of honors for me to have you at my table here tonight. I would like to take this occasion to formally acknowledge the enormous obligation that I have to your family."

The sixth duke sat, silenced and dumbfounded, as the prime minister continued with what sounded like a formal speech on the history of his debt to the Portland dynasty and of his intention of repaying it with a peerage for his stepmother.

"I come from a race," Disraeli pronounced, "that never forgives an injury nor forgets a benefit."

When the speech finally seemed to be over the duke rose to reply in similarly formal terms, but Disraeli cut him short with a curt wave.

"You must excuse me, My Lord. I have work to do," he said and left the room.

A few months later Mrs. Cavendish-Bentinck, the young duke's stepmother, became Baroness Bolsover and yet another title added itself to the family collection. In due course the sixth duke would become marquess of Titchfield, earl of Portland, Viscount Woodstock, Baron Cirencester, and Baron Bolsover. It was an awesome collection of titles to rest on such a young man's shoulders.

* * *

A year later, in 1880, Disraeli, was soundly defeated in an election
and retired to Hughenden permanently in order to return to his
novel writing. In 1881 he died and the queen was reported to be
brokenhearted.

The sixth duke settled comfortably into the Welbeck that his
predecessor had created. He became the foremost figure on the
Turf, as Lord George had before him, and filled the house with
the most brilliant members of society. He was one of sixty bachelors who launched an institution known from then on as "The
Bachelors' Ball," which led to the Bachelors' Club. Welbeck
came alive again, waking up after what had been a long period
of slumber. The house was full of voices and laughter and the
household staff found their numbers increasing to cope with the
workload.

In 1886 Lord Salisbury recommended that the duke be
appointed as the queen's master of the horse and Victoria welcomed the recommendation, remembering how her beloved Disraeli had urged her to watch out for the young man. His duties
at the Court were onerous due to the vast number of royal cere-
monies making great demands on the royal stables. He was put
in charge of the queen's state procession through London in
1887. For the queen's diamond jubilee he succeeded in forcing
the chancellor of the exchequer to pay for the replacement of the
entire state harness-work. At Welbeck the staff felt proud to have
a master who was once more playing a part in public life. The fifth
duke might have been kind to them, but he brought no honor or
glory to the estate beyond his construction work. There was a
feeling that the House of Portland was now enjoying a revival of
fortunes in the public arena for the first time since the death of
Lord George had cast such a shadow over the family name forty
years before.

Walter Druce, in his modest way, had the same problem in life that Lord George had had several decades before, along with many other younger brothers living in a time of primogeniture. As the second son of Thomas and Annie May, he was brought up on the fringes of high society. He'd inherited just enough money on his father's death not to have to work, but not enough to entirely indulge his whims. While his elder brother, Herbert, toiled to continue the growth and prosperity of the Baker Street Bazaar, Walter dabbled in this and that, as many young gentlemen of the day did. He lived an elegant but unpretentious life and caused his mother a small amount of concern with some dalliances involving a number of women whom she did not believe to be his social equal.

Not that Annie May would ever have put her foot down about such matters. She'd spent her adult life in the shadow of a man who solicited no advice or instruction from her on any subject whatsoever and she allowed this pattern to continue with her elder son, Herbert, who was headstrong and eager to make up his own mind as to what he wanted to do with his life without turning to her. Walter was less surefooted in his approach to life and Annie May sometimes worried about the standards of some of the young ladies he brought home to meet her. She feared terribly that he would one day announce he was going to marry one of them and that his life would become a misery from that day onward.

Then one day Anna Maria arrived in Walter's life and Annie May felt that perhaps now her younger son had sailed safely into port. It was not that Anna Maria lacked spirit—she was actually quite a modern woman in many ways—but she seemed highly responsible and capable of ensuring that Walter conducted the adult part of his life with the dignity befitting his slightly uncertain status. Anna Maria was a Miss Butler at the time, her father having been an agent for Lord Pembroke, a highly respected member of the aristocracy, which meant she was deemed entirely suitable socially. His Lordship had even been her guardian for a while. Although Annie May had always prided herself on never putting much store in such things as titles, she found it comforting to think that Walter was falling into safe hands. She could see that he was not a man of great determination like his father or brother. In many ways he was more like her: passive, gentle, and easily led.

Anna Maria had been introduced to Walter by his sister, Alice, who had been to school with her and greatly valued her friendship. Anna Maria liked the woman who soon became her mother-in-law and regretted never meeting Annie May's husband, who from the tales her husband told her, seemed to have been an interesting character. Those who'd known Annie May before Thomas's death told Anna Maria that her mother-in-law was now very different.

"She was the mousiest of little women when Druce was around," one told her, "although enormously pretty. Druce was quite a tyrant, you know, and many of us thought that once he'd gone she would just wither away. She seemed only to survive because of the protection he provided for her. But quite the opposite happened. Without him to shade her she seemed to blossom in the sunlight of her widowhood. She bought herself new clothes just as soon as it was respectable to remove her widow's weeds, and quite often entertained people that Druce would never have allowed in the house."

The more she heard about her dead father-in-law, the more Anna Maria was intrigued, and the more determined she became to spend time with Annie May in order to find out the true history of the family she was marrying into.

Annie May was pleased to have someone show an interest in

her. She was unused to the feeling. To have a sweet young woman asking her about her childhood and how she'd met her husband, and what their life had been like together, was flattering and she found herself saying more than she ever had before. No one who'd known him had ever dared to ask her what it was like to be married to Thomas and as the years crept by she felt more and more like talking about him and about her life. She told Anna Maria that she had originally been called Annie, but that Thomas had added the "May" as a term of endearment.

"Apparently," she confided, "he had been in love with another woman of that name in the past, an older woman. He would never give me details, but I heard about her from other people."

Anna Maria began to construct a picture in her head of how life must have been for her mother and father-in-law, and continued asking questions in an attempt to add more color to the canvas.

"Your mother said something strange today," Anna Maria told her husband one evening as they prepared for bed. "We were taking tea together and chatting about this and that and she said how hard it was to always be living in the shadows. I asked her what she meant by that phrase, thinking that perhaps she meant she was overshadowed by your father's personality, and she seemed to regret saying anything, trying to dismiss it as nothing. I was determined not to let her off so easily and asked her again what she'd meant and she said something about your father never being able to appear in society because of who he was."

"Nonsense," Walter said, only half listening to what seemed to him like idle chat. "My father simply didn't enjoy company. He preferred to be working. That was all he ever did. Just like Herbert."

Anna Maria continued to brush her hair, staring thoughtfully into the mirror. She was sure there was more to it than that, and she intended to find out what it was. The following day she was lunching with her sister-in-law, Grace, Herbert's wife, and brought up the same subject.

"Herbert has always said his father disappeared for long periods," Grace said. "Perhaps he had some secret life."

"Walter would say that was romantic foolishness," Anna Maria said.

"Yes, Herbert, too," Grace laughed. "It would be nice to think the family had some dark and exciting secret, don't you think?"

Anna Maria did think so, and so she kept working on her mother-in-law, dripping away at the stone and attempting to wear her down. Eventually, late one evening when the older woman was tired and contented from a day of playing with her grand-child (Walter and Anna Maria's infant son, Sidney), Anna Maria found out more than she could possibly have hoped for.

"He's a noble little man," Annie May said, looking fondly at Sidney as he slept in his pram, waiting for Anna Maria to take him home. "His grandfather would have been proud, however much he might have denied it."

"Why would he have denied it?" Anna Maria asked, and for a second it looked as if Annie May was going to retract back into her shell, as usual. After a moment's hesitation she seemed to decide to plunge ahead.

"My husband came from a noble family, but preferred to keep that part of his life separate."

"You mean he led a double life?" Anna Maria tried to sound as if she was only half concentrating on the subject, fiddling with Sidney's blanket to give the appearance of being distracted, not wanting to frighten her mother-in-law back into her normal state of discretion.

"Don't mention this to Walter or Herbert, or anyone," Annie May spoke hurriedly, as if already regretting her indiscretion and wondering how to get herself back into the safe territory of conversational small talk.

"Of course not," Anna Maria purred. "It"ll be our little secret.

"Thomas was actually a lord but he liked to escape the life in order to live as Thomas Druce, an ordinary shopkeeper."

Anna Maria was about to say that she didn't think the Baker Street Bazaar was exactly an "ordinary" shop, but she bit her tongue. "What was his title?" she asked instead.

"My husband was the fifth duke of Portland," Annie May said, the words tumbling out as if relieved to be finally free.

Anna Maria was now unable to hide her amazement. She stopped fussing with the baby and stared in unashamed wonder at the older woman. "So you are the duchess of Portland?"

"No, no," Annie May blushed. "That title belongs to the wife of the sixth duke. I am Mrs. Thomas Druce. No one must ever know this, Anna Maria. I'm trusting you completely with my secret."

"But you could claim your title and take your place at the very pinnacle of society," Anna Maria said. "You should be one of the richest women in England."

"I am quite content with what I have," Annie May assured her, now becoming nervous at her daughter-in-law's fervor, wondering if she had made a terrible mistake. "I couldn't claim the title. The situation is far more complicated than it seems."

"In what way?" Anna Maria wanted to know.

"In many ways, my dear."

"Do Herbert and Walter know nothing of their situation?" Anna Maria was trying to orient herself in a world so full of new possibilities and apparent impossibilities that she felt dizzy trying to separate them.

"No," Annie May was suddenly adamant, making Anna Maria jump with the strength of her reply. "Nor must they find out, ever. It would cause no end of trouble for everyone. For the sake of Walter and Sidney, you must promise me you will never breathe a word of this to anyone."

"Of course I will tell no one if that is your wish," Anna Maria assured her, aware that even if she did tell Walter what his mother believed, he would dismiss the idea out of hand as the foolish fantasies of an aging woman with too much time on her hands. "But I feel sure you should be claiming what is rightfully yours."

"Never. Promise me you will respect my confidence on this."

"Of course."

That evening Walter was puzzled by his wife's intense silence. Anna Maria was usually so full of chatter when they sat down to supper together, but she seemed to be lost in her own thoughts and nothing he could tell her about his day seemed to interest her. In the end he gave up trying and lapsed into an identical, if slightly resentful, silence. Walter was devoted to his wife, but found her moods something of a puzzle. Being a man of virtually no ambition at all, quite contented to live on the modest amount of money that his father and brother had passed his way, he couldn't understand why Anna Maria could not be similarly satisfied with her comfortable lot in life. He knew that she would have liked him to take up politics, or even join Herbert in the shop, in order to improve their financial and social standings, but Walter found that a life of modest leisure suited him.

In the coming years Anna Maria became very close to her mother-in-law. The older woman seemed to find it a relief to have someone show an interest in her past and the stories she had to tell. For so many years she had had to remain sphinxlike in her discretion, out of respect for Thomas, who never wished to discuss any of the family secrets that she found out by accident along the way. Her sons, like their father, never chose to speak of personal matters, preferring to keep their feelings and emotions in check, pretending they didn't exist. The two women would spend hours alone together sipping tea and discussing the ways of the world and the men in their family.

After just eight years of marriage to Anna Maria, Walter died in 1880 at the tender age of twenty-eight, leaving Anna Maria with even more time on her hands and providing one more bond, that of mutual grief, between his bereaved mother and widow.

When Walter died the Druce family vault was opened at Highgate Cemetery and Walter's body, encased in a coffin of lead-lined oak, was slid in beside his father's.

Thirteen years later, when the tomb was opened once more to accept the coffin of Annie May, Anna Maria stared at the coffin that was supposed to contain the remains of her father-in-law as the priest continued to pray in the background. She was already feeling sad at the loss of a woman who had become a dear friend as well as a mother-in-law, and the ritual opening of a musty vault seemed to match her melancholy mood. She felt that with Annie May's passing the family secrets had become hers in some way, that she was now responsible for the way future generations of the Druces might be regarded. If she did not speak up then the secrets would die with her and the Druces would slip into obscurity. The service passed slowly and her mind continued to wander.

She stared at Thomas Druce's coffin, trying to imagine what the body inside might look like by this time, as the priest's voice droned on in the background. Then a thought struck her as if from nowhere and she couldn't imagine how she had never seen it before. It suddenly became obvious to her that the coffin was empty, that Thomas had not died when he supposedly had; he had merely killed off his character, so that he could continue his life as the duke of Portland. The revelation made her almost breathless with excitement. If she could get the coffin opened, then she would be able to prove that her father-in-law had led a double life. If he had, in fact, been the fifth duke of Portland, then it meant that her son, Sidney, was the rightful heir to the title, since everyone knew that Herbert (Walter's older brother and Sidney's uncle) had been born out of wedlock.

She said nothing at that solemn moment, but decided to make further enquiries. She knew that she would need to have more proof than the ramblings of an old woman, who was now dead and unable to confirm anything, in order to convince the authorities to open the coffin. She needed to find someone who was willing to come forward and attest to the fact that the burial had been a fraud.

She placed a small advertisement in the London newspapers, announcing that she wished to hire a private detective to undertake some delicate family enquiries. A man who looked more like a bank clerk than a detective answered the advertisement and she explained her problem to him. The man proved to be more efficient than his appearance had led her to hope. He traced a man named Vassar, who had once been in Thomas Druce's employment. The detective told Anna Maria that it would be worth her while hearing what the man had to say.

Vassar was an elderly fellow, but his recall seemed to be sharp enough to convince anyone who listened to him. He told Anna Maria that in 1864 he had been instructed by Thomas to bring some lead into the house, which he believed was used to fill a coffin. Anna Maria was certain the lead was meant to simulate the weight of the missing body. Encouraged by this breakthrough, she rewarded Vassar for his information and told the private detective to renew his efforts to uncover as many people as possible who had seen Thomas Druce after the date when he was supposed to have been buried.

The detective, pocketing his fee, set out with renewed enthusiasm. He had a feeling he was involved in something that could turn into a very big case indeed. He could not have anticipated just how big a scandal it would soon become.

15

SIDNEY'S BIRTHRIGHT

Y ou are the sixth duke of Portland," Anna Maria shouted, her exasperation with her son finally proving too much to bear. The year was 1896 and Sidney was now nineteen years old. Anna Maria couldn't understand why he didn't seem willing to join her in fighting tooth and claw for his birthright. He was too easygoing, like his father, Walter, she decided, and not enough like his grandfather, Thomas.

"It's madness, Mother," Sidney replied, forcing himself to remain calm in the face of his mother's rage. He, above everyone, knew how much strain she had been under. He knew she'd been close to his grandmother and that Annie May's death had affected her dramatically, removing her best friend and greatest confidante. The bereavement had served to make her more insecure and strident in her attempts to exert her will on those left around her, mostly on him.

The claustrophobic atmosphere at home with his mother had been one of the reasons Sidney had decided to become a sailor and take to the sea. He loved his mother dearly, but he knew that if he remained at home she would smother him. He was tired of her telling him how she could see his aristocratic lineage every time she looked at him. Sidney didn't want aristocratic lineage; he wanted a quiet life.

"They've robbed you of your birthright, Sidney," Anna Maria was saying, as she had a thousand times before, her teeth gritted in her determination to put her case reasonably. "The money that should have come to you was divided up between the man who now calls himself the sixth duke, who is just a cousin of the family, and the Howard de Walden family who just happened to have the good fortune to marry into the family. It's your money. We must make them return it, along with your title and lands."

The de Walden family had become linked to the Cavendish-Bentincks through marriage to Lucy, one of the fifth duke's sisters. When the estate had been divided up, a substantial portion of it had been transferred to the de Waldens. They too were landed aristocrats and part of the establishment that Anna Maria was convinced was conspiring to keep her son from his rightful inheritance.

"What would Father have wanted me to do?" Sidney asked eventually. His mother fell silent and cast her eyes down. Sidney pressed his advantage. "Did you ever bring up the subject with him?"

"You know what your father was like; anything for a quiet life; never wanting to upset anyone. He was worried about your uncle Herbert and he didn't want to create a scandal around his parents' name. He had a hundred and one reasons why we shouldn't do anything, but it was just that he was too lazy."

"I think we should respect Father's wishes," Sidney suggested. He didn't doubt that his mother was right, but he was rather in favor of a quiet life himself. He didn't like the idea of seeing the family name all over the newspapers and he wasn't sure that he actually wanted to be the sixth duke of Portland. He suspected there was a great deal more to being one of the richest men in England than met the eye. If he could just be allowed to continue living the life he had always imagined for himself, traveling the world and dreaming his dreams, he would be perfectly happy. He wouldn't have had the slightest idea how to start running a vast estate, and he certainly wouldn't have wanted to become part of the public life of politics. The thought of being responsible for the livelihoods of hundreds of staff, and the upkeep of almost as many buildings, made him feel positively sick. He would be terrified of losing the whole fortune within a year. He had so many plans for places he would like to visit, sights he would like to see, and he couldn't imagine that he would be free to wander the globe in quite the same carefree way if he was a duke. His travels might be more luxurious, but they wouldn't be how he had planned them in his head.

Anna Maria, however, was not willing to let her son's lack of spirit deflect her. She might have had to bow to her mother-in-law's wish to remain silent while Annie May was alive, and she might have felt obliged to obey her husband's wishes when he was alive, but she could see no reason why she had to be cheated of her chance to be a dowager duchess by her son's docile nature. She appreciated that he was feeling daunted by the prospect of taking his rightful seat in the House of Lords, but he would have her to help and advise him. He would soon get used to his elevation to the pinnacle of high society.

"I'm going to write to the home secretary," she said, her tone suggesting that she was no longer asking his opinion. "I'm going to ask for your grandfather's coffin in Highgate Cemetery to be opened. If your grandmother is right, then the coffin will be empty, or filled with lead, because the fifth duke didn't die until fifteen years after your grandfather, Thomas, was supposed to have been laid to rest in that vault."

"What if there is a body in there?" Sidney asked, intrigued by his mother's plan despite his better judgment, and relieved to think that he would be safely back at sea while she was making her mischief. Sidney enjoyed his life in the navy. He loved his mother dearly, but she had dominated him since his childhood and now, with his father gone, there was nothing to distract her from her mission to "make something" of him. Sidney did not want to have anything made of him.

"Then either there has been some greater crime and a false body has been buried," Anna Maria replied, "or your grandmother was mistaken. I'm certain the coffin will be empty, quite certain."

She bustled from the room before her son could come up with any more questions, determined to write her letter to the home secretary before she was assailed by second thoughts.

The home secretary's office received the letter later the same day. An assistant read it first, and had to read it again to ensure that he had understood it correctly. He then went out to the home secretary's club to find him.

"What's in the letter?" the minister asked when his assistant found him half asleep in a comfortable chair, not wanting to trouble himself with looking for his spectacles so that he could read it for himself.

"The lady claims that there has been a false burial. She says that her father-in-law, Thomas Druce, the owner of the Baker Street Bazaar, who was buried in 1864, was merely a pseudonym for the fifth duke of Portland. She suggests that the duke wearied of his life in the guise of a London shopkeeper and staged the death in order to give up the personality. She says that an opening of the coffin will show it does not contain the body of Druce because he went on to live another fifteen years as the duke."

"Good God!" The home secretary had by now fully woken up and found his spectacles. He snatched the letter from the other man's hands in order to read it himself. He read it through twice to make sure he hadn't missed anything before sitting back in the chair with an amazed hiss of escaping air.

"If she's right that'll mean the whole Portland succession could be thrown into doubt," he spluttered. "This woman's son could have a claim to the whole damn estate and all its titles. It would be chaotic. God knows what would happen to the family fortune. It could all end up being spent on new dresses. Tell the woman to go to hell."

The assistant bowed his acceptance of the instruction and returned to the office to draft a more tactful version of the home secretary's reply. The home secretary, still at his club but having moved on to dinner, later signed a polite letter to Anna Maria saying that he could not consider her application to open the coffin unless legal action showed due evidence to warrant action on his part.

"Very good," he told his subordinate. "The lawyers should be able to hold things up nicely for years. No one can get past them when they're determined to block the way."

Anna Maria read the letter the following day with a determined expression. She knew the game that was being played. The home secretary was probably a crony of the incumbent duke of Portland and was protecting him from losing his title and fortune. It was the Establishment clubbing together to keep out the upstart. This was exactly the sort of response that Walter had told her she would receive if she tried to make trouble. But Walter was dead now and Anna Maria did not intend to let them get away with it. They were not going to cheat her Sidney of his birthright.

She went back to her desk and wrote two more letters, one to the cemetery authorities in Highgate and one to the Bow Street police station. She was not put off by their negative responses a few days later and continued sending a stream of letters for several weeks, finding herself with plenty of time on her hands now that

Sidney had gone back to sea. None of the authorities were willing to change their minds. It was becoming obvious that she would have to make the next move herself.

Sitting down once more at her desk, gazing out onto the busy London street outside the window as she thought out what she wanted to say, she eventually perfected an application to the House of Lords asking for the ejection of the sixth duke of Portland in favor of her son, Sidney.

The application caused a ripple of amusement at the House of Lords, with just a tinge of apprehension. One or two of them made contact with the sixth duke to find out what was going on. They wanted to know if this woman could stir up trouble. None of the aristocratic families liked the idea of people disputing titles, even if the titles in dispute weren't their own. It made them all feel uneasy, undermining their sense of security. The sixth duke appeared to be treating the matter with patience and good humor, as if he expected the problem to go away quite soon. Enquiries were made. It was discovered that Anna Maria was a widow with no apparent patron. She was of limited means and could probably not sustain a long legal battle. The Lords eventually replied to her letter to say that there was nothing they could do unless her case was properly prepared and presented by counsel. They asked that she make a deposit of £10,000 so that her case could be heard. They assumed that would be the last they heard of Anna Maria Druce. They were mistaken.

Anna Maria's next port of call was the bishop of London. The bishop received her with great politeness and listened as she explained that the burial had been false and that Highgate Cemetery had therefore been desecrated, thus bringing the matter within ecclesiastical jurisdiction. The bishop, anxious to be helpful, but not keen to become involved personally, passed her on to Dr. T. H. Tristram, Q.C., chancellor of the diocese of

London. He suggested that Anna Maria call their bluff and go to court. Anna Maria was elated. At last, someone in authority was taking her claims seriously. He did also warn her, however, that any legal path she might follow was bound to cost a great deal of money and that the Cavendish-Bentincks had the Portland millions at their disposal, while she had only the limited means of a gentlewoman and widow.

"I do not believe," she replied with more dignity than she could actually afford, "that in a country like England, justice should only be available to those who can afford to buy it."

Dr. Tristram nodded wisely, as if in agreement with her, which he probably was, but also because he knew that what *should* be happening in England and what actually *was* happening in England were many miles apart.

His comment, however, helped Anna Maria to focus her thoughts. She would need to find people who would be willing to back her financially should the battle become drawn out. It occurred to her that one of the newspapers might be interested in buying the story from her. She made an appointment to see the editor of the *Daily Mail,* who received her with enormous civility and some skepticism. He listened to her story and to her suggestion that he should lend her £20 to help her proceed with the case, and then, equally politely, declined her offer. No doubt a century later the same newspaper would have been a great deal more willing to work with someone who brought them such a major story, but these were still the early days of freedom of the press.

Word of her financial vulnerability must have spread in circles she was not aware of, because one morning she was delivered a letter inviting her to the offices of a well-known and respected firm of lawyers in the city of London. They didn't say what they wished to discuss with her, only that it would "be to her advantage" to attend the appointment.

* * *

The lawyers who received her were all elderly, heavily whiskered men who showed her no smiles and only the barest minimum of good manners. The room that she was led to was large and paneled in dark wood and had nothing welcoming about it. They informed her they could not tell her who they were representing, only that they had been instructed to offer her the sum of £60,000 if she would sign some papers guaranteeing to cease her foolish pursuit of the House of Portland. The papers were already prepared and lying on the desk that stood between Anna Maria and her putative benefactors. For just a moment the possibility of being given a sum that would more than assure her financial welfare for the rest of her life, and help Sidney to establish himself in America or Australia or wherever he chose to put down roots, tempted her greatly. Then it occurred to her that if they were willing to make such a magnanimous offer at this stage, she must have something she could unleash that they badly wished to keep quiet.

The question that sprang into her mind was, who was making the offer? She assumed that her brother-in-law, Herbert, would be very keen to silence her before she brought any more unfriendly publicity upon the Druce name. But she already knew that at the time Thomas Druce died, his entire estate had only been valued at £70,000. This offer of money, it seemed, was not coming from Herbert, or anyone called Druce, but had to have been sanctioned by someone far wealthier and with far more to lose, someone like the sixth duke of Portland or the Howard de Walden family. The offer seemed to her confirmation that they believed she was destined for success if she kept going and that was why they were anxious to buy her off.

She had fallen silent while thinking the offer over and the lawyers became restless. They had been under the impression she would accept it with gratitude, and it seemed incredible to them that she should have to give such a generous offer even a moment's thought. The woman, they decided, must be demented in some way. Eventually she spoke, thanking them kindly but declining to accept. They seemed unable to believe what they were hearing. How could anyone of modest means refuse such an enormous sum? They exchanged glances, all wondering if she had some secret backer, someone with enough money to fight such a case in the high court. Anna Maria detected a hardening in their previously deadpan expressions.

"We would not be able to increase that offer," they warned her, their voices giving the impression that they were disappointed, that they had mistaken her for a reasonable woman but that she had now shown herself to be a money-grabbing opportunist.

"It would do you no good to increase it," she replied, a little tartly. "I have right on my side. My son will be the sixth duke of Portland, I will see to that. And then you will be making offers on our behalf rather than the other way."

The men on the other side of the desk made noises that sounded to her a great deal like scoffing and then they told her the meeting was at an end. Anna Maria left the office feeling that she now stood a good chance of winning her fight.

On March 9, 1898, two years after her first letter to the home secretary, Anna Maria found herself in St. Paul's Cathedral stating her case before a tribunal at a sitting of the Consistory Court of London. The private detective she had hired had provided her with more than her money's worth of information. He'd uncovered a story so shocking and dramatic that even Anna Maria had had trouble believing it at first. She had cross-examined him rigorously, believing that he might be fantasizing merely to ensure that she would keep paying his fees. But his story seemed to stand firm under scrutiny. Anna Maria was elated. She had more than enough evidence to justify the opening of the coffin, and more than enough to convince herself that she couldn't fail to win any subsequent claims for the titles of the Portland family.

By the time she reached St. Paul's she had told the story so many times she felt like an actress performing a well-loved and familiar play upon the stage, and she injected her words with all the drama she could in order to win over the grim-faced men who sat before her. She had also given the same story to the *Lloyd's Weekly Newspaper* and the editor planned to print it four days later, a sign that despite the reluctance of the *Daily Mail* to back her financially, the media was becoming a little braver in their willingness to print stories that might upset the powerful Establishment of the day.

"The marriage that took place on October 30, 1851, at New Windsor in Berkshire, between my late husband's father and mother, and in which their names are recorded as Thomas Charles Druce and Annie May, spinster, was in reality between the marquis of Titchfield, afterwards fifth duke of Portland, and the illegitimate daughter of the fifth earl of Berkeley."

Deep in her heart Anna Maria felt a flutter of guilt at making public a confidence with which Annie May had entrusted her, but she felt it was crucial to bring as much of the truth into the public domain as possible, in order to demonstrate that she had a great deal of inside knowledge and wasn't some gold-digging nobody. Her detective, while pursuing his enquiries around Welbeck, had discovered by sheer luck the fact, as she believed it to be, that Annie May was the illegitimate daughter of the earl of Berkeley. The discovery had come after Annie May's death, and so Anna Maria had been unable to ask her about it, but she was confident it was right.

"These two had lived together for many years," she continued, "and the circumstances that led up to their intimacy and to the subsequent double life of my husband's father are of a most remarkable character, and also serve to throw a very strong light upon what had always been regarded as the extraordinary eccentricities of the fifth duke. He and his brother, Lord George Bentinck, were both in love with the same woman, but while Lord George's suit received the approbation of their father, the fourth duke not only discouraged the desire of his eldest son, but treated him with insult, and referred in very gross terms to the skin disease from which he suffered."

This was the first that the others in the room had heard about Lord John and Lord George being in love with the same woman, and the first they had heard of a disfiguring skin disease. Anna Maria paused for breath, increasing the dramatic effect of her tale. She could see she had her audience's full attention and that what she was about to tell them would leave their jaws hanging slack.

"The climax of the quarrel between the two brothers was reached on September twenty-first, 1848, when Lord George was found dead near Welbeck Abbey, it was stated, from a spasm of the heart. Whether this was the true cause of his decease can now, of course, never be known, but it is quite certain that from that time my husband's father suffered the keenest remorse and the most abject fear."

She waited again, watching their faces. They were taking in what she was saying and beginning to realize the implications of her words. She continued once she felt they had caught her up.

"Nearly always in a state of terror, he took various courses to protect himself from exposure and prosecution, and, adopting the name of Thomas Charles Druce, transferred to himself, as Druce, immense property from himself as the duke of Portland."

She now had them in the palm of her hand. All of them could

imagine clearly the importance of the accusations she was making and they wanted to hear everything that she knew.

"Everyone knows how he undermined Welbeck Abbey with subterranean apartments," she continued. "He did precisely the same thing with the Baker Street Bazaar, so that he might always have a place of refuge. But, realizing the risk of exposure he was subjecting himself to by his double existence, he determined to end his life as Thomas Druce and for that purpose caused a coffin to be buried with his, Thomas Druce's, supposed remains. Even after this, however, the duke's fears were not quieted and he determined to assume madness, in order that, should he ever be accused of any crime, he might have the plea of insanity to fall back on. Taking the name of Harmer, and conducting himself in the most extravagant manner, he caused himself to be placed under the care of Dr. Forbes Winslow, and succeeded in entirely convincing that gentleman of his madness, but after about a year of incarceration he was permitted to leave."

She waited while one of the men whispered something into the ear of another. She strained to hear what he was saying, but it was impossible. She thought about challenging him to speak out loud, but decided to press on.

"As to why my husband's father and mother did not marry for so long, it is impossible to say accurately; but probably the desire to conceal the facts surrounding the lady's birth had a great deal to do with it. As to the opening of the grave, I have today received a letter from the cemetery company saying that they will not open it without my son's written authority. My son is currently in Australia, farming, so there will be a delay, but I do not despair in the least. It is on his behalf that I mean to win. If you could see him you would see the extraordinary likeness he bears to several members of the Bentinck family and also to the portrait produced here of Thomas Charles Druce. I may add, though it is not a pleasant thing to say, that my younger daughter suffers, though of course in a lesser degree, from the same skin disease that affected her grandfather. I have been offered sixty-thousand pounds for my claim, but have refused it. Every obstacle has been put in my way but I am absolutely confident of success, and now that the case has at last come before the public, have no doubt as to its ultimate result."

Anna Maria went on to list the many people who claimed to have seen Thomas after the alleged day of his death, and included an experience of her own, when she claimed she met "Dr. Harmer" during his sojourn in the madhouse and recognised him as being her father-in-law from pictures she had seen.

Dr. Forbes Winslow, who ran the madhouse that Dr. Harmer had been in, was brought into the court and shown a picture of Thomas Druce.

"That would seem to be a picture of Dr. Harmer," he confirmed. "He was a lunatic without a lucid interval. Mrs. Harmer would visit him and paid for his keep."

The worthy men of the tribunal let out an audible sigh of amazement as Anna Maria finally fell triumphantly silent, her case successfully presented. One or two of them exchanged stunned looks. They had been aware of the woman's claim to the Portland fortune—everyone in society had heard about it—but they were staggered by the suggestion that Lord George had been killed by his elder brother, and the suggestion that Annie May was the illegitimate daughter of the earl of Berkeley sounded most unlikely to all of them. In fact the smallest amount of research later revealed that the Annie May in question, the one fathered by the earl, would have been a great deal older than both the brothers and highly unlikely to be the object of their shared desires. The tribunal dismissed that particular suggestion as pure hearsay, although it didn't stop the story from spreading through the country as if its truthfulness had been proved beyond any shadow of a doubt. In cases of this kind people often believe what they choose to believe, which means they believe the story that is most dramatic, most shocking, or most interesting, and not always what has been proved to be true.

Despite the sensational embroidery that Anna Maria had indulged in, the tribunal could see that the woman had a possible case. Dr. Tristram, chancellor of the diocese of London, agreed there was enough evidence that Thomas had survived beyond 1864 to throw doubt on the fact that his body lay where it was reported to be, and granted an order for the vault to be opened and the contents of the coffin to be examined.

"It certainly is a very curious case," he said, "but what strikes the court is that the certificate of death does not contain the name of the medical gentleman who purported to certify the cause of death. This is a very serious omission."

Anna Maria was elated. There was no doubt in her mind that once the coffin had been opened all the world would be able to see that she was speaking the truth. She had won.

Anna Maria was right to be optimistic, but not right to think that she had achieved her goal. A few days after her case was reported in the newspapers, as she waited for the paperwork to come through for the opening of the grave, a letter was received by the editor of the *Times* from a firm of solicitors purporting to be representing Mrs. Harmer. Their client, they informed the editor, had been surprised to read in his pages that her husband had in fact been Mr. Druce and that she, by default, was therefore Mrs. Druce. Their client wished to publicly deny that her late husband had been anyone but his unfortunate self. She asked to meet Dr. Forbes Winslow who, she was sure, would be able to identify her since they had met often during the time of her husband's illness.

Dr. Forbes Winslow could do nothing but agree to meet the lady and immediately recognized her. He then felt compelled to make a long statement in the *Times* explaining that he disclaimed all responsibility for the alleged identity beyond confirming a striking resemblance between Harmer and the picture of Thomas Druce.

Anna Maria read the statement with mounting horror. The sighting of the man she had thought to be Thomas, but who had called himself Harmer, was her only personal, firsthand knowledge of the case. The collapse of this argument couldn't help but deal a serious blow to her credibility and to her chances of success.

Her lawyers asked for a meeting and when she arrived at their offices, she discovered that things had grown worse. The judge had insisted that anyone who might have an interest in not opening the coffin must be informed of what was planned. The person who had the greatest interest in maintaining the status quo was Herbert, who by then had been running the business he had inherited from his father for over thirty years and did not want to have his whole inheritance called into question by a sudden revelation that the father who had left it to him had in fact not died when everyone had assumed, but had merely gone back to being someone else.

"The damn woman's a menace," Herbert exploded to his wife, Grace, when he was informed of the actions of his sister-in-law. "If Walter was alive he wouldn't be allowing this nonsense. He would no more allow her to rummage around in our father's coffin than I would. I will absolutely not permit it to happen."

Without sending a note to announce his approach, he went round to see Alexander Young, a friend of his father's who was the last surviving executor of Thomas's will. The old man, who had been a member of a well-known firm of accountants, had also heard about Anna Maria's quest and had been expecting to hear from Herbert sooner or later.

"We can stop it," Young said, "if we act quickly. I'll apply to the chancellor for a caveat to prevent the opening of the grave and then for leave to intervene. That'll buy us several weeks, during which time we can brief the solicitors and have a stop put to her antics once and for all."

At the end of the month the chancellor, Dr. Tristram, was called upon to justify his decision to open the vault. The case came down to a matter of legal technicalities, which infuriated Anna Maria, who could only see the mighty injustice that was being done to her and the obviousness of the solution that lay before them all. If they just opened the coffin the case would be proved either way. If the body was in there and looked like Thomas Druce, she would be unable to pursue her cause. If it was empty then the fight could really begin. At the end of all the arguments she had once again won. The vault could be opened as soon as a license could be obtained from the home secretary.

"It's another delaying tactic," she raged at her solicitors once they were alone. "They think if they keep finding one more obstacle I will eventually give up. We must attack them simultaneously from another direction; we must not allow them to become complacent. They must see that I am not just going to go away. I am not some little housewife who will bend her knees simply because some aristocrats wish it. They must have something to hide. If Herbert believed his father was in that grave he would open it immediately in order to discredit me. He could destroy my case just like that!" She snapped her fingers to show how easily she could be got rid of. "But only if the body is there. So they must either know something, or they must be fearful that I might be right."

"What is it you want to do?" the solicitor asked, unable to keep the weariness from his voice. He was beginning to think that taking on Anna Maria's case had been a mistake. A number of very senior people in the legal profession had made a point of having a word in his ear over the previous few months, all of them suggesting that he would be unwise to continue working for a woman who was making so many enemies in high places. He was a man of sufficient character to withstand such pressures if he believed his client to be in the right, but he was beginning to wonder if she might not be a little demented.

"Challenge the will!" Anna Maria announced.

"It's all rather a long time ago now," the solicitor demurred.

"Are you saying it can't be done?" There was a dangerous glint in the woman's eye.

"We could issue a writ to revoke the probate," he said reluctantly. "If he didn't really die on the date claimed then there would be a case for revocation."

"Then do it," she commanded.

The solicitor did as she instructed, causing Herbert to curse Anna Maria all the more roundly when he found out.

"We need to go to the court of appeals," Herbert announced when he heard that yet another judge had upheld Anna Maria's right to open the grave. "Before the home secretary has time to issue his licence."

His lawyers agreed but were mistaken in their belief that the Court of Appeal would overturn the decision. That court also agreed that Anna Maria should be allowed to go ahead with the opening of the coffin.

The letters between the lawyers and judicial figures continued to rain down, while the home secretary remained uncharacteristically quiet about issuing the license. Anna Maria applied to the chancellor once more, this time asking for leave to serve a citation on the cemetery company. The citation was served and another band of lawyers was moved onto the chessboard, this time representing the cemetery company. Nothing could move in any direction. It was a stalemate; nobody was winning apart from the many lawyers' offices, which were continuing to send out their bills to a variety of interested parties, including the increasingly impoverished Anna Maria.

The pressures were building inside her mind as the weeks ticked past. With Sidney in Australia and her husband and mother-in-law both dead, she felt quite alone in the world. She knew that her financial resources were running out but could see no way to replenish them without pressing on to win the case. She was also horribly aware of just how vast the resources working against her were. The opposition, in the form of both her brother-in-law, Herbert, and the Cavendish-Bentinck and Howard de Walden families, had bottomless pits of money and legal expertise on their sides. Anna Maria was more than aware that the sixth duke could quite easily request an audience with the home secretary and be granted it within an hour. He could patronize and manipulate virtually anyone in the country if he so wished, so great was the wealth and power of his family. All she had on her side was the support of the part of the general public that enjoyed watching a great romantic tale unfold before them, and those members of the legal profession who she could afford to pay. It was not a position that allowed her many nights of comfortable sleep.

By May of that year she had started to believe that all the forces ranged against her were planning to break into the vault and remove the coffin, so that when she finally won the right to open it no one would be able to find it. She would make daily visits to the cemetery to check that there were no signs of anyone breaking and entering. It was in June that she saw the grave diggers at work and decided they were trying to tunnel into the vault on the orders of their superiors.

After the incident in the cemetery, when she was once more sitting with her lawyers, unusually subdued by the events, Anna Maria made it clear that no matter how many barriers they put in her way, she would continue to fight for her rights.

"They've called me a fraud and a swindler," she said, with not a trace of a tear in her eye. "They've been very hard on me, but I will not cave in just because they want me to. My son is the duke of Portland."

The lawyer nodded his agreement, his heart going out to the aging lady before him, knowing what a fight still lay ahead of her.

16

LIFTING THE STONES

W e must win possession of the grave!" Anna Maria
announced.

These ideas came to her every so often and when
they did she would cling to them like the wreckage of some ship
that had come to grief in rough seas.

"They must give it to Sidney. His father was the only legitimate
son of Thomas Druce, since Herbert was born before the marriage of his parents. So he should own the grave."

"It might be a case worth putting," her lawyer agreed, reluctant to raise her optimism to unrealistic levels. He couldn't help
but admire the woman's perseverance; no matter what obstacles
were put in her way she refused to give up her dream of one day
winning the title for her son. Like most people, the lawyer was
privately divided in his opinion as to whether she was wise to sacrifice her life, her money, and her health to this one cause, but he
was constantly amazed by her tenacity. Every time she was
knocked back he expected her to finally admit defeat, but she
would be back in his office within days with some new idea of
how they could proceed, how they could circumnavigate whatever new obstacle had been found to block their path.

"Please proceed then," she instructed, and left before he could explain to her the many reasons why it might not be a wise way forward. The lawyer sighed as the door closed behind her; some clients were impossible to advise. He would never be able to show her the error of her ways, so he would simply do as she asked. Sometimes he actually believed she might ultimately triumph, her perseverance wearing away the opposition.

When this case came up it occupied three days in the City of London Court in August 1898, at the end of which the judge dismissed Anna Maria's claim and the cemetery company obtained an order prohibiting her from taking any more actions against them. The lawyer wished he had tried a little harder to dissuade her from pursuing that route.

"They can't do that!" she shrieked when she heard the court's decision. "They've refused me access to the vault in which my parents-in-law and husband are buried. I'm entitled to that access! We'll take an action against them to recover the value of the vault."

Once again the lawyer opened his mouth to advise against it, and once again she was gone before he could find the right words. When the courts rebuffed her this time, Anna Maria's grasp on reality slipped a little farther beyond her reach. She ranted and raved in the lawyer's office for at least an hour before he managed to persuade her that it would be better for her to return home and rest, so that she might conserve her energies for another day.

The newspapers were deeply grateful to Anna Maria for her doggedness in providing them with an endless story that continued to grip the attention of their readers. They covered every twist and turn in the plot with ill-concealed glee, no longer willing to toe the line of discretion that once would have prevented them from embarrassing a family like the Cavendish-Bentincks in public. If the Establishment wanted to show Anna

Maria up as a fraud, the editors argued in their leading articles, then let them open up the coffin and show the world what was inside. That way, if they were right in their claims, she would be silenced once and for all.

The *Daily Mail* was particularly sympathetic:

> *Whatever may be the merits of her case, we may be sure that Mrs Druce, struggling in poverty against wealth and power, driven from pillar to post, harassed, and worried yet ever persevering, has the sympathy of the great majority of her countrymen. Let those who are opposing Mrs Druce consent to the grave being opened so that the matter may be set to rest once and for all.*

"How can they be so blind?" Herbert moaned as he read the newspaper for the third or fourth time. "Do these people really think that I would only stand in Anna Maria's way because I'm frightened she may be right and my father's body might not be there?"

"She's a deluded woman," Grace said, trying to comfort him. She was personally saddened by the whole business, not only because of the worry that she could see it was causing her husband, and the embarrassment for the children of having their family secrets exposed in public, but also because Anna Maria had been her friend and she could think of no way to help her to find peace of mind.

"Can none of them imagine," Herbert fumed, "how they would feel if they were asked to dig up the remains of a beloved parent? Do they not understand that to disturb the rest of the dead is the worst of desecrations and no son would undertake such a task lightly? It is because I'm convinced his remains are in the box that I will not let her touch it with her money-grubbing spade, not because I fear she is right. If I thought for a moment the box was empty I would let the damned woman take an ax to it."

"Yes, dear," Grace said, trying to calm him, anxious that such displays of indignation might damage his heart. "Why don't you write to the papers?"

"I will. I will do that!" Herbert spluttered, going straight to his study and penning half a dozen furious letters to various people in authority as well as the editors of all the papers. He mailed the letters.

The editors duly printed his comments and then replied that they believed Herbert and his friends were desecrating the remains of his father far more by squabbling over them in court after court, and for year after year, than by spending five minutes in inspecting them. Herbert's wife did her best to keep the papers from him on the days the articles were printed, pretending they hadn't been delivered, but Herbert was a man of unbreakable habits and if he had no newspapers delivered to the house he would go out and buy them and spend the rest of the day bellowing furiously at anyone who crossed his path.

Anna Maria's poverty was proving to be the most pressing of her problems. Her greatest fear was that she would run out of money before achieving her goal of opening the vault and would therefore be unable to continue with her fight. The support of the newspaper editors gave her heart, and also an idea: if so many members of the public were now beginning to believe that she might have a case because of the number of obstacles being put in her path, perhaps they could be persuaded to take a gamble on the outcome of the case. If she could persuade the public to invest in her case, she could offer them a share of whatever she managed to win in the end. If she were able to get hold of the Portland millions, she could offer a handsome return on any money loaned to her now.

She put the idea to her lawyer. Since it had been beginning to worry him as to where his client was going to find the necessary financing to meet his bills, he jumped at the idea. In the summer of 1898, shortly after the incident with the grave diggers in Highgate Cemetery, she issued a quantity of Druce-Portland bonds. On Saturday November 12, 1898, a newspaper called the *Anglo-American* printed what they called "The Whole Story," with the subheading "What is the position now? Six judges on the side of Mrs Druce and Three Courts already in her favour."

The story, which illustrated just how confused the public and the press were by that stage about what was proven and what was not, ran as follows:

Bonds will be issued in a few days time for the purpose of raising money to meet the legal and other obligations of Mrs Anna Maria Druce, mother of Sidney George Druce, on whose behalf it is claimed that he is the lineal descendant and heir of the Druce and Portland Estates and Properties which were owned by his grandfather, the late Thomas Charles Druce, otherwise the fifth Duke of Portland.

What has become very popularly known as the "Druce Case" has been so prominently before the public of late that little need be said in this prospectus as to the merits or demerits of Mrs Druce's claim to the Druce and Portland Estates.

It is alleged, however, that the fifth Duke of Portland lived a double, if not a treble, life; that whilst in one character he was the Duke of Portland and enjoyed the estates and emoluments of the Dukedom, in another sphere of life he was the commoner Thomas Charles Druce, and as such carried on various gigantic commercial enterprises, the principal of which was the Baker Street Bazaar, a property which alone is estimated to bring in at the present time no less than £350,000 a year to the present possessor.

It is also alleged that the Alexandra Palace, the Agricultural Hall (Islington), and the Portman Rooms and other similar great undertakings were the outcome of Mr Druce's enterprise.

To gather a fair conception of the extraordinary character of the late fifth Duke of Portland, it will be necessary to go back to September 1848 when the two sons of the fourth Duke—Lord George Bentinck, and his elder brother, the Marquess of Titchfield (the latter being the man who, Mrs Druce alleges, afterwards sank his identity under the name of T.C. Druce) were walking home together accompanied by two gentlemen.

Strange to relate, both these men were in love with the same woman, who, passing as Annie May, was in reality an illegitimate daughter of the fifth Earl of Berkeley, and therefore a relative of the Cavendish-Bentincks.

This gave rise to jealousy between the two brothers which culminated in a fatal quarrel on the evening in question, Lord George being found dead near Welbeck Abbey, and, as is alleged, on what is supposed to be indisputable evidence, the Marquess of Titchfield was his murderer.

The facts of the murder at the time were concealed but they seemed to have preyed upon his mind to an extraordinary extent, and from about this period his eccentricities, if not his temporary insanity, dates.

As Mr Harmer, he became a patient of a private lunatic asylum under the care of Dr Forbes Winslow and this expert and other witnesses of repute are prepared to swear that Mr Harmer, Mr T.C. Druce and the Fifth Duke of Portland were one and the same person.

On October 30th, 1851 at New Windsor, Berkshire, the marriage took place between the surviving brother and Annie May.

The public invested in droves, such was their confidence that Anna Maria would ultimately win the case. They ignored the fact that the stories about a woman called Annie May who was the illegitimate daughter of the earl of Berkeley, and about Dr. Harmer also being the fifth duke, had both been discredited. They wanted to believe that it was all true.

Another of the newspapers that had been following the case with interest was the *Weekly Dispatch*. The editor, Frederick Carson, was a man with a keen nose for a story and all the enthusiasm for the hunt. He felt that even if Anna Maria was deluded and wrong in her claims, there were almost certainly more murky secrets to be found in the family histories of the Cavendish-Bentincks and the Druces. Thomas Druce in particular seemed a fertile ground for investigation. Carson called John Benson, his youngest and sharpest reporter, into his office and explained his thinking.

"If you could prove that the fifth duke of Portland and Thomas Druce were the same man," the editor said, "you'd be able to name your price at any newspaper in the land from the moment we printed the story."

"Yes, sir," the young man said, nervous at being called into his editor's office, but anxious to do whatever he was asked.

"Do you think you have it in you to root out the truth?"

"It's what I came into journalism for," Benson assured him.

"Good man. Take these files and study them." Carson pushed across details of the various court cases and background on all the characters involved. "If you want my advice you won't waste too much time on the Cavendish-Bentincks. They're too rich and too powerful. They've been covering up skeletons for too many centuries to let a young whippersnapper like you dig them up. But Thomas Druce's past may not be so well protected. You'll need to go around lifting some stones.

"All anyone seems to know about him is that he arrived in London already in his mid-thirties, as the owner of one of the biggest stores in the city. Where did he come from? Nobody knows. How did he make his money? Nobody knows. If you can find out what Thomas Druce was doing in the years before he came to London, you're quite likely to discover whether or not he was the duke of Portland. The public all want to know the truth, so let's see if you can find it for them, shall we?"

"Yes sir," Benson said, clutching the bulky files to his chest as he left the office, desperate to start his research, to crack the case that everyone was talking about, and thereby stake his claim as the best young journalist in England.

John Benson was not a prepossessing man to look at, small and thin and rather rodentlike in his facial features. But he had a determination about him that Frederick Carson had recognized when he agreed to take him on. Carson had a feeling that the future of the British press would fall into the hands of men like Benson, who were willing to keep searching and hunting until they had managed to unearth the truth. Carson wasn't sure that he was comfortable with the idea, but if it was going to happen he wanted to be sure that Benson was on his payroll and not the opposition's.

Once John had read all the material, familiarizing himself with the claims that Anna Maria was making, he began his inquiries. He needed to find all records of families by the name of Druce in England in the first half of the century. Initially, the number of names seemed daunting, but as he continued to compare and cross-reference them the patterns became clear. There were a few dozen families named Druce and they centered on various parts of the country. There was nothing for it but to start traveling and meeting as many of them as possible.

Being a thorough young man, Benson prepared a plan to get to each family in the minimum amount of time. He ran the plan past Carson, who would need to approve the expense of the trip, not to mention the amount of time that his reporter would be unavailable for other stories. After studying the plan for a few minutes, Carson had to admit, if only to himself, that he was impressed.

"Very well," he said eventually. "But make sure you come back with a story."

Benson was unable to hide his joy. This was going to be an adventure. In his inexperience he was unable to envisage the many days he would spend in railway carriages or bumping over potholes in coaches and carts without springs, being jostled and pushed for countless hours against people he would prefer never to have spent so much as a minute with. He couldn't imagine the filth of the rooms in some of the inns and taverns where he would have to stop for food and sleep, or the blisters and sores he would develop on his feet as he walked to places accessible only on foot.

All he saw at the beginning of his journey was a successful end, returning to the newspaper with incontrovertible proof that Thomas Druce and the duke were one and the same person.

That vision kept him going over the following months, together with the fear of having to admit to Frederick Carson that he had failed to get the best story in the country. Failure was not a possibility for him; he had to keep searching until he succeeded.

He was amazed by the contrasting circumstances that the different Druce families lived in. Some were prosperous pillars of local towns, running shops or inhabiting professional offices, others were farming families living in the remotest of areas. Some of them had heard of the celebrated Druce/Portland case while others responded to Benson in suspicion and puzzlement. Some would welcome the weary traveler with hospitality; others would keep him outside their houses and shake their heads to every question. Occasionally, he would strike what he thought was a seam of gold, hearing about some twenty- or thirty-year-old man with the family name who had disappeared from sight. He would follow up each lead, but there was always some reason why it couldn't possibly produce the man he was searching for.

By the time Benson reached a village about twenty miles from Bury St. Edmonds he was beginning to feel despondent. When he was told that all the Druces in the area had moved away years before, his spirits sank even lower. As he had in every other place in his search, he visited the local graveyard, hoping that perhaps a gravestone would render some vital piece of information.

Many of the markers were covered by ivy or lichen and it took Benson some time to discern all the engraved names, but none of them was Druce. Feeling tired, hungry, and miserable, he made his way toward the warm lights of the vicarage across the lane.

A pleasant-faced man answered the door. "I was looking for the vicar," Benson told him.

"You've found him," the man replied, extending a welcoming hand. "What can I do for you?"

Benson explained what he was looking for and the young man took him to the kitchen where his wife was preparing supper. The couple sat him down and fed him as he regaled them with the endless tale of his travels around the country in search of Thomas Charles Druce.

"I'll tell you what we'll do," the vicar said. "We'll make you up a bed here for the night and in the morning we'll go through the parish records together to see if we can find any trace of your man."

Benson gratefully accepted the offer. He felt at the end of his tether and had a terrible feeling that he might return to London empty-handed. He doubted if he would keep his job after he'd broken the news to his editor. Once in among the soft feathers of the vicarage spare bed, Benson sank into a sleep so deep he didn't stir until past ten the following morning. When he arrived downstairs he found the vicar's wife already preparing lunch. But she made him some breakfast, refusing to let him out of the room until he'd eaten every last scrap, and then directed him to her husband's office, where the vicar had been hard at work on his behalf for some hours.

Benson found the vicar sitting at his desk amid a heap of files and records. The man's face was alight with excitement.

"Come in, come in," he crowed. "Did you sleep well? Good, good. I think I may have found your man."

The vicar pulled a rickety wooden chair up beside him so Benson could share in his find and began opening page after page as he blurted out the story he had managed to unearth.

"It seems your Mr. Thomas Druce arrived in the area at the age of sixteen. No one knew where he came from, but he was obviously a boy of some character. Despite his age he managed to persuade a young lady called Elizabeth Crickmer to marry him, in St. James's Church, Bury St. Edmonds. It seems it was all a bit hurried, so it may be they eloped without her parents' consent. She was only sixteen as well. Two star-crossed lovers, no doubt, a veritable Romeo and Juliet."

The vicar took off his glasses, giving them a quick polish. He seemed to have been affected by the romance of his own story.

"Anyway, they lived in the area and Thomas Druce was extremely active in local affairs for the church and for local charities. He seems to have been something of a stalwart of village society, despite being away for long periods, serving in the army.

"The couple had three children. I've listed their names and

dates of birth for you here." He passed over a piece of paper. "Two boys and one girl. Then something went terribly wrong. Thomas Druce vanishes completely from the records. Elizabeth, it seems, was left with three children and no money whatsoever. She had to be moved into a house provided by the local authorities and lived off handouts from several charities. I suspect life must have been very hard for the poor woman."

"What happened to the children?" Benson asked.

"I don't have any records of them, but I dare say you could trace them down in London. They would be very elderly indeed if they are still alive, but they might have left offspring of their own who would be able to tell you a tale or two."

For the rest of the day Benson sat at the vicar's desk painstakingly recording every piece of information he could dig up: every date, every name, every address that he could find. The next day, having risen earlier than usual due to a state of considerable excitement, he went around to the houses that Elizabeth Crickmer and Thomas Druce had lived in, either together or apart, taking copious notes of the impressions they made on him. He could feel the story building, although he knew he needed more evidence if he was going to claim that this Thomas Druce was the man who appeared at the Baker Street Bazaar fifteen years after leaving Elizabeth Crickmer.

Three days after arriving at the vicarage in virtual despair, Benson set off back to London in high spirits, believing that he was about to give Frederick Carson the most sensational story in the country. If this was the same Thomas Druce, and he could hardly bear to think that it wasn't, then it changed everything about the case. If, as Anna Maria claimed, Thomas Druce and the fifth duke of Portland were one and the same, then Elizabeth Crickmer's eldest son was the legitimate heir to the Portland millions, not Anna Maria's deceased husband. If any of Elizabeth Crickmer's children had produced sons, then they, not Anna Maria's son, could step forward and claim the title and money.

While Benson's discovery would almost certainly ruin Anna Maria's chances of making her son the duke of Portland, the evidence he had uncovered about Thomas Druce did nothing to rule out the suggestion that he led a double life. In 1816 he'd appeared near Bury St. Edmonds from nowhere aged sixteen, the age when the young Lord John would have been free to come and go from Welbeck Abbey. He'd left his home with Elizabeth for long periods of time, supposedly serving in the army. He could easily have been appearing somewhere else in the world as Lord John during those times. He then vanished from sight for fifteen years, from 1820 to 1835, during which time he could have been living at Welbeck Abbey as the marquess of Titchfield and preparing for his life as a businessman in London by transferring funds into the name of Thomas Druce.

Once he was back in London, Benson resisted the temptation to go straight to Carson's office and blurt out what he'd found. He wanted to make sure he had every scrap of proof possible before presenting his story. Armed with the names and birth dates of Thomas and Elizabeth Druce's three children from the local records at Bury St. Edmonds, he went back to the national records in London and renewed his searching. It took two more days before he discovered that one of the sons, Henry, had emigrated to Australia, while Charles and Frances Druce were registered as dead. Frances had died an unmarried spinster, but Charles had produced several children. Benson tracked down one of his sons, William, and went to see him.

The man was intrigued to be approached by a reporter. He'd read about the case in the papers but had assumed it was a different branch of the Druce family, not having any idea how many people bore the same name in the country and knowing little about his own ancestors. Once Benson laid the case out for him, however, William Druce racked his memory for stories he'd heard as a child, and a jigsaw puzzle began to fit together through the mists of half-remembered family anecdotes.

"I was always told," he said, "that my father, my uncle Henry, and aunt Frances were abandoned by their father when they were young. Their mother brought them up on her own, which was very hard, and then their father came back to get them when they were teenagers. I was taken to meet my aunt Frances when she was very elderly. I don't think she and my father had seen each other for years. I remember her telling me how puzzled she was that her father seemed to be so rich, when her mother had always been so poor. Her father told her that her mother was dead and that she would be living with him from then on. He housed her with a woman he said was her aunt, I think. She only discovered much later that her mother hadn't died when her father said she had. But by the time she found out it was too late because our grandmother was truly dead."

He paused and reflected for some time. Benson didn't interrupt his thoughts.

"So you think the Thomas Druce in the Druce Portland case is my grandfather?" he said eventually.

"Yes, I do," Benson told him. "I most certainly do."

"That would mean that if Anna Maria Druce is right about the connection with the duke of Portland, then my cousin Charles would be the sixth duke of Portland, as the eldest surviving son of Henry, who would be the fifth duke's eldest son?"

"Yes," Benson nodded enthusiastically. "I believe that's true. Do you know where I would find your cousin?"

"I'm not certain," Druce admitted. "We've not really kept in close touch. His father, my uncle Henry, emigrated to Australia and he was born out there. I guess they still live there."

As soon as Benson felt he was out of sight of the house, he gave a small skip of joy. He had his story and it was going to make his reputation. Everyone was going to read the words he was about to commit to paper. He still lacked solid proof of a connection between Thomas Druce and the fifth duke, but he had managed to unearth a completely new angle on the story, which was bound to make the public want to buy any paper that carried his report.

The following morning he was waiting in Carson's office when the great man came in. The editor raised an enquiring eyebrow and Benson passed him a sheaf of papers with trembling fingers. Carson sat down and read them through with painful deliberation, then rose to his feet and shook Benson warmly by the hand.

"Young man, you have a great future ahead of you at this newspaper."

17

REVELATION UPON REVELATION

On February 26, 1899, Anna Maria read, along with much of the rest of London, the headlines of the *Weekly Dispatch*. Even in her troubled state of mind she was able to see they purported that her case had collapsed. John Benson's story, by the standards of the day, was sensational in the extreme. Not only did the public thrill to the idea that there were now yet more potential claimants for the title of the sixth duke of Portland, they were also able to read about shameful past behavior among the wealthy and powerful. Even if the connection between the Druces and the Cavendish-Bentincks was not proven, there were still plenty of revelations to titillate the casual reader. Thomas Druce, it now seemed, was not only a shopkeeper with curious personal habits; he was also a bounder and a scoundrel, a man who was willing to leave his former child bride living in poverty while he built himself a business empire and lived in sin with another woman, a woman who was herself accused of being the illegitimate daughter of an earl. Never mind what the truth of the situation might be, the possibilities were delicious enough on their own. The nation was once more enthralled by the unfolding narrative.

"I will not be giving up the fight," Anna Maria told anyone

who would listen, her eyes wide with outrage at this new attempt to keep her from the title that she so coveted. "They cannot defeat me this easily."

But everyone else could see that if this story could not be disproved quickly her chances of success were now dashed on the rocks of the evidence. Everyone now wanted to know who else from the Druce lineage would step forward and replace her in the front line of assault on the Portland estate.

Herbert Druce also learned about his father's earlier marriage and family for the first time in the newspaper that day. His wife wondered why he'd fallen so silent at the breakfast table. He usually read choice bits of news to her as he came across them, or denounced some new government foolishness that he'd discovered in the dense newsprint; quiet concentration was unusual. But Grace knew better than to interrupt him while he was reading. Eventually Herbert put the paper down and she saw that something had shocked him deeply. She was about to ask him what the matter was, when the look of surprise on his face changed to one of amusement. The poor woman was startled to hear a sound that had not emitted from her husband in all the years she had been married to him, that of laughter.

When his mirth eventually subsided he waved the newspaper at his wife.

"That should shut Anna Maria up once and for all," he choked. "Some reporter has discovered that my father was married before he even met my mother. He had children by this first wife. If Anna Maria is right and he was also the duke of Portland, then they're the potential beneficiaries, not her precious Sidney. She's finally been ruined by her own madness and greed."

"Another family?" Grace couldn't find it in herself to join in Herbert's merriment. "You mean you have other brothers and sisters?"

"Two half brothers and one half sister, apparently," Herbert replied, the thought sobering him markedly. "Apparently they're all dead."

"You had no idea your father had been married before?"

"None at all. But that's hardly surprising. I knew virtually nothing about the man. I was his son, not his keeper. He didn't confide anything in me."

He took a sip of his tea and stared at the paper, which now lay on the table beside him. Grace could see that the information was beginning to seep deeper into his mind. She was well aware that her husband had not had an easy relationship with his father and the discovery that his whole childhood had been lived beneath such a gigantic lie was bound to be a shock. The thought of the hurt he might feel made tears start in her eyes, but she knew Herbert would shed no tears. For over half a century her husband had been learning how to suppress emotions, like all gentlemen should. As long as she lived she would not be able to fathom the relationships that men formed, particularly fathers and sons.

The story didn't stop at the shores of Britain. As soon as the boats could make it to Australia with the news, it was pounced upon by the newspapers of the New World.

George Hollamby Druce was not an avid reader of news from Europe. He was an Australian born and bred and had enough to think about in his own daily life without worrying what might be happening on the other side of the world. His father, Henry, had left a sizeable mining business when he died, which had been divided between George Hollamby and his older brother, Charles. Both boys had enjoyed privileged childhoods. Eventually there were many houses on the outskirts of Melbourne and a number of servants. Henry had been away from home a great deal on business and the sweet-natured Rachel had not been able to exercise as much control on either of her boys as might have been appropriate. They fell in with a set of other young men who spent most of their time hunting, drinking, and gambling. Life in Australia was simply too easy. The sun shone, the food was plentiful, and life was good. The boys could not understand their father's drive to work all the time. Unlike him, they had nothing in their pasts to escape from. When Henry died and the business fell into their hands neither of them had the slightest idea what to do with it, nor any inclination to run it. Two years after they gained control, when they had already allowed it to halve in its value through negligence, they gave up even pretending to care, and sold it to a British company that was buying up all the mineral rights they could lay their hands on.

Rachel was brokenhearted to see Henry's company—the one he had spent so many years creating and building—vanishing overnight. Charles used his share of the money to buy himself a sheep farm, and George Hollamby used his to buy himself a smart house in the newest of Melbourne's suburbs, equipped with the trappings of a gentleman bachelor. His life was just as he wanted it, with all the freedom he needed to drink and gamble with his old friends, but the money was not going to last forever. In his few sober moments, George Hollamby realized that sooner or later he was going to have to find a way to earn some more. Each day he would put off the decision as to how he was going to do that by telling himself that maybe tonight he would be lucky at the card table. On some nights he was lucky; on most he was not.

It was during one of these card games that another of the players drew his attention to the newspaper carrying John Benson's story.

"Your father was called Henry, wasn't he?" the man enquired.

"What of it?" George Hollamby wanted to know, his attention

divided between his cards and the young woman standing beside him, watching him play.

"Seems like you might be a member of the English royal family, then," the man laughed, passing the paper across to him.

When the game finished George took the girl and the newspaper to a settee and called for another drink as he looked at the article. At first he read it in the same humorous spirit as his friend, but as the words sunk into his brain he began to sober up. He felt a stirring of excitement in his stomach. All the facts seemed to fit. If his distant half-cousin by marriage, Anna Maria (a woman whose existence he had known nothing about until that moment), was correct about who his grandfather really was, his elder brother, Charles, was possibly the legitimate heir of the fifth duke of Portland.

"Streuth!" he muttered when the realization dawned on him. "Charlie could be the richest bloody man in the world!"

Several days later George Hollamby had crossed a large part of the Australian continent to show his brother the newspaper and to suggest that they might go to England and stake a claim to their family fortune.

"You could be a bloody duke, Charlie," George Hollamby pointed out as they sat on the porch with beers, watching a pair of dogs playing in the dust.

Charles shook his head thoughtfully and read the article again before responding. "I don't know, George. It's a long bloody way to England, and supposing we lost the case? We could be well out of pocket."

"Where's your sense of adventure, man?" George Hollamby wanted to know. "You could be a duke. Imagine what a time you could have with all that money."

"I'm pretty happy the way I am, you know, George. I don't think I would suit being a duke."

George Hollamby looked around the ramshackle ranch building and had to admit, if only to himself, that it was hard to imagine his brother living in an English stately home. Himself, that was a different matter. He was a man of style, a man who would know how to comport himself around the fashionable areas of London.

"I tell you what, Charlie," he said eventually. "It seems a pity to waste an opportunity like this. Why don't you sign the rights to the title over to me, and I'll cut you in on the money as soon as I get hold of it. You can have whatever you need to do this place up a bit. That way there's no risk of it costing you any money if it doesn't work out. It's a risk-free venture for you. What do you think?"

"I don't know about lawyers, George. They're all slippery devils, fleecing you of your money as soon as they look at you."

"Don't worry about a thing, Charlie." George Hollamby slapped his brother reassuringly on the back. "I'll take care of everything. All you'll have to do is sign on the dotted line and work out what you're gonna do with the money."

The nineteenth century passed by and the wheels of the law ground slowly on. No one in the legal profession was in any hurry to reach a conclusion in a case that was creating so many rich pickings in legal fees. It wasn't until 1901 that Anna Maria was back in court pleading her case, by which time the British public had heard that George Hollamby was also going to be staking his claim to the Portland millions. She cut a sorry figure now. Everyone except her could see that she no longer stood a chance of benefiting from proving that Thomas and the fifth Duke were one and the same person. If she now succeeded in getting the grave opened and the coffin was empty, as she still insisted it would be, the rewards for her years of struggling against the authorities would almost certainly go to descendants of Elizabeth Crickmer.

To those who witnessed her performance in court her mind seemed to be wandering. For five years she'd been monomaniacal, battling alone against the entire British Establishment and the strain was taking its toll on her health. When asked in court about George Hollamby Druce, she began to rant.

"He's an impudent, audacious and absolutely ignorant impostor, foisted upon me by the people, whose name I won't mention, to keep me in a state of ferment. This man is a miner by occupation, now in the Antipodes, and must be brought over by the extradition court at Bow Street and, together with his solicitors, be incarcerated in jail to teach them a lesson they won't forget."

The judge and the lawyers attempted to continue a professional dialogue about the opening of the grave but Anna Maria, tired of their legal jargon and procrastination, kept leaning forward and interjecting, as if playing an elderly duchess for all the world.

"I am the plaintiff," she would announce loudly, "and the duchess of Portland, remember that. Prove your pedigree."

The lawyers attempted to continue as if she wasn't there and for a few moments she was silent, before bursting forth once more.

"I won't be robbed of everything I have in the world, to the value of this lead pencil!"

The lawyers waded on for a while and Anna Maria's patience snapped once more. She was brazenly determined now to prove that the two Thomas Druces, her father-in-law and George Hollamby's grandfather, were different men, desperate at the thought she might have put in all these years of effort just to see someone else walk off with her prize.

"Let him produce his form of pedigree," she yelled. "I have

it, but the onus is on him. He is the grandson of Thomas Druce, a draper at Bury St. Edmunds, who was born in 1785, and was thirty-one years of age when he married in 1816. He is no relation of Thomas Charles Druce, fifth duke of Portland, who was born in 1800 and could not, therefore, have been married in 1816."

No one took any notice, it having already been established by the records that Thomas was sixteen when he was married to Elizabeth Crickmer. Anna Maria was finding it increasingly hard to make herself sound lucid. A few weeks later, she cross-examined Catherine Bayly, who nursed her husband and his siblings as children and then became Thomas's medical nurse. Miss Bayly said she had locked the door of the room in which Druce's body was supposed to have been laid out. Anna Maria pounced on her with near-hysterical enthusiasm.

"Why did you lock the room up—to keep out the devil? What was there in there—a corpse? A skeleton? What was in this wonderful Bluebeard chamber—an effigy, ha! Ha! A wax figure ha! Ha! A face, or what?"

She went on to accuse the witness of perjury and the defense lawyers of bribery and corruption. She called counsel liars, submitted a printed newspaper as a specimen of handwriting, and a blank piece of paper as an indenture. When the judge pointed out this last mistake to her, she exclaimed:

"But I swear it is; and therefore it is so."

Later in the same day, when giving evidence, Anna Maria described again how she had met her supposedly "late" father-in-law.

"It was in 1874, two years after my marriage. I met him in Maidenhead walking with a groom in the service of Dr. Forbes Winslow. The groom told me his companion was a patient in Dr. Forbes Winslow's asylum at Hammersmith. I was driving in a carriage and pair [of horses]. I recognized T. C. Druce by his photograph. My husband was with me and the groom spoke to him. I understood that he was then passing under the name of Dr. Harmer. I only saw him on that occasion."

A sad silence fell upon the court as they listened to the witness rambling on, everyone knowing that it had long since been determined that Dr. Harmer was not Thomas Druce when the real Harmer's wife was brought into court and recognized by Dr. Forbes Winslow, the owner of the madhouse. Everyone in the room knew how many years Anna Maria had been crusading to achieve what she saw as simple justice and all their sympathy went out to her, none of them having the heart to stop her babbling.

"About the will," she ranted. "Yes, yes, the witness Henry Walker is also a mysterious person, like T. C. Druce. He is not dead at all, but lives at Forty Bernard Street, Bloomsbury, where he keeps a lodging house. He has been for many years employed to stoke the fires in the underground palace at Welbeck. I have seen him alive, so he cannot be buried in Highate cemetery, and I wish to open his grave. I said, 'You're Henry Walker.' He said, 'I'm not.' I said, 'You're a liar, you are living in the same house as he lived.'"

Her words rang around the silence of the courtroom, making no sense to any of the listeners there and making it plain that Anna Maria Druce had finally lost her grip on reality.

Despite their sadness on her behalf, the jury that day found against Anna Maria without even withdrawing to discuss it. There was no need for any deliberation. They held that the original will was valid. They believed Thomas Druce had died on December 28, 1864, as family members such as Herbert had originally claimed. Two weeks later Anna Maria applied for a new trial on the grounds that she had new evidence, but no one ever got to find out what it was. The judge told her to go to the court of appeal but she never went. Her exhaustion temporarily got the better of her and she retreated into her house and closed the door behind her, there to fight her demons in private.

People still brought her news of what was going on and when she heard that George Hollamby Druce was almost ready with his own case she flew into a terrible rage, swearing that she would never cease pursuing her case through the courts.

Alone in her house one evening, her servants long since having been fired as an economic measure, and muttering to herself in a way that had become habit, Anna Maria answered the door to an imposing-looking doctor with two attendants. The expressions on the men's faces were grim. The doctor was dressed in black from his top hat to his boots and the attendants seemed to be poised to catch her should she try to make a run for freedom. They asked to be allowed into the house to speak to her. Despite their forbidding appearance, Anna Maria no longer felt she had anything to fear in life. What more could they do to her? They'd taken all her money and her good name; they'd refused her everything she felt she was entitled to by law. Feeling she had nothing else to lose, she invited them in. She was wrong. There was still something they could take from her—her liberty.

The doctor told her she was to be committed to an institution where she could be helped to cope with her persecution mania and megalomania. Not an unkind man, he assured her that she would be a great deal happier once she had received some treatment. Anna Maria didn't believe him and, garnering all the strength her tired, fifty-year-old body could muster, beat her fists against his chest in an explosion of pure fury. The two attendants stepped forward and restrained her with straps before carrying her out to the waiting carriage. The doctor went quickly around the house to make sure there were no pets that would be locked in and that all the windows and doors were secured and then followed them out, slipping a few small valuables into his pocket and locking the front door behind him. Anna Maria would not personally be able to make a nuisance of herself again, although her legacy was to live on for several more years yet.

The courts had decided, based on her continued delusional behavior, that Anna Maria now needed medical help rather than legal.

18

GEORGE HOLLAMBY'S CASE

Mr. Druce," said the distinguished lawyer, Mr. Atherley-Jones, K.C., M.P. (King's Counsel and Member of Parliament), as he peered at George Hollamby over his glasses. The year was 1900 and Atherley-Jones had a feeling that George Hollamby was a man of the twentieth century, not the nineteenth. Atherley-Jones's look was one that was meant to intimidate men of lesser education than himself. It would have taken considerably more than that, however, to dent the confidence of George Hollamby, who had now set his sights on becoming the next duke of Portland. He had even bought himself a new set of clothes on arriving in London, in order to fit in among the many fine legal gentlemen he knew he would be meeting. Unfortunately, the clothes looked far too new, and far too well cut, to belong to a real gentleman, who would always be just a little shabby in order to show that his money, like his clothes, was not newly acquired. But George Hollamby did not know that, and so his confidence remained undimmed.

"Yes?" he replied, wondering why lawyers always had to indulge in such dramatic pauses, even when they were talking to their clients in private. "What?"

"What is to be done about Charles Edgar Druce?"

"My big brother, Charlie?" George Hollamby was nonplussed. "What's this got to do with him?"

"The laws of primogeniture mean that titles such as this one pass down the male line."

"I am the male line."

"But so is your brother, Charles Edgar. And he is older than you and therefore the first in line."

"But he doesn't want the title. He's signed the whole thing over to me."

"He's signed it over to you?" the lawyer enquired, finding it hard to believe that any sane man would do such a thing, although he could imagine that George Hollamby could be very persuasive when he wanted to be, like a persistent salesman.

"Charlie's a modest man. He's happy with his lot in life, know what I mean? A few hundred sheep, a few horses and dogs and a pleasant woman to come home to, that's all Charlie wants. He said he was happy for me to take the responsibility off his shoulders." George beamed proudly at his own benevolence. "I'll make sure he wants for nothing once the money comes through, don't you worry about that. Charlie's my flesh and blood. I wouldn't do anything to cheat him of his rights."

"And you have all the relevant paper work to prove this?" Atherley-Jones enquired.

"Certainly do," George Hollamby replied, slapping the papers down on the desk between them.

"Which brings us," Atherley-Jones said, "to the question of how you are going to fund this case."

"Fund it?" George Hollamby looked a little perplexed for a moment.

"I take it you're not a wealthy man."

"I do all right," he replied defensively, "but I guess I'm not wealthy by the standards of most of your clients. I don't own any of the counties of England, if that's what you mean."

"Quite. So how are we going to underwrite the many months and possibly years of work ahead of us, before we can hope to unlock any of your rightful inheritance?"

"I don't know. You got any ideas?" George beamed happily, confident that a man as grand as Atherley-Jones would know his way around these sorts of problems. George Hollamby had managed to get himself included in enough card games over the years when he never had the stake money to start with, to know these things were always surmountable.

"It's possible that you could do something like your cousin, Mrs. Anna Maria Druce. You could incorporate a company that would own all the assets of the estate should you win, and you could then sell as many shares of that company as you needed to finance yourself over the coming years of preparation."

"I don't want to give the whole damn lot away before I've even got my hands on it," George Hollamby protested. "I couldn't do that to old Charlie."

"You could hold back by far the majority of the shares in your own name, or the names of your wife or children."

"How do we do that?"

"I can arrange for you to meet some businessmen who will advise you."

"How long is all this going to take?"

"It would be foolish for you to rush into it. That was the mistake Mrs. Druce made. If she had done a little more research before going to the courts she would have saved herself a great deal of time, money, and anguish. She might even have saved her sanity. It may take a few years before we're ready to fight our case effectively. You must be aware that you're taking on some of the wealthiest and most influential people in the country. Look what they've done to your cousin."

"My cousin was a woman alone," George Hollamby said, puffing out his chest. "I'm not going to be so easy to brush aside. We must take as long as necessary to make sure we get justice for our family."

It was, in fact, five years from the moment he set foot in London before the outside world saw the first signs of George Hollamby stepping forward to claim his inheritance. In that time a great deal of work needed to be done in preparation. None of his legal advisers wanted to make any mistakes. The money was surprisingly easy to raise from a public still keen to see the story continue and to take a punt on the possibility of owning a piece of the Portland millions for themselves.

On July 22, 1905, a company named G. H. Druce was incorporated with a capital worth of £11,000 divided into ten thousand shares of £1 each and twenty thousand shares of one shilling. All the shares were held by George Hollamby himself, except for his statutory nominees. He had to start selling them immediately in order to raise money just to live. He had sold two thousand shares by the end of the year and by the end of 1907 he'd disposed of a total of ten thousand shares.

In the indenture, on which the company was based, Druce conveyed to the company all his rights and benefits arising out of his claim upon the Portland estate. There was also an indenture between George Hollamby and his brother Charles Edgar, clearing the way for George Hollamby to inherit the dukedom. The conditions of this indenture were kept strictly secret.

It became obvious that the G. H. Druce Company was not going to provide enough money for the prolonged battle and toward the end of 1907 two more companies were incorporated, The Druce-Portland Company and the New Druce-Portland Company. Both these corporations would also be rewarded with commission if the bid for the dukedom was successful.

George Hollamby and his advisers had learned a great deal by studying Anna Maria's mistakes. The Portland and Howard de Walden estates were thought to be worth approximately £16 million. If George Hollamby was successful in his claim then the New Druce-Portland Company, according to its prospectus, would be entitled to claim 10 percent of the money, or £1.6 million. That would make each five-shilling share in the company worth £16, or sixty-four times the amount subscribed. This promise brought in £30,000 to the New Druce-Portland Company from investors, which immediately falsified the prospectus, since sixty-four times £30,000 comes to £1.92 million, considerably more than the £1.6 million that the company was supposed to be worth. Nobody seemed to worry about such details, either because they stood to make money or because the sums were too complicated to work out. When there were such heady sums being bandied around it might have seemed churlish to complain about the odd £320,000.

During the years of preparation George Hollamby's Australian solicitor, a Mr. Coburn, traveled up to work alongside his friend and protect him from the "sharks" that he claimed inhabited the London legal sea. Coburn then wrote an article for the *Daily Express* explaining what they were hoping to achieve. George Hollamby himself wrote a piece for a magazine called *The Idler* detailing his life and the claims he was making. The magazine's editor took the bold step of offering a reward of £100 to anyone who could produce Thomas Druce's birth certificate, in order to clear up the mystery and dissuade any more claimants to the title from coming forward. Had anyone been able to do so George Hollamby's entire case would have collapsed since it would have proved conclusively that Thomas Druce was not the same man as the fifth duke. No birth certificate was forthcoming.

While using the years 1905 to 1907 to raise money, George Hollamby's team was also poring over the existing evidence and searching for new proof that Thomas Druce and the fifth duke were the same man. They combed the mountain of material already collected from Anna Maria's court cases, but didn't rest there. They left nothing to chance, interviewing everyone who had ever met either Thomas or the duke and compiling minutely detailed records. Eventually they managed to uncover enough new witnesses, they believed, to stand a good chance of winning where Anna Maria had failed.

Over seventy witnesses were found in Australia, New Zealand, and America, all places that took weeks to reach by mail boat. It was a long and slow business but the team was determined not to give up. The ultimate prize was simply too tempting. For George Hollamby there would be untold riches, and for his legal team there would be the glory of winning the most celebrated case of the day against awesome opponents.

The most compelling evidence was based on existing pictures of both men taken from family collections. Each picture had been wrongly identified by people who knew either Druce or the duke. In other words, people who knew the duke well by sight had sworn that a picture that was in fact known to be of Druce, was that of the man they knew, and vice versa.

Nearly all the independent witnesses had described both men in nearly identical terms, claiming them to be arbitrary, unap-proachable, austere, unbending, and impatient when contra-dicted. Again this evidence came from witnesses who knew one or other man but not both.

Some people claimed that both men had a skin disease that gave them a jaundiced appearance and made them avoid sunlight and favor red blinds. Many of the Druce descendants were simi-larly afflicted, as Anna Maria had already pointed out to a number of judges. Druce and the duke had also been described as being of similar height and strong build.

Both men were known to be abstemious regarding drink and tobacco, spare eaters with an objection to butchers' meat and a partiality for fish and chicken.

They were both described by those who knew them as being secretive and reserved, to enjoy subterraneans wanderings, and to possess a passion for building and altering things. A great many architects had been employed by both of them, yet they had then overseen the work themselves. They both wore a wide variety of wigs and had a restless, untiring energy. Methodical in their habits, both men chose a peculiar style of closed carriage to travel in with injunctions of secrecy lain on their coachmen when they went on their mysterious journeys. Both of them had a habit of turning up unexpectedly after long, unexplained absences. They disliked company and had only a few menials as close confidants.

A number of workmen had been employed by both men and claimed to have been sworn to confidentiality about anything they might have seen or heard while working for Thomas or the duke. Neither man would allow any discussion of their personal or family affairs. They were fastidious about the arrangement of their belongings and liked to do all their business by deputy. They were cautious and suspicious of those around them, not liking to be saluted or spoken to unless they had spoken first and both had a partiality for the fair sex. They often frequented the same house in London and both had access to great wealth. It was beginning to look as if no one could dispute the fact that they were one and the same man.

"It has to be true," George Hollamby said one evening as he and his legal team sat in Atherley-Jones's office with large glasses of brandy after another hard day with the files. "I mean the appearance of one of them always tallies with the disappearance of the other. Never were both of them around at the same time."

"That still isn't necessarily proof," Atherley-Jones pointed out. "There are many men who choose to lead secretive lives with their mistresses while maintaining a married front. It doesn't mean they are taking on different identities."

"But to have two men so similar in so many ways disappearing, sometimes for years at a time, is beyond a coincidence," George Hollamby insisted. "Do you not think that a man who is the son of the fourth duke of Portland would be mentioned somewhere between the ages of sixteen and nineteen? Wouldn't he have been at a university or a school or something? Why would he just disappear and then suddenly reappear in the army? It doesn't make sense; unless he was off marrying Elizabeth Crickmer and calling himself Thomas Druce.

"And why wasn't he at his father's funeral? It was an event that would make him one of the richest men in the world, for God's sake, and he didn't even bother to turn up? I don't believe it. But if he actually was Thomas Druce then he wouldn't have been able to show his face at a high-profile funeral a few streets away from his shop, where anyone in the street might spot him and make the connection. He never seemed to turn up to any of the Cavendish-Bentinck family bashes, even when he was head of the clan. He's never mentioned in any books about his house or his relations.

"And this Thomas Druce, how come there's no birth certificate? And where did his money come from to start the shop? A man can't just appear from nowhere and already have thousands in the bank. It just isn't possible!"

"So let's summarize what we have." Atherley-Jones stood up and paced the room, counting the years off on his fingers. "From 1816 to 1820 there are no records of the future fifth duke but plenty of Druce because he marries Elizabeth Crickmer and makes himself known in the Bury St. Edmunds area. From 1820 to 1835 there are no records of Druce but plenty of the duke because he became a Member of Parliament. From 1835 to 1864 nothing on the duke, plenty on Druce with the success of the Baker Street Bazaar, and then from 1864, after Druce has been killed off, the duke becomes extraordinarily active at Welbeck."

"How can we lose?" George Hollamby spread his arms wide and lit a cigar, as if already celebrating a victory.

"Easily," the lawyer snapped back. "We may have the law on our side, but they have the lawmakers on theirs."

George Hollamby took a long swig of brandy and drew thoughtfully on the cigar. "But we have all these great new witnesses who are going to blow apart every argument the opposition can put up."

"There's something else we need to talk about," Atherley-Jones said, ignoring the interruption.

"What's that?" George Hollamby asked.

"We've been made an offer."

"By whom?"

"It's anonymous, brought to me by another lawyer."

"Well, are you going to tell me how much?"

"Fifty thousand pounds. You will receive fifty thousand pounds if you drop the claim."

"Yahoo." George Hollamby jumped to his feet and did a war dance around the room, his cigar clenched between his teeth, certain that the making of the offer proved the opposition had something they deemed worth hiding. "We've got the buggers on the run!"

"So you will not be accepting the offer?"

"Tell them to stuff the offer up His Majesty's backside!"

"I think we should perhaps give this a little more thought." The lawyer's voice was noticeably monotone in comparison to George Hollamby's whoops of delight.

"What's to think about?"

"If the Portland and Howard de Walden estates are willing to pay fifty thousand pounds just to make this go away, imagine how much they would be willing to put into fighting it. The money we've raised so far could be sucked up in a few months if we try to take them on headfirst."

George Hollamby collapsed back into his chair and refilled his brandy glass. "So what do you suggest we do?"

"I suggest we tackle it from another angle. I suggest we go for Herbert Druce. He's wealthy enough to want to protect what he's got, but not so wealthy it would be impossible to match him."

"What have we got against him, apart from the fact that he won't let anyone open the vault? We don't want to take that approach. Otherwise we could all end up locked up in the padded cell next to Anna Maria." George Hollamby let out a coarse laugh, which made the others avert their eyes.

"I think we might be able to get him for perjury," Atherley-Jones suggested.

"How would that work?" Edmund Kimber, George Hollamby's British solicitor, asked.

"Well, during one of the cases against Anna Maria, Herbert swore he'd seen his father's corpse immediately after his death and again in the coffin. Now, unless they substituted a corpse so like Thomas Druce that even his son was fooled, he must have been lying because we are now certain Druce didn't die but merely went back to being the duke. Herbert committing perjury gives us another reason to reopen the case with a very reasonable chance of winning. Once Herbert's integrity has been damaged, the judge will be forced to accept the possibility that he was also lying about other things and will allow the opening of the grave. Once the grave is opened the cat, so to speak, is out of the bag."

There was a long pause as the other men in the room allowed the idea to soak past the clouds of brandy in their heads.

"Bloody sensational, mate!" George Hollamby exploded. "Let's go for him! Old Uncle Herbert won't know what's hit him!"

19

SENSATION UPON SENSATION

S
o it was that in 1907 poor Herbert Druce was dragged
once more from the orderly routine of his life running the
Baker Street Bazaar, so that he could answer charges of
perjury. George Hollamby and his team had nothing personal
against Herbert, but they had to sacrifice him in order to stand a
chance of gaining access to the grave of Thomas Druce and consequently to the Portland millions.

Marylebone Police Court can seldom have seen such a distinguished gathering of astute legal brains as came together for the
first day of the hearing. Horace Avory, K.C., the greatest criminal
lawyer of his generation, was in charge of the team defending
Herbert Druce against charges of perjury. In the gallery a legal
representative of the duke of Portland and Lord Howard de
Walden hung on every word spoken by both sides. Word was out
that George Hollamby, Atherley-Jones, and their team had
uncovered some sensational new evidence and the whole world
wanted to hear it. Every seat in the court was filled with fashionable people; the sixth duke of Portland himself sat among them,
smiling and nodding to acquaintances, apparently unconcerned
about what was about to unfold.

He had managed, in the twenty-eight years since he had

inherited the title, to make himself a popular figure, among both his fellow aristocrats and the local people of the areas that he owned. While he was not prone to the lavish eccentricity of his cousin and predecessor, he had proved himself to be a fair employer and a kind man. There was nobody who wished him any personal ill from the case, although there were many who hoped to see the title awarded to a common man, just for the sake of the upset and the excitement.

Herbert Druce looked less at ease in the courtroom. He sat, stone-faced, speaking to no one and consulting his watch at regular intervals as if worried about missing an appointment elsewhere.

Atherley-Jones opened the proceedings by laying out the facts of the case once more to a silent and attentive courtroom. Everyone knew the background anyway—they'd been reading about it for years—but that didn't make it any less fascinating. It made them feel as if they were part of the story. It was like a serial from a popular magazine come to life before their eyes. In public houses all around the country there were arguments about the rights and wrongs of the case, and money was laid down as to the outcome. If Anna Maria had been the introduction, this was the climax; the tough working man from the New World returning to England to claim his rightful inheritance. Some wanted to see him triumph while others wanted to see him crushed for his impudence. It was a fight everyone wanted tickets for.

"I shall call a considerable number of witnesses," Atherley-Jones said once he'd reached the conclusion of his briefing, "but there are three people of very signal importance whose testimony, if true, will successfully prove that Mr. T. C. Druce had another identity to that of the owner of the Bazaar.

"The first is Mr. Robert Caldwell, who has just arrived in this country from New York, where he's been practicing as an accountant and living since 1871. In 1855 he was suffering from

an unpleasant complaint and, having consulted a medical gentleman in India, he came to England and was introduced to the
duke of Portland, who had a similar complaint. The introduction
took him to Welbeck, and he accompanied the duke from time to
time to the Baker Street Bazaar. As a result a confidence arose
between them, and the duke disclosed to Mr. Caldwell that he
enjoyed a dual personality. He manifested himself to Mr. Caldwell
as proprietor of the bazaar, and also at Welbeck as the duke.

"After 1864 the duke determined to destroy this dual personality, and communicated this desire to Mr. Caldwell. This gentleman's evidence goes to the root of the whole matter. He will
tell the court that in 1864 he carried out, in conjunction with the
duke, the simulation of death and the mock funeral; that he
assisted in providing certain lead to place in the coffin; that he saw
the lead placed in the coffin; and that he saw the funeral leave the
bazaar and return by a circuitous route.

"Mr. Caldwell saw a reference to these somewhat dramatic
proceedings in the *New York World* and thereupon communicated with the solicitor appearing for the complainant in the
matter, and as a result he has during the last few days arrived in
this country."

There was a ripple of impressed conversation around the court
as people exchanged whispered views on the importance of this
revelation. No one had heard of Robert Caldwell before, but if his
story were true then Anna Maria Druce's original claims would be
proven once and for all. The fact that he came from America, a
land still seen by many in England as largely lawless pioneer
country, made some of the more nationalistic minds a little suspicious, but they were willing to be mollified by the fact that he was
an accountant, the steadiest of professions. George Hollamby
smiled to himself as the speculation swirled around the courtroom. The magistrate looked irritated, scowling around the crowd

like a teacher in a classroom full of inattentive children. Atherley-Jones waited for the voices to subside before continuing.

"There's also the evidence of Miss Mary Robinson. She's the daughter of the owner of a tobacco plantation in one of the southern states of America. Owing to the Civil War she came to England and one of the places she stayed was the Star and Garter, Richmond. Her father was acquainted with the late Charles Dickens. Having left this country she returned in 1868 and was employed by Mr. Druce. She can tell a story that will seem incredible but for the fact that it's supported by the diary that she kept. She tells how she used to meet the duke of Portland in the grounds of Welbeck Abbey, and perform duties as amanuensis and a sort of typist. A girlish intimacy sprang up between them. She eventually received large benefits from him and is at the present time living on the personal property that was given to her.

"She continued to see the gentleman called Mr. T. C. Druce up to 1878, a year before he died, and she saw him as the duke of Portland. If her evidence is correct, it disposes clearly of the story of the death of Mr. T. C. Druce in 1864. It's curious that while she lived near Welbeck Abbey, by the duke's request she passed in the quaint name of 'Madame Tussaud,' letters being addressed to her in that name." Atherley-Jones paused to allow a ripple of laughter to pass through the room. He could feel the crowd was on his side. They wanted more. These were new characters in the drama, new eccentricities to marvel at, new and confusing shafts of light into the mystery.

"There is also a Miss Stewart, who afterwards became a Mrs. Hamilton; she"ll give evidence supporting this state of affairs, and she was told by Mr. T. C. Druce to call him 'Scot.' Mr. Druce lived at the time on Gower Street and she recollects his calling to see her father and hearing a conversation between them. She remembers hearing the duke saying to her father, 'You know, Stewart, I never intended to kill him. I only fought back.'"

Atherley-Jones paused for a moment for the crowd to catch up to him before continuing, wanting them to cast their minds back to the accusation that the fifth duke of Portland was responsible for the death of his brother, Lord George. He waited, like a performer, for the crowd to grow quiet again.

"These are the three main witnesses, and there are others in support of the summons, among them a photographer. I would also like to read out some extracts from a statutory declaration made by a James Gray Smeaton, the grandson of the late Robert Gray, city architect to the corporation of Edinburgh and himself a consulting engineer."

Atherley-Jones held the letter aloft in a dramatic gesture and then scanned it for the relevant passages.

"I am the nephew of James Gray, the senior partner of the late firm of Gray and Ormson," he read, "horticultural architects and builders and engineers of Chelsea, who were in a very large way of business and did a great deal of work for a large part of the aristocracy. I was a draftsman to them, and occupied a confidential position in the firm, and was present at many interviews between the partners when it was openly stated that Mr. T. C. Druce of Baker Street Bazaar was identical with His Grace the fifth duke of Portland.

"On one occasion, when Mr. Ormson, my uncle's partner, had been instructed to proceed to Baker Street Bazaar in order that he might there receive instructions as to certain work to be carried out at Welbeck in connection with some engineering work there, illness prevented his attending, and Mr. Ormson then sent for me, and in the presence of his confessor, Father Bond (he being a Roman Catholic) and Dr. Sanderson, said to me: 'I believe I am about to die, and I wish therefore to declare to you the fact that Mr. Druce of the Baker Street Bazaar is, in reality, the duke of Portland; I am fully in his confidence. I tell you this in order that when you learn the fact yourself, as you undoubtedly would, through being brought into contact with him, both at Baker Street and Welbeck, you may not be surprised into betraying the secret, for should you do so the firm would lose the business.' I then went on to Mr. Druce at the bazaar and, having stated that I came from Mr. Ormson, was conducted to his private room. His manner was not that of an ordinary tradesman, being, although courteous, very haughty. He declined to discuss any matters with me, saying he would wait until Mr. Ormson, who knew all about it, could come personally.

"Shortly afterwards I went down to Welbeck Abbey, where I saw the duke of Portland. He was the same individual whom I had seen at the Baker Street Bazaar as Mr. Druce.

"Mr. Ormson recovered and on several occasions repeated the substance of the communication made to me. He bound me by solemn promise not to disclose the fact of Mr. Druce and the duke being one and the same person during the lifetime of the said individual."

Atherley-Jones lowered the piece of paper and allowed his eyes to scan the court. George Hollamby looked as if he was about to jump on the table and cheer, while the sixth duke of Portland had his head bowed and was rubbing his eyes as if tired but determined to stay awake for a little longer, if only out of politeness. Atherley-Jones then sat down with a flourish and Mr. Avory, for the defense, stood, asking for more time to prepare his case, since he had only just been given the case by his client. George Hollamby let out a snort of derision at such an obvious tactic but the magistrate ordered a postponement for a fortnight.

Mary Robinson, who had traveled all the way to England from New Zealand to testify in the case, was extremely nervous about the safety of her diary, the one that Atherley-Jones had referred to in his opening speech. On arriving in England she'd handed it to Edmund Kimber, George Hollamby's British solicitor, but had later transferred it to her own solicitors for safekeeping. She was particularly nervous because several original letters from Charles Dickens and the duke of Portland had been stolen from her on her journey from New Zealand.

To prepare herself for the evidence she would be asked to give when the court resumed, she recovered the diary from her solicitors and copied certain passages. She was determined to keep the book in her sight at all times, and even took it with her in her handbag when she went out shopping. Gazing into a shop window at some bonnets, she was shocked by a passerby who kindly warned her there was a spider on her shoulder, offering to remove it for her. Mary accepted the offer gratefully, blushing a little at the touch of the man's hand on her coat. It was only once the stranger had gone, satisfied that she was safe from the spider, that Mary realized her handbag had also departed.

The news reached Atherley-Jones and his client within an hour and they traveled together to Edmund Kimber's office, where a clerk proudly showed them a copy of the diary he had made by hand before handing it back to Miss Robinson's solicitors.

"Will they accept this as evidence in court?" George Hollamby wanted to know.

"Let's hope so." Atherley-Jones looked doubtful. "But it's bound to have less impact and to raise suspicions."

"What can we do?"

"I'll go on the attack. There's obviously foul play here and I shall say so, forcefully. Then we just have to pray."

True to his word, Atherley-Jones brought the subject up when the court reconvened, reading from letters between Edmund Kimber and Herbert Druce's solicitors, Freshfields.

"This is now the sixth theft that has taken place upon my client and his adviser and witnesses of important documents supporting his title," he read from a letter written by Kimber. "And the information I have been able to gather points to the instrumentality of some agents employed by your clients in collusion with the agents of the duke of Portland and Lord Howard de Walden."

A rumble of amazement rose from the crowd of onlookers. For anyone to suggest that men of the stature of the sixth duke of Portland and Lord Howard could be involved with common thieves was outrageous, and titillating in the extreme. Both men were in court and all eyes flickered in their direction. Neither showed any sign of emotion. They didn't look furtive or guilty, but neither did they seem outraged at the suggestion that they might employ thieves. George Hollamby noted their expressions and was glad he had never met either of them across a poker table. Lord Howard was whispering something into the ear of the man next to him and the duke of Portland seemed absorbed in picking a stubborn piece of fluff from his trousers. It was as if they hadn't heard the accusation at all.

Mr. Avory rose immediately on behalf of the defendant, positively steaming with righteous indignation. "I need hardly say that Messrs. Freshfields and my learned friends with me treat this suggestion with the contempt that it deserves. I wish to point out to Mr. Edmund Kimber that there is a point at which excessive zeal becomes professional misconduct, if not something worse."

No matter how much Avory blustered, the minds of the crowd were already imagining the army of agents that Herbert Druce, the duke, and Lord Howard had in their employ, and telling themselves that such strings of thefts and losses were more than mere coincidence. Everyone knows that there is never smoke without fire. The picture being painted was too fascinating for anyone to quite banish it from their minds, however fair-minded they wanted to be. Atherley-Jones's ploy had worked in distracting attention from the loss of the original diary, and it would now be easier to convince the court with readings from the clerk's copy.

Atherley-Jones then put Robert Caldwell on the stand. Caldwell cut a frail figure at seventy-one years of age, and it was hard to imagine that he had once been a farmer and a mill owner in Ireland before moving to America and taking up accountancy. The room fell completely silent as he told how, fifty years ago, he left his native Ireland and, after two years in London, traveled to New Zealand where he had heard there was a doctor who could treat a nasal disease, which he was suffering from. The doctor's treatment failed and the young Caldwell returned to London, where experts told him his condition was incurable.

"When in London I heard of some gentleman in India who had a cure for the malady. In consequence I consulted with my father and went to India. This affliction made my appearance unsightly. I saw the gentleman. He was a captain in the British Army—the Buffs. His name was Arthur Wellesley Joyce. Subsequently I married his niece. He affected a cure. On my return to London I contacted Sir Morell Mackenzie, who had previously pronounced the condition incurable, and he introduced me to the duke of Portland. That was in the early part of 1864 at Welbeck Abbey. Sir Morell accompanied me to Welbeck.

"The duke was suffering from a similar malady to what I had. On subsequent occasions I went to Welbeck. The duke ultimately submitted himself to the treatment. Sir Morell Mackenzie went with me twice to Welbeck Abbey after I'd commenced treatment. At the request of the duke, Sir Morell ceased to come, as he did not think it necessary. I stayed at Welbeck Abbey. On the second visit I stopped there for a night. Afterwards I stopped other nights. I cured the duke in about sixty days. After the cure I stayed at the abbey. I stopped there for two or three weeks at a time. The greater part of the cure took place at the bazaar in London. I became on intimate terms with the duke. I traveled with him from Welbeck to London. We traveled in a peculiar carriage to Worksop, and then in a carriage of his placed on a wagon to London. When the carriage reached the terminus there was a relay of horses to take it to the Baker Street Bazaar. The duke went into the bazaar to his private office. There were bedrooms there. I have slept there. I believe the duke was stopping there. I was his guest."

"Did anyone at the store address him by name?" Atherley-Jones enquired.

"I heard him addressed by his manager as 'Prince'; that was, however, behind his back. I never heard anyone address him but his manager. I heard him speak to the duke, but not by name."

"Did you know the duke by any other name?"

"Yes, Thomas Charles Druce."

"Did he live at the bazaar?"

"I believe so."

"Did you meet any members of his family there?"

"Yes, his wife, and I was introduced to her by the duke."

"Any others?"

"Yes, her children. I saw some children there, and the duke introduced them as his sons."

A picture of Annie May was produced and Caldwell identified it as the duke's wife.

"I received remuneration for the care of the duke from Sir Morell Mackenzie," he continued. "I received five thousand pounds. I received presents from the duke amounting to nearly ten thousand pounds. I heard the lady, his wife, addressed as 'Mrs. Druce.' He called her 'Annie May' also. She addressed him as 'Mr. Druce.'"

The magistrate leaned forward and interjected at this point, "Did he address her by any other name? It seems a little stiff."

"Not that I'm aware," Caldwell replied. "After a fight he would address her as 'Liz' or 'Crick.'" There was a buzz of laughter in the courtroom as onlookers imagined the repercussions for Druce of calling his second wife by his first wife's name, which the magistrate quelled with an angry look. "The duke lived at the bazaar occasionally. The lady lived there sometimes and also the rest of the family. I employed a carpenter while residing at the bazaar at the request of the duke."

"What did you employ him to do?" Atherley-Jones enquired.

"I asked him to make a box or coffin.

"What was the shape?"

"Almost the shape of a coffin, but not so much tapering at the end."

"The carpenter made it?"

"Yes."

"Where?"

"Oh, a short distance from the bazaar. The carpenter brought it to the bazaar the following morning. It was brought, I believe, on December twenty-seventh, but I won't be certain. I went to a store and purchased some lead at the duke's request. It was sheet lead, and the weight was about two hundred pounds."

"Why select two hundred pounds?"

"That might be the weight of a person said to have died."

The magistrate broke in again. "To represent the dead body of a person?"

"Yes," Caldwell replied and an audible hiss of excitement passed through the crowd.

"What was done with the lead?" Atherley-Jones asked.

"I put it in the box assisted by an old man, one of the employees of the store."

"Where was the duke at the time?"

"I could not tell. On the following day a funeral took place.

The hearse came to the bazaar. I ordered the hearse from a livery-stable keeper near."

"At whose request did you order the hearse?"

"The duke of Portland's."

"Did you order other mourning coaches?"

"Yes, by order of the duke also."

"Was the coffin put in the hearse?"

"Yes."

"How many coaches were ordered?"

"I believe about fifty."

"Did you see the funeral?"

"I saw the people in the coaches."

"Did you see the coffin put into the hearse?"

"Yes. I assisted to put it in."

"Was there any body in it?"

"No, only some lead and brass to keep it still. I put the lid on with the assistance of the old man and the carpenter put screws in."

A gasp of shock went around the court and Atherley-Jones raised his voice to be heard above it. "Did you see the duke on the day of the funeral?"

"Yes, at the bazaar."

Caldwell went on to give more details of the duke's behavior, how he would put on false beards when he wanted to become Thomas Druce, which set the courtroom laughing once more. Atherley-Jones then asked him if he knew anything about Thomas Druce's will.

"The first or second day after the mock funeral I asked if Mr. Druce, so called, had made a will, and the duke seemed surprised at his own stupidity at not making a will. He said he must have a will made. I asked him how about witnesses. He replied: 'Can you draw up the will?' I said, 'No.' He asked if I knew of a lawyer who could be trusted to draw a will. I said no."

There was a loud burst of laughter from the crowd at the expense of all the lawyers in the room, only some of whom showed any hint of amusement at the comment.

"Don't take that as my general impression," Caldwell added. "He became excited and said, 'Of course, I must have a will made.' I waited, expecting to see him the next morning, but didn't see him for two days. He said he'd got everything connected with the will settled to his satisfaction, and thanked me for reminding him about it."

There wasn't a person in the courtroom who hadn't stolen the occasional glance at the sixth duke of Portland and Herbert Druce during that speech. Still, neither man had shown a flicker of emotion. Druce kept his eyes steadily on Caldwell as he spoke, neither smiling nor frowning, giving nothing away; the duke looked down at the gloves he was holding in his hands, apparently lost in thought.

20

GREAT BARRISTERS IN BATTLE

The acclaimed Mr. Avory rose from his seat like an avenging angel as the court settled down to see if he would to be able to discredit Caldwell's story. To their surprise he started to talk about another scandal in America in which Caldwell had been involved. Like the Druce case, it involved disputed wills and disappearing bodies. Onlookers had to concentrate hard to follow this apparent change of tack. What did this have to do with the case in hand? Caldwell admitted there had been a story about a different case he'd tried to sell to the *New York Herald* for $10,000 at an earlier, unspecified date, but that the editor had declined to buy it. For the first time onlookers began to wonder if Mr. Caldwell was all he claimed to be; trying to sell stories to newspapers was not the actions of a gentleman. Avory had succeeded in sowing a seed of doubt as to the reliability of Caldwell as a witness. Atherley-Jones and his team were busily passing notes to one another as if unaware of what was being said in the witness box. In reality, of course, they were listening to every word and their notes were on exactly that subject. Their star witness, it seemed, was not all they have hoped he would be.

With a flourish, Mr. Avory produced a more recent article from the *New York Herald* and began to read the headline out loud to the court.

"'Mysteries to Him as Plain as the Nose on his Face,'" he read, pausing for dramatic effect before continuing. " 'Robert Caldwell, "Great American Affidavit Maker," Reveals Another Secret—This Time in the Guise of a London Cablegram.'"

The *Herald* went on to say that the story Caldwell was swearing to, which related to the Druce case, rivaled in sensationalism the unpublished story that he had brought to them before, and that some persons regarded Mr. Caldwell as the most accomplished romantic humorist. They called him the "Great American Affidavit Maker" because he was always willing to sign oaths swearing that his claims were true. Mr. Avory paused again and looked at the witness rather as a long-suffering schoolmaster might look at a disappointing pupil.

"The article is a bundle of lies," Caldwell protested in confident tones, suggesting that no one of intelligence ever took seriously what they read in the papers.

Avory turned back to the audience and pressed on with his reading as if no one had spoken. "'Mr. Caldwell Deals Only with Men Who Are Dead.'" He lowered the paper and swiveled to face Caldwell again. "Have you noticed that peculiarity about your affidavits?"

"No, sir." Caldwell stared back at him, as if determined to show that he would not be bullied by anyone.

"The gentleman who wrote this article does not seem to think much of you judging from what he writes," Avory suggested.

"I think as much of him as he does of me," Caldwell snapped back.

Avory continued to suggest that Caldwell was only involved in the case for the money, which Caldwell continued to deny, and then Avory changed tack.

"You say in your affidavit that in 1855 you consulted Sir

Morell Mackenzie. Are you aware that Sir Morell was only seventeen or eighteen years of age at the time?"

Gasps and chuckles circulated the room. It seemed that Mr. Avory was going to make Mr. Caldwell look a fool.

"I do not mean to say that I saw Sir Morrell then," Caldwell replied, apparently unruffled by the news. "I'd been given a recommendation to him in 1857 and carried it around with me for several years before presenting it."

"Waiting for him to grow up, I suppose?" Avory suggested, raising sniggers from the crowd. He waited again before casually asking, "Your nose was horribly disfigured?"

"Yes." Caldwell touched his nose with his fingers, as if to check that it was still there.

"And you say the duke of Portland was similarly disfigured?"

"Only not quite as bad as me."

"But a disfigurement that everyone must see?"

"Yes."

"Did it appear to be a disfigurement of long standing?"

"Nearly two years, I believe."

"Did Sir Morell—or Mr. Mackenzie as he then was—go down with you to Welbeck on his own account?"

"I believe it was at the duke's invitation. It was common rumor that the duke had a bad nose, and he was very glad to know anyone who could cure it."

"How long did the treatment take?"

"About an hour to remove a hair from his nose. That irritated him, and he did not behave very quietly." Caldwell smiled, hoping to win back the sympathies of the room with an image of an elderly duke fussing like a child over a minor discomfort. No one laughed; they were too anxious to hear what would come next.

"You said you slept at the Baker Street Bazaar," Avory said. "Where was the bedroom?"

"On the second floor at the back of the house."

"You said the wife and five children slept there?"

"That was my impression."

"Why did you believe so?"

"Because they were there for breakfast the next morning and wished me good night the previous night."

"Did you dine there?"

"Yes."

"Where was the dining room?" Avory was firing the questions like bullets, apparently not wanting to give Caldwell any time to think up appropriate answers, trying to trip him up with his own tongue.

"Upstairs on the second floor."

"The same floor as the bedroom?"

"Yes."

"Where was the kitchen?"

"I don't know; I didn't go prying about the kitchen." Caldwell laughed at the very idea and the onlookers joined in. They were enjoying the back-and-forth action as much as if they had been watching a tennis match. "The food might have been brought in."

"Was it pretty hot?"

"It was."

"How many servants were there?"

"Two maid servants and half a dozen men in livery."

"They waited on you at dinner?"

"Two did."

"What were the others doing?"

"Do you think it possible for me to tell?"

Avory took a deep breath and stared at the ceiling as if thinking the evidence through for the first time. "If there was no bedroom, kitchen, or dining room at Baker Street Bazaar," he said eventually, "your story must be untrue?"

"I should say so," Caldwell agreed.

"I throw the servants in, too. Supposing there were not any. Your story about them must be untrue?"

"Yes."

"At what station did you alight when you traveled with the duke? Was it Euston? Was it a terminus?"

"I think it was a wayside station."

"And then you drove to Baker Street?"

"Yes."

"The duke alighted and walked into his office and became Mr. Thomas Druce?"

"Yes."

Avory then turned his mind to the coffin, asking Caldwell a number of detailed questions about its construction and size.

"What were you having a mock funeral for," he asked, "with fifty coaches and a hearse, and starting from Baker Street and going to Highgate?"

"That was to pretend someone was dead," Caldwell replied, as if the answer should be obvious to even the dimmest of people. "I believe it was the pretense of the duke."

"Who was supposed to be dead?"

"Thomas Druce, who was the same person as the duke."

"Why was there no inscription on the coffin if it was pretended that Druce was in the coffin?"

"I did not pretend anything. I don't know why there was no inscription."

Avory then began to question Caldwell on the false beards and whiskers that the duke and Thomas Druce would wear, showing him photographs of both men.

"And you suggest that the duke walked about at Welbeck in his own abbey, among his own servants, with false whiskers?" he asked once Caldwell had finished painting this particular picture for them.

"Yes," Caldwell nodded.

"When did he generally put them on—at breakfast or dinner?"

"I cannot say, but I have seen him with them at breakfast and dinner."

"Did you say he had a large stock of whiskers and beards at Welbeck?"

"I cannot say that."

Avory went on to ask questions about where at Welbeck Caldwell had he slept and whether he had dined with the duke while there.

"Sometimes I did, but I did not really want to be with the duke. In fact, I wanted to get away from him, but he wouldn't let me. He wanted a companion. He would talk to me by the hour and he had all the talk to himself. I couldn't get a word in edgeways."

"Did you know about the underground rooms under the house, under the abbey?" Avory asked.

"No, not under the abbey."

"Did you ever go into the ballroom, a fine room about a hundred feet long?"

"Yes."

"And the picture gallery?"

"Yes."

"Did you notice any of the pictures?"

"I cannot remember them, but I understood it to be the most valuable collection, perhaps in the world."

The sixth duke sighed and leaned back in his seat, discomforted by yet another reference to the wealth that the witnesses were suggesting he had acquired from his cousin under false pretenses. He was a modest man by nature and did not like people to think that he was boastful about his wealth. He was well aware that he had only earned it by being born to the right parents. Luck was nothing to be proud of. He was proud of the way in which he managed the affairs of the estate, but embarrassed by all references to its immense value. He closed his eyes, giving the impression that he was either falling asleep or was trying to concentrate more fully on what was being said. Herbert looked equally uncomfortable at such vulgar statements being made in public.

Avory showed Caldwell a picture of the duke reproduced in a pamphlet, taken from a portrait in the gallery at the abbey, and Caldwell identified it as one he had seen on his visit.

"Now listen to me," Avory said, lowering the volume of his voice and making everyone in the room strain to hear what he said. "Suppose these underground rooms, picture gallery, and ballroom were never constructed until 1872. Your whole story must be untrue?"

"Well," Caldwell smiled back. "I am not to suppose anything at all; but I do not accept it as a fact."

"Suppose the portrait of the late duke when marquess of Titchfield were not painted until after his death. Is your story untrue?"

"It might be another. All I know is I saw a picture exactly like that."

Avory straightened up and raised his voice again, as if getting back to the real business at hand.

"You said you saw the duke at the bazaar on the morning of the mock funeral in the office?"

"Yes."

"Did you sleep there?"

"Yes, I was in my bedroom."

"Did you have breakfast there?"

"No."

"No appetite, I suppose," Avory smirked and the crowd

laughed appreciatively. They were beginning to come to the opinion that Caldwell was not being completely honest with them. "Was the duke walking about on this morning attending to his business?"

"He was."

"So that Mr. Druce was in his office at the Baker Street Bazaar superintending the arrangements for his own funeral the same day?"

The crowd laughed again.

"He was superintending the arrangements as the duke of Portland."

"With the whiskers and all?"

"Yes."

"Black ones perhaps, for the funeral?"

"No, they were gray."

"Did you see him at the bazaar the same night?"

"Yes."

"So that he was walking about his own office attending to his own business after the funeral."

"That is quite silly," Caldwell muttered, becoming irritated with the repetitiveness of Avory's questioning.

"I should have thought it was, and I am wondering that you are telling us this story."

"I saw him in the dining room."

"Taking a hearty dinner, I suppose, on the strength of it."

Avory then appeared to change the subject, asking Caldwell about his life in New York.

"Did you know a gentleman, Mr. Ballantine, who is in court today?"

A man stood up to be identified and Caldwell shook his head, indicating that he did not. He then peered more closely at the man and seemed to change his mind.

"Are you Mathew Ballantine?" he asked.

The man nodded.

"I knew his brother, Tom," Caldwell told Avory, "who I believe served time in a penitentiary."

Avory asked some questions about a man named Christy and Caldwell began to become annoyed. "I know what you're driving at," he exclaimed. "I had a brother who was for some years with Christy. It is a case of mistaken identity."

The crowd had fallen silent, unsure where the line of questioning was going but aware that Caldwell was no longer his jocular self; Avory appeared to have uncovered something that was making him uncomfortable.

"Was he a twin?" Avory asked.

"Not that I'm aware of," Caldwell replied, attempting to regain his confident air. "My brother's name was William and mine Robert. As neither of us liked our names we exchanged. My brother went to America in 1871."

There was a hum of disbelief around the room and a glint of panic showed in Caldwell's eyes. He had utterly lost the sympathy of the crowd. He seemed to be making stories up on the hoof.

"Did your brother embezzle Mr. Christy's money before he went away to America in 1871?" Avory pressed his advantage.

"I do not know. Most positively no." Caldwell seemed to have been tipped off balance.

"If it was you who did it you would know something about it?" Avory's voice was all sweet reason.

"Yes, I should."

But Avory was not giving up. He produced a string of questions, making it clear that there had been complex and unethical financial arrangements and some doubt as to which brother was responsible for which arrangement.

"It is a case of mistaken identity to put any of this down to me," Caldwell insisted. "My brother wrote like me, talked like me, and looked like me."

The crowd laughed mockingly. For a few moments they'd forgotten the reason for their being there in the first place, as they watched Avory playing cat and mouse with the witness who had had them eating out of his hand just a short time before.

"Your evidence about your brother is as true as that you have given about the duke?" Avory suggested.

"All my evidence is true," Caldwell replied.

"That is for others to decide," Avory said. "I have no more questions."

There was a unmistakable look of smugness on Avory's face as he sat down. He had managed to make Caldwell sound unsure and unreliable, deeply damaging his credibility as a witness. He had struck a vicious early blow for the defense.

Atherley-Jones then spent a day reexamining the witness and winning back the confidence of the onlookers by explaining in more detail the relationship between Caldwell and his brother. Then Avory tried once more to discredit him by pointing out the confusing manner in which the two brothers had led their lives. He then finished his questions by returning to the matter of Druce's coffin.

"Supposing the grave was opened at Highgate Cemetery tomorrow?" he asked. "And an inscription 'T. C. Druce' was found on the coffin. Would that shake your faith that he did not die in 1864?"

"It would not. It must have been put there since, if there is one."

Next on the witness stand was Mary Robinson, fifty-six years of age and apparently respectable in the extreme. She told the court that her father was the owner of a Negro plantation in Virginia in the second half of the nineteenth century, where they grew tobacco.

"I remember the Civil War breaking out. My father took part in it and died. Shortly after the war broke out I came to this country. I attended school and was introduced to a variety of people by an aunt and other ladies, including a Mr. Thomas Druce of the Baker Street Bazaar. I knew him also to be the duke of Portland. He told me he lived at Nottingham and kept tame foxes running about the wood.

"In April 1862, during my Easter holidays, I went to stay at the Star and Garter in Richmond. Mr. Druce came to visit with some other friends, including a young lady who was blind. The lady sang at Mr Druce's request. She sang 'Ivy Green.' Mr. Druce said it was a song composed by a friend of his, Mr. Charles Dickens, the novelist. Mr. Druce accompanied the lady. It was a duet.

"There was a children's party and Mr. Druce was there and took part in the festivities. There were private theatricals. 'Little Red Ridinghood' was played and Mr. Druce was the grandmother. He had on a nightdress with a grandmother's cap tied with strings. He sang a song after jumping into bed. He sang 'Johnnie Sands.' He was encored and he then sang 'I am ninety-nine.' He made a profound impression on me. I've never forgotten him.

"We went to the exhibition with him at Hyde Park and a little girl fell into the lavender water fountain. Mr. Druce pulled her out and it caused enthusiasm on the part of the spectators."

The audience in the courtroom laughed, delighted by this glimpse of gentler, pleasanter times.

Mary then went into details of how she returned to America and met Charles Dickens in Boston. Dickens suggested she should return to England and visit Druce in order to be an "outside correspondent." Druce, Dickens told her, was now living at Welbeck. The year was 1868. The audience was obviously puzzled as to what her duties as an "outside correspondent" might be, but waited patiently to be enlightened.

"I was eighteen when I returned to England, this time with my mother. We traveled to Worksop and stayed in lodgings with a widow who used to take us for drives through Welbeck Abbey.

"They were making alterations at the time and we saw a place where they were digging an underground tunnel. The next day I went on a walk on the estate with Mr. Dickens. We went into the park, where there were some beautiful oaks, and Mr. Druce was there, waiting."

"Did you know at that time he was the duke of Portland?" Atherley-Jones asked.

"Not for a certainty."

"Did you know him again?"

"I knew him, notwithstanding he had blue spectacles on."

"Did he say anything?"

"He said I was to come the next day at about four o'clock."

"Did he give you any instructions?"

"He told me I was to carry a blue silk umbrella and was to put it up."

"Did you meet Mr. Druce?"

"Yes."

"Was he wearing blue spectacles?

"Yes."

"Had he any hair on his face?"

"No, none."

"Did he have any when you saw him in London?"

"At Richmond he wore a beard."

"At Welbeck his face was hairless?"

"Yes."

"What did he say to you?"

"He gave me instructions that I was to receive letters and to post letters. The first one I posted was to Amsterdam. Others were to Denmark, Switzerland, and Russia."

"Did you receive any money on this occasion?"

"Yes, a five-pound note."

Mary went on to describe how letters for the duke would arrive at her lodgings, addressed to Madame Tussaud, and she would pass them on, and how he gave her a piano and some furs as a thank-you payment for her work.

Once, while visiting Welbeck Abbey, she met two men from Amsterdam who asked to see the duke, although she couldn't remember exactly which year. She informed them she would see if he was available and went to tell Druce the two men were there. Druce asked her to say the duke was indisposed but that she would pass a message on. When she returned to the men they didn't wish to leave a message but talked about money they were owed. Mary told the court she didn't bother to pass that message to Druce. The men remained in Worksop for a fortnight and she knew they were watching her. They expected her to convey a check to them from the duke, but she never did and couldn't fathom what the mystery debt was about. When she mentioned the matter to Druce, he told her the men were frauds and that she had acted correctly in ignoring them.

A whisper went around the courtroom as people remembered the story of the two men who'd been reported as being with Lord George and the marquess of Titchfield on the night that Lord George was found dead in 1848. Was it possible that these two had been blackmailing the duke, threatening to expose him as a murderer? The magistrate ordered the crowd to be silent once more so that Mary could continue her testimony.

She talked of other jobs that Druce sent her on. Once, when she was in York, Druce came to visit her, saying he was getting out of the way of the Dutchmen. On another occasion she met with Charles Dickens in London and, as a result of what he told her, she went to the village of Bray in Berkshire where Druce was staying at the Hind's Head, and remained with him in a private room. Then they had an argument.

"I told him I didn't understand why I should receive these letters in the name of Druce, when Mr. Dickens told me that he was the duke of Portland," she explained to the court. "He was short in his manner, and said he would tell me another time now that he had confidence in me. He said he'd tell me something he'd never told me before."

Druce, she said, would often come to visit her in different places. One time he brought her a brooch. "It was painted," she explained, "with two ladies and a dog, very small and beautifully done. Mr. Druce stayed and talked about people he'd known when he was young. He said he knew the Duke of Wellington, and spoke of his funeral, and that he had a model of the carriage at the Baker Street Bazaar. I think he stayed about a fortnight on that occasion. He spoke of Princess Charlotte's funeral and had a slight recollection of Nelson.

"And on another occasion he told me he was the duke of Portland; that he bore the name of Druce because he'd been married twice in that name. He said he had children by both wives. These wives, he said, were both of low station, and therefore he did not look upon them as wives—they were 'below par.' He said he continued to use the name of Druce because of things that had happened in his family."

Everyone in the room began speculating as to what these revelations might mean. There were more murmured references to the mysterious death of Lord George and then the magistrate roared for them to be silent or he would have them all removed from his court.

"He told me," Mary continued, once she could be heard, "that he had told Mr. Dickens to break the ice to me."

"Did he tell you anything about his wives?" Atherley-Jones asked.

"He told me in reference to the first wife that it was a boy and girl marriage, and was forced upon him by the female side. He also said he had three children by her."

"Did he tell you when his first wife died?"

"I can't remember. He told me when he married the second one."

"Did he say anything about her?"

"Yes, he gave her a very good character."

"She was 'above par,'" the magistrate interjected, raising a laugh from the spellbound audience.

Mary went on to explain how she started traveling after the duke's death, ending up in New Zealand. When she read about the Druce case in the papers she managed to make contact with Mr. Coburn, George Hollamby's solicitor in Australia.

There was more discussion about the false beards and wigs that Druce and the duke used to don, before Mr. Avory stepped forward once more.

"Did Mr. Druce ever tell you he had pretended to die in 1864?" he inquired.

"Oh no," Mary replied.

"Did you ever hear before you came over to this country in February last that Mr. Druce, of the Baker Street Bazaar, was supposed to have died in 1864?"

"I never heard it mentioned."

"How came you to meet Mr. Dickens?" Avory asked after a little more discussion on the topic of false hair.

"My mother took me to his hotel to see him."

"You were then seventeen years of age?"

"Yes."

"And do I understand that at that first meeting it was arranged you were to come over here as what you call 'outside correspondent' to Mr. Druce?"

"Yes, it was arranged by my mother," Mary said, lurching to one side, holding on to the side of the witness box as she swayed precariously. The crowd gasped as if they were watching a high-wire artist, and Mary suddenly fainted. The case was adjourned to the following day.

Mary seemed to have recovered when the court reconvened and Avory began questioning her about Druce's nose and whether there was, in her opinion, anything particularly wrong with it.

"I couldn't say," Mary replied.

"Do you know what a bulbous nose is?" Avory asked.

"No."

Avory described what it was and Mary told him that she recollected Druce's nose being powdered over and that it appeared to have warts on it.

"Enough to disfigure him?"

"Yes."

Avory had a photograph of the duke handed to her and asked if she saw any warts on the nose. She said that she did not but she could only see one side of the nose.

Avory asked about her travels around the world with her mother and then returned to the question of her duties as "outside correspondent" for Druce.

"Your duty was to post the letters?"

"Yes, to post and receive them."

"You posted them at Worksop Post Office?"

"Yes."

"They were addressed in his own writing?"

"Yes."

"Then he might just as well have given them to his servants to post?"

"He knew best what he wanted. He never associated with his

servants or workmen. He knew his own business best. He would not have paid me wages if he did not require me."

"How were your private letters addressed?"

"In my own name."

"You had two names at the lodgings?"

"Yes."

"You had two sets of letters coming there?"

"Yes."

"Otherwise you would have opened the duke's letters?"

"Mr. Druce's letters, yes."

"Did you ever open any of the letters addressed to Madame Tussaud?"

"I see you are in a fog," Mary said, not unkindly, "and I am not going to expose other people's affairs. There were two covers. The underneath one was addressed to Mr. Druce. I only took the outside cover off."

"You mean the sealed letters to Mr. Druce were delivered inside envelopes which were addressed to you as Madame Tussaud?" Avory clarified for the benefit of the court.

"Yes."

Avory changed his tack and asked her about the mechanics of her meetings with Druce before returning to the subject of Charles Dickens and his part in getting her the job as outside correspondent.

"Mr. Dickens knew Mr. Druce and his business," Mary confirmed.

"Are you aware that it has been publicly proclaimed by the Dickens family that Mr. Dickens had nothing to do with the duke?" Avory asked.

"When?" Mary asked.

"A few days ago."

"I get the paper, but did not see it."

Avory pressed her for more details of her meetings with the famous novelist.

"I cannot collect my thoughts," she said, rubbing her forehead vigorously with her fingers. "My memory is going."

It looked as if Mary was going to faint again but she pulled herself upright just in time. The magistrate suggested she might like to step outside and take some air. When she came back in she was still complaining of feeling unwell but Avory continued with his grilling.

"Was there any secret or doubt that the gentleman living at the abbey was the duke of Portland?"

"I do not really think there was," she said.

"Then if it was generally known, why was it he was very much annoyed when you told him Mr. Dickens had informed you who he was?"

Mary looked down at her hands and did not answer.

"If everybody knew he was the duke of Portland," Avory persisted, "why should he be annoyed at your knowing it?"

Mary took a number of deep breaths and raised her eyes to the high-vaulted ceilings before replying. "I suppose it was because he'd not told me himself. He was also annoyed when he heard that people called him 'Resurrection.'"

Avory reminded her that at a previous hearing she'd stated that Druce had told her he had asked Dickens to break the ice to her on the subject of his being the duke.

"That conversation took place after Mr. Dickens's death," Mary said.

"Then why, if that is so, should Mr. Druce have been very angry at Mr. Dickens's having told you?"

"I do not know," Mary confessed.

"Nor do I," remarked Avory.

The noise of the crowd rose as Mr. Avory sat down, everyone discussing what they had just heard. Any mention of a name as famous as Charles Dickens was bound to hold the attention of the listeners, but Mary's story had seemed far-fetched and her tendency to faintness had undermined the strength and confidence of her delivery. No one was sure what to make of her.

When Atherley-Jones stood once more he questioned Mary again on her relationship with Dickens and then asked permission to read a piece from a magazine called *Anglo-Saxon Review*. He was granted permission.

"'And in Kensington Gardens,'" he read, "'I caught my last glimpse of Charles Dickens as a living man. It was only a week before his death, and he was strolling down one of the paths under the trees. His companion was a girl of tender years and manifestly humble circumstances, to whom the Master was talking with that animation of mood and manner which had never failed him to the last.' Did that description correspond to you?" he asked. Mary cast her eyes down and said nothing. "Was he generally animated?"

"Yes."

"Were you in receipt of a salary at that time as an amanuensis?"

"Yes."

"Did you assist your mother with a portion?"

"Yes."

"What was your salary?"

"A hundred pounds a year."

"At that interview in Hyde Park you said you had a conversation with the duke?"

"Yes."

"Did you tell the duke what Mr. Dickens told you in Hyde Park?"

"Yes, I did."

"What did you tell the duke? Was it after Mr. Charles Dickens's death?"

"It was after Mr. Dickens's death. I told him that he had spoken about his private life. I told the duke that he said Mr. Druce and the duke were one man. He asked why he thought so. I said over this Van Aish coming. Van Aish was one of the men from Amsterdam whom Druce described to me as being 'the curse of my life.' I wished to know the man I was working for, I said. The duke had told Mr. Dickens to break the ice to me. Mr. Dickens said that I was to be careful what I did in the duke's presence. I did not like going through the tunnels and places because they were like the catacombs of Paris. I spoke about his family, and he said that he would explain that another time. I was careful what I did say. I picked out the sweetest parts."

"Did the duke say anything about Druce, that is, about himself."

"I think he said that when he was a young man he took the name of Druce for the purposes of business and other transactions he had in hand, and his marriages. He changed his name and came to live at Welbeck as the duke of Portland. That was his home, he said. He told me more, but I forget what it was. He told me about his family affairs."

Atherley-Jones's questions had bolstered Mary's credibility in the eyes of the onlookers, building her confidence once more. George Hollamby's case was not off the rails yet. Herbert Druce was shaking his head in disbelief that others in the room seemed to accept what seemed to him to be patent nonsense.

The third witness to be brought before the court that day was Mrs. Margaret Hamilton, who said she lived in Kensington. She was a woman in her early seventies who claimed that one of her godfathers was the fourth duke of Portland. Her father, Robert Lennox Stewart, was somehow related to a distinguished soldier called General Scott and the fourth duke had been married to one of Scott's daughters, a great heiress. General Scott, therefore, was the grandfather to the fifth duke of Portland, his three brothers, and five sisters.

"Did you know the son of the fourth duke?" she was asked by Mr. John Goodman, a colleague of Atherley-Jones.

"Yes, Scott-Portland. Sometimes we called him Willie, but mostly Scott." There was a ripple of laughter in the courtroom; they had already heard the fifth duke referred to as the marquess of Titchfield and Lord John, not to mention Thomas Druce and Dr. Harmer, and now they were learning of yet more names.

"These were the family names that you knew the fifth duke of Portland by?" Goodman asked.

"That's right."

"Did you know a gentleman named Druce?"

"Yes, of course, he was Druce as well as the duke."

"Where did this gentleman named Druce live?"

"Sometimes at the Baker Street Bazaar and sometimes at Welbeck Abbey."

"Did you see Mr. Druce at the bazaar?"

"Yes I did. My father was on the Continent at the time. I needed somewhere to stay in London and did not know how to contact my father so I went to the bazaar to see the duke. When I found him, calling himself Thomas Druce, he said 'Madge, what are you doing here, child?' So I told him. He said, 'Well, I must take you somewhere to stay a little time.' He then considered a little and said, 'Come along,' and we went through many turnings to a house, and he knocked at the door and a person opened it."

"What was her name?"

"Mrs. Harrison. I stayed with her until my father returned from the Continent."

After her father returned, she explained, she lived with him in London.

"Did Mr. Druce ever come on a visit to you or your father?" Goodman asked.

"Yes, very often."

"Was that the same gentleman you knew as Scott-Portland?"

"Yes, of course; he was the duke of Portland. I remember that gentleman taking me to have my portrait done."

Mr. Goodman then moved on to the subject of the wigs and beards. Mrs Hamilton confirmed that the duke would keep a beard in his pocket at all times.

"Do you remember saying anything to this gentleman about his false beard?" Goodman asked.

"Yes. I many a time asked him why he wore it."

"What did he say?"

"Sometimes he would say, 'Never mind why I wear it, child.' Then he used to say, 'Well, of course you know I am Mr. Druce when I put that on.' I also said to him, 'What do you want with the bazaar? You have got so much; it's ridiculous.' He said, 'Oh, it is a very good thing, It makes a lot of money' or something like that. I accompanied my father to the bazaar, but he would not let me go inside."

"Did you ever hear of a house called Harcourt House?" Goodman enquired.

"Oh yes; that belonged to the duke. Mr. Druce asked me why I did not go there, and I said my father would not let me. He said, 'You could come by yourself,' but I said, 'No, if my father says no.'"

"Is it right that the duke used to say he would marry you? Did he say that in your presence?"

"Yes, and in the presence of my father, and my father got into a passion about it and told him to go out."

"What did he say to the duke?"

"He said, 'You shall never have my little girl.'"

"Anything else?"

"He said, 'Of course you must marry Annie May, that is the woman you must marry.' Mr. Druce said, 'Bother Annie May,' or something like that."

"Did you ever see Annie May?"

"Only once. She was a very pretty woman. My father took her to the theater, and of course the duke and he had some words about it. I don't think he would have married her but for my father. My father went to their wedding."

"Did you ever know if he was married before?"

"Yes, he told me he had been married before. He said he was very young when he married Miss Crickmer."

She went on to describe her early visits to Welbeck around 1856 or 1857, and remembered the duke telling her of his plans to build a riding school. Later, when the school was built, he took her to see it and pointed out a coffin-shaped sentry box and told her that when the riding was going on he could go in there and see without being seen.

"Did he ever speak about any of his children?"

"Oh, yes, but I forget how many he had by his first wife. I think he called one Fanny."

"Did he mention any son?"

"He mentioned a son, Herbert, and a younger son. He said he was going to leave him one thousand pounds. My father said, 'Why not six or seven thousand pounds?' and he replied that one was quite enough for him."

"Did you ever hear of a house in Hyde Park Gardens?"

"Oh," Mrs. Hamilton clapped her hands in excitement, "where the coffin was on the roof. Oh, yes, and I heard my father say he had seen the coffin many a time. He said the duke did not believe in being placed in a coffin underground, and that people ought to be put in their coffins on the roof. My father said, 'I suppose they want a lot of fresh air.'"

Later in her testimony, Mrs. Hamilton described another conversation between herself and her father and the duke. The duke said, 'Madge, I'm going to die.' I said, 'Well, you don't look like it.' He replied, 'Oh, but I am,' and then my father said, 'Oh, well, you know he's going to cease to be Druce.' I said, 'How can that be? What is he going to do?' He said, 'Well, he's going to have a funeral.' The duke said to my father, 'Why, you know, I think we could get a corpse at either the workhouse or one of the hospitals.' My father said, 'Don't talk of such a thing. That will never do. Put whatever you like in the coffin, Scott, but don't do that. Put in bricks, mortar, lead, or anything, but not a corpse.' The duke said, 'Very well, I don't think I will do that.' My father went to the funeral. He said it went off better than he'd expected considering they had no certificate. Scott said he was glad it'd gone off well. He said it'd cost him thousands, I suppose to bribe everyone, officials and others at the cemetery. No doubt they were bribed or they would never have taken the coffin without a doctor's certificate."

Mrs. Hamilton went on to describe another encounter between herself, her father, and the duke.

"The duke pulled a whole bundle of handkerchiefs from his pocket and said to my father, 'Look here, Roby, look what my wife has done. She's taken my handkerchiefs and put my coronet on. When I married her I made her promise she would never use my coronet and never go to Welbeck, and by so-and-so she never shall.' He then asked me if I had any scissors. I handed him a pair and he cut off all the corners and threw them into the fire. I said, 'Oh what a pity it is!' Of course most of them were burned, but after he'd gone I picked up one that happened to have fallen underneath a shovel, and I kept it. I later destroyed it, along with many other things."

Later in the day, when George Hollamby's legal team had finished their questioning of Mrs. Hamilton, Mr. Avory asked her how she first came into this court case.

"It was in consequence of an advertisement I saw in *Lloyds* paper asking for people who knew anything about the Druce case. I came to London and saw a gentleman connected with *Lloyds* who told me he was going to get a big 'screw' out of it. He asked me to come forward for the sum of twenty-five pounds, but I declined, and he then said, 'I know there will be a big sum, and whatever they give me I will give you half.'"

"Did he give you anything?"

"Never, but he borrowed half a sovereign off me. I made an affidavit for Anna Maria Druce, but Anna Maria said she couldn't call me because she thought I was dead. I thought this was a good thing, because I didn't want to know her, as I thought she would be a nuisance to me."

"Do you know," Mr. Avory asked, "that she also told the court you were really the duchess of Abercorn?"

"I heard so."

"But you are not, I suppose, are you?"

"Oh dear, no."

"Did you ever meet or hear spoken of Robert Caldwell?"

"No, never. My father spoke of a Mr. Cardwell; I suppose it must have been Mr. Caldwell. He thought he was going to do good things for his nose, he said. I said 'His nose!' and he said, 'Yes, those lumps.' I said, 'Oh, I thought they were natural things. I thought they'd always been on his face.'"

"Did you ever hear the duke speak of an 'outside correspondent'?"

"A secretary, but he didn't mention her by name. My father said it was a woman. I said to him 'Secretary?' He said, 'Some young woman. I don't know what he wants with her.'"

Once his legal team had finished with Mrs. Hamilton, George Hollamby was having to fight the urge to punch the air in triumph. It seemed she had saved the day, her own credibility rubbing off on Caldwell and Mary Robinson. Numerous other witnesses were called to give a clearer idea of the world of fifty years before, including a draper who worked on Baker Street at the time and was familiar with Thomas Druce. He admitted he'd heard that Druce was dead but had seen him after the funeral.

"And, according to your story," Mr. Avory put to him, "you saw a man who was supposed to be a corpse walking about Baker Street after that?"

"Yes."

"You were astonished?"

"Not at all."

"You are accustomed to seeing corpses walking about Baker Street?"

"No, but this corpse was. At the time I didn't think much of it. It was general knowledge throughout Baker Street at the time that the funeral was false."

"And general knowledge that he was trying to conceal the fact that he'd ever been Druce?"

"I suppose so."

"For four years after he was supposed to be dead you saw him walking about on Baker Street?"

"I've seen him standing at the door, but more often I've met him out."

But another tradesman, a fishmonger who owned a shop opposite the bazaar and claimed to have known Thomas Druce well up until 1864, gave evidence to the effect that he had never seen him around Baker Street again after the funeral.

A tailor who had served the duke was called, and attested to how they would make frock coats for His Grace in sets of three, each one fitting snugly over the other so that they could all be worn at once. A gardener came forward and attested that he had seen an attractive young "American lady" coming to Welbeck on a number of occasions, carrying bundles of letters.

Atherley-Jones eventually announced that the prosecution would rest. Although he could find at least twenty more witnesses to confirm what had already been heard, he didn't want to waste any more of the court's time on repetition. He then stunned the court by disowning one of his own witnesses, Robert Caldwell. It was obvious from the grim set of George Hollamby's jaw that this was bad news from his point of view, all signs of his previous optimism had drained away. Finding Caldwell and bringing him over from New York had been a time-consuming and expensive business. To now have to discard his evidence was a bitter pill, made even worse by the knowledge that Caldwell's exposure as a man of dubious character had reflected on the way all their other witnesses were viewed by the court. Atherley-Jones told the Court that he and his clients had lost faith in Mr. Caldwell's evidence during his cross-examination, but were confident that the evidence of the other witnesses was reliable enough without Caldwell's contribution. Although it was a terrible blow for the prosecution's case, putting in doubt the whole story of the false funeral that was so important to making the case for opening the coffin, the benefits of disowning Caldwell outweighed the harm it did.

In his summing up, Avory, finding it hard to suppress his personal jubilation at this turn of events, was quick to attack the surrender of Caldwell's testimony.

"This fiction was first put forward in 1898 by a woman named Anna Maria Druce," he reminded everyone, "who is now where she ought probably to have been long ago—namely in a lunatic asylum—a fiction that from that time has been fostered by a certain section of the press, which, with no regard for the feelings of people who might be wounded by such publications, would publish anything that would afford sensational copy; a fiction that has now developed into a fraudulent conspiracy to swindle the public or rather that section, that foolish section of the public, who are ready to believe anything they see in print, especially when it is illustrated by pictures that are falsely and libelously described as authentic portraits of the late duke of Portland. We hope to once and for all expose the falsity of the story that has been put forward about the mock funeral and about the duke of Portland and Mr. T. C. Druce being one and the same person.

"As to the Druce-Portland Companies," he took a deep breath as if about to run a long race, "nobody in their senses believes that George Hollamby Druce, the claimant, is himself alone responsible or that he was furnishing the funds to maintain the prosecution. We should point out, therefore, that every one of the promoters and every one of the subscribers to these companies is at this moment liable to be put into a criminal dock and charged with champerty [financing a litigant for reward in the event of a successful outcome], and maintenance, and there could be no answer if they were so charged. They would eventually find themselves charged with conspiracy, which, I suggest, undoubtedly underlays the proceedings in this case, a conspiracy to prefer a false claim to these estates and a false charge against Mr. Herbert Druce, and a conspiracy to swindle the foolish public who have subscribed the shares and bonds of these companies."

Avory went on to suggest that George Hollamby and his legal team had waited to bring the case to court until many of the people who might have supported Herbert's case were either dead or too infirm to make an appearance.

"There was Dr. Shaw, the doctor who attended T. C. Druce for months before and at the time of his fatal illness, and who actually saw him lying dead and helped to lay his body out. There was a Dr. Blasson, who also had attended Mr. Druce shortly before his death, and who deposed in the previous case to the character of the illness from which he was suffering. There was the nurse called Bayly, who had been in the service of the Druce family for years, since she was fifteen years old and had helped to bring up the children, including the present defendant and who deposed to being actually in the room when T. C. Druce died. Then there was Alexander Young, the executor of T. C. Druce's will, who deposed to the fact of his taking up the office of executor and knowing as he did that T. C. Druce died in 1864. All these witnesses were called and a special jury who investigated the case was satisfied and found as a fact that Mr. T. C. Druce did die in 1864."

What Avory did not mention was the fact that despite the presence of so many medical people in Druce's life, there was no signature by any of them on the certificate of death.

"Fortunately," Avory continued, "in the interests of justice, Nurse Bayly was still alive and able to give evidence to the same effect she did in 1901."

In the many weeks that the trials had been going on there had been various slips made by witnesses that hadn't been part of the main evidence. Avory started to list them, first mocking the testimony of Mary Robinson, and pointing out that she had been hired as a secretary but had shown in court not to recognize the duke's handwriting or to know how to spell "Tussaud," the name she had supposedly been addressed by. She had claimed that certain pieces of jewelry were gifts from the duke, but examination had revealed them to be cheap and worthless baubles. She'd started out claiming she'd received nothing by way of inducement to give evidence and later had had to admit to being paid £250. He poured scorn on the idea that a man of Charles Dickens's character and standing would become involved in such a grubby conspiracy and dismissed the idea that the missing diary had ever existed.

He was initially more inclined to be charitable toward Mrs.

Hamilton, he said, describing her simply as a "crazy old woman," but in the course of listening to her evidence had changed his mind. Either, he suggested, she had been taken advantage of by others who should be ashamed of themselves, or else she was a "very crafty, cunning and deceiving old woman." She had been shown to have improved, touched up, altered, and embellished her evidence in order to suit the circumstances of her case.

"If there is one subject that has appealed more than another to the man in the street since the inquiry first started, it is the question of opening the grave in Highgate Cemetery. My learned friend has more than once referred to the fact that Mr. Herbert Druce is the proprietor of the grave and has refused to allow it to be opened. I wish to say it is a pity that everybody who has formed or expressed any opinion on this subject did not put themselves in Mr. Druce's position for the moment. Here was a gentleman who saw his father die in 1864, who saw him buried, who has no interest whatever in this claim that is being made by somebody else to be the duke of Portland, and who from the outset in 1898 said what I should have thought every man of decent feeling would have said under the same circumstances— namely, 'I am not going to have my father's grave desecrated to satisfy either public or vulgar curiosity, nor am I going to have it opened to satisfy the whim of a person who chooses to make a claim to an estate I am not interested in and who has put forward a claim that I know to be untrue." Therefore he has taken the attitude that he would be no party to any desecration of his father's grave.

"When this prosecution was first started it was obvious that one of the points to be made was this refusal and Mr. Herbert Druce placed himself entirely in the hands of his advisers. They advised him that if it should become necessary in the interests of public justice that the grave should be opened, he should subordinate his personal scruples and his own sentiments in the matter, and he willingly agreed to this course.

"Now the position is a little curious. The only man whose evidence seemed to call for such a step being taken was Robert Caldwell, who has deposed to a coffin filled with lead being taken to Highgate Cemetery and there interred. The whole of his evidence being withdrawn, there now appears to be no evidence that calls for any extreme step on the part of Mr. Herbert Druce and, speaking for myself, I hesitate to advise him that it is necessary in the interests of public justice that he should take a step so distasteful to himself."

All eyes turned to Herbert, who was listening impassively from the back of the room, occasionally nodding his agreement with what was being said. No one could have told from the fixed look on his face what he was feeling. In fact he was forcing himself not to become optimistic. There had been too many occasions in the previous years when he had believed he'd heard the last of the whole stupid business, only to find it rising up once more.

"It is a matter now of public knowledge that Robert Caldwell has fled from the country to avoid, if possible, the fate he knows he so richly deserves and that I hope may yet overcome him. It may be that the interests of justice may yet require that this step should be taken so as to demonstrate the falsehood that Caldwell told in this court. Certainly, when the need does arise, Mr. Herbert Druce is perfectly willing to have the grave opened in order once and for all to get rid of the story that has got about, and for which Mr. Caldwell is apparently alone responsible, that there was lead in that coffin."

Atherley-Jones was unshaken by Avory's summary when he came to make his own closing address. He said Caldwell had merely gone home to New York, not into hiding, and could be extradited if that was necessary, and he completely disagreed that

Mary Robinson and Margaret Hamilton had been inconsistent in their evidence. He accepted that their memories might have failed them once or twice, but that was not of consequence. He was also puzzled by the suggestion that the prosecution had cast any aspersions on the conduct of Charles Dickens.

"The matter might be solved if they would consent to have the grave opened," he said.

"Are you prepared to abide by the result if the grave is opened?" the magistrate asked. "Would you take it as a conclusive step or not?"

"I am here, strictly speaking, as representing the Crown," Atherley-Jones said. "And I do not think it would be proper on my part to say that the ends of justice should not be pursued independently of the fact whether Mr. Herbert Druce consented or not. An order for the opening of the grave was granted long before Caldwell was heard in connection with the case."

The following day it was the turn of Mr. Avory to call his witnesses for the defence. The first was Catherine Bayly, the Druce family's nurse. She told the court how her employer had been ill with a painful complaint for at least three months before he died.

"Did Dr. Shaw attend him right up to his death?" Avory asked.

"Yes."

"Was he in the house the night he died?"

"Yes."

"Holding his hands?"

"Yes."

"How long had he been in bed unable to move?"

"Three weeks."

"Had Sir William Fergusson operated on him shortly before he died?"

"Yes, ten days."

She went on to say that two other medical men, James Smith

and Michael Blasson, had also attended him, along with hospital nurses.

"I had been left alone in the room with him when I saw a change come over him. He spoke to me. He knew he was dying. Herbert Druce, who was a boy at the time, came into the room just as he was nearly gone and he remained in the room. Mrs. Druce looked into the room but did not stop. She was ill herself. The complaint that Mr. Druce was suffering from made it very unpleasant to remain in the same room."

Many eyes turned to look at Herbert Druce, to see what effect this remembered scene from his youth was having on him. Herbert kept his eyes on the floor and made a show of blowing his nose with a well-pressed handkerchief.

"I laid the body out with Dr. Shaw and a nurse. Because of the offensive condition in which the body was, chloride of lime was put into the sheet in which the body was wrapped. The next day an undertaker came from a street near the bazaar and brought a shell and I saw them put the body into that. The shell was put into a leaden coffin, which was placed in a coffin of oak with black handles. The lead coffin was immediately soldered up and it was all taken through to the drawing room. Three or four days later the funeral took place. I saw the coffin taken from the drawing room and placed in the hearse. I myself had been keeping the key to the room that the body had been in. I saw the procession start and there were very few people—there were nothing like fifty carriages."

Nurse Bayly confirmed that she would give exactly the same answers as she had done when Anna Maria had first raised the case, and Mr. Avory proceeded to read the evidence previously given by the doctors.

When Atherley-Jones took over the questioning, he discovered that Nurse Bayley had been under the impression that Fanny, who had visited Druce at home occasionally, was an adopted daughter, and that there had been an adopted son also. She had known nothing about a previous marriage. She then answered a few questions about the Druces' domestic arrangements.

"Mr. Druce went to business by omnibus when living in Hendon, but afterwards had a carriage. His wife used to call at the bazaar for him sometimes. She had two carriages, and her sons had saddle horses. At one time she took Mr Druce's lunch regularly to the bazaar accompanied by one of the little boys. There was a little room there where I was told the attendants used to cook their food, but Mr. Druce did not have his lunch there."

"You've always taken an interest in the story of the mock funeral?" Atherley-Jones inquired.

"It was very disagreeable to me."

"You don't believe in it a bit?"

"No, as I saw him die I'd heard the matter talked about, and Mrs. Anna Maria Druce pretended to cross-examine me in the previous proceedings."

"You knew long before Mrs. Anna Maria Druce came on the scene that people talked about a mock funeral?"

"Never." The elderly Bayley, who had previously seemed rather nervous beneath Atherley-Jones's questioning, was suddenly adamant, not to say indignant. Atherley-Jones pressed a little harder.

"Well," she said eventually, "I don't know if I remember it, but I suppose I did hear some talk about the sham funeral."

"Do you remember who spoke of it?"

"Silly, gossiping people. I just heard some of the servants and outside village people speak about it, and would not listen to it."

"Were they the Hendon people?"

"They were the Hendon folk, and I don't believe they themselves believed the wicked things they said about him."

"Can you tell the magistrate when Mr. Druce was first seized with his fatal illness?" Atherley-Jones asked.

"I cannot tell the date," she replied, "but it was about six or seven months before his death. During the whole of the fatal illness Drs. Shaw and Blasson attended him alternately. Mr. Druce was confined to the house about a month or longer before his death."

"Do you know what the illness was?"

"Fistula."

"Who told you that?"

"Sir William Fergusson. He was attending him for some time and then operated."

"You've said Mr. Druce was very regular in attendance at the bazaar. Did he never go out of town?"

"Yes, the family went out together. He never went away by himself. Mrs. Druce and the children and myself always went with him."

"Did he never go away by himself on business?"

"No. During the whole time from 1848 to 1864 he never once, to my knowledge, slept out of the house except when he was with his family."

"But might he without your knowledge?"

"No."

Atherley-Jones pressed on and pointed out that Nurse Bayly had changed her story about when she had called the doctor for Thomas Druce from six years previously, when she had first been called into a witness box. The elderly woman, her voice growing quieter and quieter, justified her changes of story, saying she had previously been mistaken.

"None of his children or wife was with him when he died?" Atherley-Jones asked.

"Not at the last."

"Was the hospital nurse with him?"

"He begged me not to have her in the room."

"Then you were alone in the room when Dr. Shaw arrived?"

"Yes."

"It would not be correct to say the hospital nurse was alone in the room when Dr. Shaw arrived?"

"There was no necessity. I'm sure I was there and she was not."

"Did Dr. Shaw find fault with you for not laying him out?"

"No. The hospital nurse had refused to assist. The complaint was so painful no one cared to come in."

"Who put the chlorate of lime in the sheet?"

"The doctor."

"Was Herbert Druce in the room after Dr. Shaw arrived after the death?"

"Yes, he was."

She then told the court there were two coffins altogether.

"That wants clearing up," the magistrate said. "Last time you told us there were three."

Nurse Bayly mumbled something that sounded like agreement, but her voice could hardly be heard.

"Did you see the fastened-down shell put into the lead coffin?" Atherley-Jones persisted.

"Yes. The doctor was there. And when the lead coffin was put into the oak one he was there watching."

"Did you lock the bedroom?"

"There was a worry that the servants would go in. Mrs. Druce suggested the door should be locked to keep them out."

"Was the coffin kept locked when it was moved to the drawing room?"

"No."

"Listen to this," Atherley-Jones kept a kindly tone in his voice, not wishing to give the impression that he was bullying a frail old lady. "Did you not say in your examination in chief that you had the keys of all the rooms in which the coffin lay?"

"I cannot tell you any more." A silence fell over the room as the nurse collected her thoughts. Eventually she went on, every ear straining to catch her words. "I cannot say whether the room was locked or not."

"The 'adopted' daughter, Fanny, did she come to the house after the death and was she refused admission?"

"Not so far as I can remember."

"Did Mr. Charles Crickmer-Druce, the 'adopted' son, go to the house and create a disturbance because he was not allowed to see the coffin?"

"I don't believe that ever happened."

When asked about the funeral Bayly said again she thought there were only two or three funeral carriages. She said that Annie May Druce did not go to the funeral, but that Herbert did.

Avory came back to question the nurse about Anna Maria.

"She told me she was 'going to be the duchess,'" Bayly told him. "She said she would share everything with me."

"Was there anything eccentric about Mr. Druce?" Avory asked.

"Nothing at all. I never heard him speak of Welbeck and I never noticed anything peculiar in his dress. He never wore three coats at once."

"Did he ever have any warts on his face or any skin complaint?"

"No eruption whatever."

"Did you ever hear him speak of Charles Dickens, or of Mrs. Hamilton or Mr. Stuart or Miss Robinson?"

"No. It was true, however, that he went to Mr. Marks's shop for his fish."

The more questions the lawyers asked the more muddied the waters became. None of the witnesses, it appeared, had even vaguely similar recollections of the time surrounding Thomas

Druce's death. It was a puzzle that would never be solved to everyone's satisfaction unless the coffin was opened. There were few people in the country who did not now believe that Herbert should agree to have the contents of the coffin examined so that either his father could, finally, be allowed to rest in peace, or a terrible injustice could be put right.

21

OPENING THE COFFIN

Poor Anna Maria, locked away in her padded cell, still furious with a world that had cheated her of her birthright and destroyed the life she had, was not able to see the workmen setting about bringing her dreams to fruition. Herbert Druce, ten years after Anna Maria first started her campaign, had finally bowed to the advice of his legal team and allowed the vault in Highgate to be opened. No one informed her of what was happening. As far as her attendants were concerned she was just one more lunatic they had to feed and clean each day; they had no interest in what might be going on inside her head. Those among them who had read anything about the happenings in the courtroom and cemetery in the winter of 1907 would not have thought to pass the news on to her.

The usual quiet of the graveyard was shattered for days by the crashing of hammers and the shouts of the workmen as they erected a three-hundred-square-foot shed over the Druce vault. It was a shed of very specific design. Because of the level of interest the public showed in the contents of the coffin, it had no windows. Whatever was revealed to be in the coffin would be viewed only by those allowed inside. Such precautions only added to the drama and a crowd of onlookers gathered every day just to watch the construction rising before their eyes.

"It's to be lit by skylights and artificial lights," curious onlookers were told by the officials who periodically asked them to move back and allow room for some new delivery of wood.

On the morning of December 30, 1907, a crowd of several hundred people gathered around the shed, in the knowledge that behind its makeshift walls several tons of stone were being moved aside to allow the investigation of the coffin to take place.

The activity had started before dawn, when a small group of official-looking men had arrived and taken possession of seats opposite the main gates of the cemetery. A biting cold wind was carrying rain and sleet almost horizontally, cutting into the faces of the curious, making them rub their hands and stamp their feet in attempts to keep warm as events unfurled before them. At five A.M. the main gates were opened for the electricians who were responsible for the special lighting arrangements. Two hours later a covered van arrived, carrying the men who had the tools necessary for opening the coffin. Three more vehicles followed with more men of importance, including Chief Inspector Tom Dew, who held a warrant for the arrest of Robert Caldwell should the remains of Thomas Druce be found.

Small platoons of police, including a mounted patrol, arrived at each of the cemetery gates. There was a buzz of expectancy in the air, which heightened when a carriage brought George Hollamby Druce to the cemetery superintendent's lodge. George Hollamby descended from the carriage with a nod toward the watching crowd and disappeared inside the lodge. Despite the fact that he was now so short of money he was reduced to living in lodgings in North London, he had bought himself a new hat and a new coat for the event, and had a large cigar clamped in his mouth, looking for all the world like the prosperous man-about-town that he no longer was. Whatever money had been raised by the share offerings had long since gone to the lawyers or been spent in the casinos of Mayfair. The crowd speculated on what must be happening inside the building as they waited. George Hollamby reappeared a few minutes later and was immediately surrounded by pressmen firing questions.

"I've been refused admission to witness the exhumation," he announced to the crowd, "and I've lodged a protest."

The news passed through the crowd and they speculated what this could mean. It seemed that the Establishment wished to find out in private what the coffin contained, before deciding how to break the news to the rest of the world. If they let George Hollamby in he would be announcing their discoveries to the world the moment he left the shed. Even now, the crowd feared they might be kept from knowing the truth of what was happening behind those windowless wooden walls. Would anyone ever let the truth of this case be known? Some thought yes and some thought no. The debating helped to distract them from the cold and wet.

"Do you intend to go farther and repeat your demand at the main entrance?" a reporter asked.

"No," George Hollamby shook his head, causing a spray of rainwater from the brim of his hat, "it's useless to do so."

But standing in the rain doing nothing seemed foolish so he decided to make one more attempt. Rebuffed a second time, he climbed back into his carriage and ordered the driver to take him home. There was a limit to the humiliation he was willing to suffer at the hands of the authorities. He would hear the results soon enough, he was sure about that.

Only two representatives of news agencies had been authorized to witness the opening, while other reporters had to wait outside. All those who went inside found the building brightly lit, making the grass and stones look as unnatural as a stage set.

The atmosphere among the gathered officials was reverent, almost like being in church. Once everyone who was invited had arrived, word was given to commence operations. A tarpaulin was spread over a portion of the floor and two pairs of trestles, with a tabletop placed over one pair, were laid on top. The earth and mould sticking to the stone was removed and workmen with crowbars then eased up the mighty flagstone that covered the vault, moving it away on rollers.

Inside the vault the white-painted walls reflected the glare of the electric light, which the workmen lowered on the end of a cable. The shadows danced to the movement of the bulb as it swung like a pendulum, illuminating the second tier of slabs and Annie May's coffin, lying on top of the one purported to hold the remains of her husband. It was a very different scene than the one Anna Maria had once described in court, in which she'd claimed that when attending the burial of Annie May, she had noticed that the weight of her husband's coffin had broken the lid of her father-in-law's, which lay below it. She'd cited this fact as further evidence that her father-in-law's coffin must be empty. Either she had been mistaken, or the coffins had been moved around.

The workmen lowered a ladder over the edge and descended, passing ropes beneath Annie May's coffin and raising it to the surface. Helpful hands lifted it out and placed it to one side of the opening.

The workmen descended once more into the vault and numbered the slabs they planned to move, so they could be sure to replace them in exactly the same order. Then, cutting the cement in the joints, they began to lift the stones, disclosing the top of the coffin supposed to contain the remains of Thomas Druce. One of the men started to clear the dust off the nameplate but a command barked by an overseer stopped him in midmovement. They were ordered to concentrate on removing the rest of the slabs. The chisels caused one or two of the slabs to break and sent pieces of lime down onto the coffins below, making it impossible for the moment to decipher the inscriptions on the lids.

The slabs removed, the workmen climbed back to the surface and laid planks across the hole. A camera was brought up and placed on the planks to take a picture of the caskets supposedly holding the mortal remains of Thomas and Walter Druce as they lay in dust and grime. The officials were recording every move. No one wanted there to be any doubt about the sequence of events on this day.

The home office officials arrived, including a Mr. Augustus Pepper, and the workmen went back down into the vault with their ropes, putting them around the coffin of T. C. Druce, hauling it to the surface with the utmost care. It was old-fashioned in appearance, covered with cloth and studded with brass nails. One of its six brass handles had come off but otherwise all that was amiss was some fraying of the cloth and little wasting of the edge of the lid.

Careful measurements were taken and the officials made detailed notes. Orders were given for the nameplate to be washed and the inscription was laid bare, reflecting the sparkle of the lights.

Thomas Charles Druce
Esqre
Died 28th Decr.,
1864,
In his 71st year.

Above the inscription was a brass cross. A photograph was taken and the grave diggers left. Two workmen employed by the undertakers then entered the shed, unscrewed the lid with powerful pliers, and revealed the lead inner coffin, which carried the same inscription as the outer one. Further measurements were taken and noted. A workman cut through the lead all around the outer edge of the upper surface and the lid was removed, bringing away with it the top of the innermost wooden shell that was attached to it.

The crowd of officials could see in the shadows of the casket a shrouded human figure, which proved to be that of an aged, bearded man. A small elderly man named Thackrah was brought to the front of the crowd and leaned forward to stare at the face of the corpse. People asked one another who he was, but no one recognized him, not even those who had attended any of the court cases.

Later that day Edmund Kimber, George Hollamby's solicitor, made a statement to the press.

"I cannot deny that the remains of a man's body were found in the coffin opened today, but we are still without legal evidence to prove conclusively that the corpse is actually that of T. C. Druce. In fact, the opening of the coffin strengthens our case rather than weakens it."

"So, no doubt the case is now ended?" a contradictory reporter ventured.

"Oh, dear me, no," Kimber chortled in a patronizing manner, "it is only just beginning."

During the following two days George Hollamby, Kimber, Atherley-Jones, and Coburn, the Australian solicitor, held lengthy consultations. Coburn let it be known to a crowd of waiting reporters at the end of the meetings that his client was satisfied that the body found in the coffin was not that of T. C. Druce.

Investigations were made into the layout of the vault to check if there was any other way into it, but none was found. At the final hearing a few days later Mr. August Joseph Pepper, surgeon and adviser to the home office for the Metropolitan Police, told what he had witnessed.

"Inside the shell there was the shape of a human body covered by a shroud of white cambric."

"Was there anything over the face?" Avory asked him.

"A linen handkerchief about the size of a pocket handkerchief."

"Any mark on it?"

"The initials TCD and the figure 12."

"On removing the sheet in which the body was wrapped what did you find the body to be?" Avory asked.

"A male body, aged."

"By 'aged,' what do you mean?"

"I should say from sixty-five to seventy-five."

"And about what height?"

"The actual length of the body as it lay in the coffin was five foot seven inches and allowing for shrinkage after death would make it five foot eight inches to five foot nine inches in life."

"Speaking of it generally, what was the state of preservation?"

"It was extremely well preserved. The skin was only broken in one part of the body."

"Was it sufficiently preserved for the features to be recognized?"

"Oh, quite easily."

"Before you describe the details, tell me, had you on you at the time this photograph?" Avory held up a photograph of Druce in a standing position.

"Yes."

"With that photograph in your possession did you form, Mr. Pepper, your view as to the identity of the body?"

"There was a striking general resemblance. Upon comparing particular points the resemblance was also marked."

"How would you describe the face and head to be?"

"The head was covered with scanty reddish-brown hair, with a small part white. It was parted neatly on the left side. One side was brushed slightly over the forehead. The eyebrows were rather thick and wavy. He also had a mustache, reddish-brown in color and dropping straight over the upper lip. The whiskers and beard were of a reddish-brown color, with a good deal of white, and the beard was very bushy. The hair was coarse."

"The whole of this hair on the head and face that you are describing was natural hair?"

"Yes, it is exactly as shown in the photograph. It had the appearance as if he had been shaved in the upper parts of the face."

"To put it another way, it commences in a distinct line?"

"Yes, exactly as shown in this photograph."

"Upon examining the body, did you find any difference in the lower region—in the state of preservation?"

"Oh, yes. In the lower region of the trunk there was extreme decay."

"Is that what you would expect to find if the man had suffered from fistulas and abscesses in that region?"

"It is quite clear he had suffered from some destructive disease of that kind."

"Is the cause given on the death certificate consistent with the appearances that you found?" Although Thomas's certificate of death had never been signed by a doctor, the description of the cause of death had coincided with the description that Nurse Bayly had given in court.

"Yes. The only thing is, there is no mention made of the part affected. What I saw indicated that there had been gangrene in that part of the body."

"Having made this examination and your notes upon it, did you witness the replacement of the body in the coffin?"

"Yes."

"And the return of the coffin to its original place in the vault?"

"I did."

"With the exception of the lead of which the lead coffin was composed, was there any lead found in or about his coffin at all?"

"No."

"Or in the vault?"

"No. Of course the other coffins were not disturbed."

"Was Mr. Thackrah present with you at the time the coffin was opened?"

"He was."

When Atherley-Jones rose to question the surgeon he assured the court that he did not intend to ask anything in a critical spirit, but for the purpose of fuller elucidation.

"Will you tell me," he said, "whether you made any investigation to discover whether there were any traces of chloride of lime?"

"There were marks about the middle of the body that might have been chloride of lime."

Avory then called George Thackrah, a partner in the business of Messrs. Druce and Co. on Baker Street who had first entered the business in 1860, employed by Thomas Druce. His job, the court was told, had been to attend on Mr. Druce at the Baker Street Bazaar and carry out his instructions. Mr. Thackrah told the court that the face of the body in the coffin had been distinctly recognizable as that of the late T. C. Druce, a man he had known for four years.

"You recognize him beyond a shadow of doubt?" the magistrate asked.

"Oh yes, beyond a shadow of doubt. There is no doubt whatever about it."

Avory then closed his case, pointing out to the magistrate that every word Herbert Druce had said with regard to the details of his father's death and burial had been demonstrated to be absolutely true. People looked around to see what Herbert's reaction might be, but he wasn't there. He had no wish to be seen to be crowing over a victory that was so distasteful to him. He'd been forced to unearth the remains of his father and he had no wish to appear in any courtroom ever again. The sixth duke had also decided to stay away. He'd heard that the body of Thomas Druce had been discovered in the vault and saw no reason to spend any more time on the affair. George Hollamby was too drunk to be able to make it to the hearing.

Atherley-Jones then announced to the court that he would be withdrawing from the case and made a speech assuring all those who were listening, which was the majority of the English population, that he had complete confidence that George Hollamby had acted in good faith, truly believing that Druce and the duke were one and the same man and that the funeral had been a sham.

After the conclusion of the case a letter was published in the *Times* from Edmund Kimber, which included the following passage.

> *The person buried in 1864 was on the tombstone alleged to be seventy-one years of age. According to the census returns of 1861, "T. C. Druce of Baker Street Bazaar" was then only sixty-two. If he were the same man as the man buried, he could not have been seventy-one. All parties have endeavoured at great expense—and so, I believe, has the Press—to find out the date and the place of birth of Thomas Druce who married Elizabeth Crickmer in 1816, who is alleged to have been T. C. Druce alias the late duke of Portland, but as yet without success.*

22

THE FATE OF THE WITNESSES

Robert Caldwell, who had been staying with relatives of George Hollamby in London during the court case, was already on board the Kaiserin Auguste Viktoria and sailing for America via Europe when Atherley-Jones announced in court that he was jettisoning his evidence. The day after Atherley-Jones's announcement, a warrant against Caldwell for perjury was issued at the Bow Street Police Station and Caldwell read the news in the ship's daily newspaper.

The shock of becoming a wanted man just a few days after being a star witness for the prosecution shook him more profoundly than he could have expected. The authorities arrested him in Hoboken, Belgium, on 21st of December 1907, upon the request of the British authorities, who wanted to bring him back to England if the body of Thomas Druce was found in the coffin. He was hauled before a court in Belgium. The court appointed doctors to inquire into his physical condition. It seemed obvious to all who saw him that the elderly Caldwell was in a bad state of health, shaking and making little sense as he spoke.

He was released for a fortnight on $5,000 bail, during which time more doctors studied him, pronounced him gravely ill and unlikely to survive more than a few days, and said that extradition was therefore out of the question. Within days they realized that his condition was mental rather than physical and he was certified as suffering from paranoia. The doctors added in their report that they believed he had been suffering from the condition for over a year. He was declared insane and committed to an asylum, just like poor Anna Maria. The British authorities would not allow him to slip through their fingers, however. Despite his alleged mental state they threatened proceedings. But they failed to get him back and Caldwell eventually died in the asylum three years later, in January 1911.

Mary Robinson was arrested on a charge of perjury. At Bow Street she was sentenced on April 10, 1908, to four years in Holloway prison. There, in her cell, she was persuaded to write a statement containing the following descriptions of how she came to be involved in the case. Her frail fingers soon hurt with the effort of writing so much, but the warden who sat with her kept goading her to continue.

"I saw an account in an Australian newspaper in 1906 of the Druce case. I wrote to Mr. Druce in Melbourne and said I knew the duke and had seen him many times," she wrote, remembering sadly how badly her life had gone over the previous two years.

"Three weeks or a month afterwards a man called at my house in New Zealand and said his name was Druce. He said, 'I have an offer to make to you." He said that the Druce case was in want of funds; that he had made some inquiries about me, and I was just the person he required. He said he'd heard I was clever at writing, and if I would write what he wished and do as I was told, I should receive £4,000.

"I said, 'What am I to do for the £4,000?' He told me he wanted a book written in my own handwriting of the history of all I knew about the duke and surroundings; to make it as attractive as I could, so that they could raise money on it to meet their expenses. The expenses, he explained, were to enable the firm in favor of Druce to claim the dukedom of Portland. The man Druce said—I think he was the brother of Mr. Druce in London—that he claimed to be the grandson of the fifth duke of Portland."

She straightened up her aching back and flexed her fingers. The warden indicated that she should keep working.

"He also told me that his father came out to Australia at the time of the gold diggings, that he had £1,000 given him by the duke in '65 to enable him to live out there. I asked him what Druce's father was, and he replied, 'A perfect gentleman and a well-educated man, but a gold-digger.' He then asked me what I knew about the duke, I told him, and he said he wanted me to write in pamphlet form all I could say or invent about the fifth duke of Portland. I said, 'I'm not going to expose myself to everybody." He said, 'Say you come from America. We have another person coming from there. He's writing to say so. You won't be alone in writing.'

"Before this occurrence I had seen a few scraps in the newspapers concerning the Druce case. This same man asked me if I knew the Baker Street Bazaar, as he said the duke of Portland was the owner.

"I then wrote on sheets of paper just what I thought would do for it. About the beginning of November 1906, I heard from England, but before this I'd finished the history on paper by about September and, not hearing from Australia, I thought they'd made a fool of me."

The wardens in the cell changed over, but Mary kept her head down and continued to write, her memories flooding back.

"Before I finished my history I received by post from England six pamphlets, two at a time, one called *Portland Millions* and another *The Druce Case*. Some of these I used for wastepaper and some I saved. I was disgusted when I read *Portland Millions*. I got the pieces of paper on which I had written the history and transferred it into an old diary book. When I transferred it I kept the sheets of paper already written on. The contents of this diary I compiled alone at the request of the man from Australia, as I thought I was going to have the £4,000.

"They then wanted to know if I would come to England and bring the diary with me. There was nothing in these letters that would implicate them; they were too artful. I wrote saying I would come over and Druce cabled me £250. I left in February last. Mr. Coburn and Mr. Kimber met me at Plymouth. The first thing Mr. Kimber asked me for was the diary. I said the captain had got it. Mr. Kimber asked the captain for it, but he wouldn't give it to him and Mr. Kimber kicked up a regular row. Mr. Kimber had four or five men with him but Mr. Coburn didn't stir from the launch.

"I then went to the captain, and he at once gave me the things, the diary and various other little articles. I told Mr. Kimber that I'd lost a package, which was some letters. He said, 'Stick to your tale. Stick to your tale.' He said, 'We want to make a sensation; there is nothing done without it.'

"In the train Mr. Kimber and Mr. Coburn had a long talk about the Druce case. They told me Mr. Druce would be the duke of Portland very soon, and referred to him as 'His Grace.' Mr. Coburn said to me, 'You'll get your £4,000 without a murmur, perhaps £5,000 if you stick to your guns.' As soon as the captain handed me the diary and the other things Mr. Kimber took possession of them.

"Mr. G. H. Druce told me this time they were doing well with the diary and were receiving plenty of money on it, and any time that large shareholders came they had to be taken to Mr. Kimber's office to see the diary.

"Mr. Coburn asked me to try to obtain my diary from Mr. Kimber, and also any papers I had had given to me by Mr. Kimber, or any other papers that had anything to do with the case. Mr. Kimber refused, saying the diary was at his bankers. I think I gave Mr. Kimber a few papers, but I can't remember what they were. I think I gave him the piece of paper that I'd written in New Zealand after the man Druce had called on me. Mr. Coburn laughed very heartily when I gave him this, and said they had made a lot of money in Australia over this, and all they wanted now were good witnesses. He told me they would have to depend on their witnesses, as they didn't intend to say anything themselves.

"The next time a Mr. Balham came and said they'd had a cable from Mr. Kimber in America saying he would be back in a few days but that the man was not coming with him as Mr. Kimber hadn't the money to pay him. I was told this man was Caldwell and the next thing I heard was Caldwell and his solicitor were arriving and there was a great dinner to entertain them, I think in Liverpool. I never did see Caldwell in my life until I saw him in the Police Court at Marylebone when I went to swear my information.

"I think Druce introduced me saying, 'This is the lady who has come from New Zealand and who wrote this wonderful diary that has caused so much sensation and raised so much money.' Caldwell said he hoped he would be able to do as much for them as I had done, and said he would bet his life that he would have Herbert Druce in jail.

"I had a letter from Mr. Kimber saying that Scotland Yard was after me, and that I was a bad character, and had been chased out of New Zealand by the police there. When I got this letter I thought Mr. Kimber was drunk. After that Mr. Druce brought my money.

"About a week before I went to Marylebone to swear on

information, I had a letter from Mr. Kimber and a document, typewritten, about some evidence I was to give. I did not like this and I sent it to my solicitors. They told me not to swear to anything I objected to. Coburn came after this and said he wanted me to go to court and swear about some lead in the coffin. I told him I would not swear it for anyone, as I knew nothing about the lead in the coffin.

"The day after this Caldwell's solicitor called upon me. He told me he was a detective. I said, 'I thought you were a solicitor.' He said, 'So I am in America.' He asked me about my diary, and said he should like to get hold of it. He called me several times, and asked if I had got my diary, as if once it got into his hands he could make some money out of it from the newspapers. They were all at this period trying to get my diary. It was at this time in the hands of my solicitor, who got it from Mr. Kimber, so that I could read it over before I went into court. I wanted my tale in the witness box to appear a little feasible, even if it was all lies.

"The first thing I did on getting the diary was to read it to see that it was all there. We bought a couple of exercise books. It took me three days to copy it. I did not make the copy exactly as the original diary. I did not copy some of the pages. I did not have time. I did not leave out much. The reason I hurried so was that I wanted the original out of the house.

"The story I have already told as to the loss of the diary is a true one. I never actually told any of them that I had manufactured the contents of the diary, but I think that they knew it from what they said and the manner they treated me. They were always telling me I should be run in or poisoned. I was not questioned by anyone as to how I knew what I was going to swear. They took it all for granted.

"All I care to say about the duke of Portland is that I knew him and he knew me well, and he was very kind to me when I lived at

Worksop with my husband. I never saw Mr. Atherley-Jones and Mr. Goodman until they examined me in court. I never had any letters from the duke of Portland. But I did have two from Charles Dickens. These were missed in transit from Wellington on the boat.

"I never came to swear that T. C. Druce was the duke of Portland—only to say what I heard of him. When the man called on me he said, 'Say T. C. Druce, of the Baker Street Bazaar, was the same person as the fifth duke of Portland.'

"With regard to copies of letters found at my flat purporting to come from the duke of Portland and from Charles Dickens, those from the duke were written for my amusement. The one from Dickens is practically a copy of a letter received by me from him. I did know Charles Dickens."

She paused for a moment to think as she wrote, a small smile on her lips as she remembered the letters she'd written to herself, pretending they were from the duke. She could still remember them well enough to quote them.

"'My dearest Mary,'" she wrote, "'I remember this, that, though you were not the wife of my youth, you are the joy of my life. You are the most worthy of all my earthly comforts. You possess what I most admire in a woman—sweetness and cheerfulness, mixed with kindness of manner. For your study I recommend some of the most useful parts of mathematics. In my eye, they're a special object of interest. Farewell my dearest, from your affectionate and dearest friend.'"

With a sigh she forced herself back to the reality of the cell where she was sitting under the gimlet eyes of her warden, and continued with her statement.

"The last time Mr. Kimber came to see me here in prison I told him I should plead guilty and show the lot of them up. He said, 'You must not do that. If you do you will get seven years.' Then

I made up my mind I would tell the police all about all I knew. My father was a police sergeant in Mortlake in England, not a plantation owner from the American Deep South, and I thought I would rather tell the police than anyone else."

Mrs. Hamilton was also arrested and tried for perjury. She was sentenced to eighteen months' hard labor.

"But for your great age," the judge told her (she was seventy-eight), "and infirmity, the sentence would have been much more severe. It is one of the most serious and cruel cases to have been brought before a court of justice during the last century."

23

RETURN TO THE STATUS QUO

U pon his return to Australia, George Hollamby made it a priority to stay drunk for as much of the time as possible. He sold his house, and what little money was left from his father's efforts vanished into the tills of bars. His friends and relatives grew tired of hearing his tirades against the British upper classes, who he believed had cheated him of his rightful inheritance. In the end his brother, Charles, gave him a home in one of his worker's huts.

The sixth duke of Portland, finally free of the onerous legal work and expense, which had been required to keep his title, was able once more to turn his attentions to his tenants and other good causes. The ordeal, which had been going on for over ten years, seemed to have aged him twice that amount. In August 1908 he was due to give a speech at the annual show of the Bothal Tenant Agricultural Society. The members of the society felt deeply honored that he should spare them the time from his busy schedule.

Such an event would not normally have excited much curiosity beyond those interested in local agricultural matters, but this was the first time the duke had been free to speak in public about the case linked to his family name for so many years. There was also political interest from the public in his views of a finance bill then being discussed in Parliament.

The duke, as president of the National Union of Conservative Associations, had made Welbeck the scene of many political gatherings in recent years. In 1904 Joseph Chamberlain, who had just left the government on the Protectionist issue, launched his tariff reform scheme before a concourse of ten thousand people in Welbeck's riding school.

So, when the duke rose to speak on that warm summer's day, a larger crowd than would usually have been found at a country event fell silent and attentive.

"The Druce-Portland case," he said, with a slight smile, "was a wonderful and ridiculous fabrication. I can only hope that the more or less ridiculous proposals and impostures contained in the finance bill might be completely pricked as has been the case."

A polite murmur of amusement went through the crowd as they squinted against the bright sunshine, straining to hear His Grace's every word, pleased to be in the company of such an illustrious man, comforted by the sense of continuity that a family like the Cavendish-Bentincks brought to the area. Imagine, they said to one another, what would have happened if such an illustrious title had fallen into the hands of an Australian adventurer, quite forgetting how fascinated they had all been for so many years at the prospect of just such an event occurring.

"The latter originated in the diseased brain of a poor, crazy old woman," the duke continued. "I do not know from whose brain the finance bill originated, but somehow or other the two get muddled up in my mind, possibly because they appear somewhat alike."

There was a respectful ripple of applause and those listening agreed among themselves that it must have been a terrible ordeal for His Grace and that he and his family must be relieved the whole thing was over once and for all, so that now things could get back to normal.

The British public might have enjoyed watching their entrenched class of leaders suffer for a while, but most felt a sense of quiet relief as life settled back into its familiar pattern. One of the reasons the Empire had grown and flourished as successfully as it had was that everyone knew their place and their role within the hierarchy. At the pinnacle of the Empire had sat Queen Victoria, placed there by the money of the great families and the guile of Disraeli. Beneath her, but only just, were the great families themselves, amongst whom the Cavendish-Bentincks ranked high. Among the vast mass of people that strived and struggled below the aristocracy were the solid middle classes and those merchants and professionals who might, with enough ambition and hard work, succeed in creating the new great families of the future. Thomas Druce, wealthy proprietor of a mighty department store, would have been just such a one.

When a certain woman from the aspiring class, Anna Maria Druce, attempted to change the status quo, she not only provided a fine show for the general public to watch, just as Roman citizens might have watched gladiators fighting for the right to live; she also lifted some curtains and allowed the common people to glimpse inside the lives of those who ruled them, lives so different from their own as to be almost unrecognizable.

This spectacle had all taken place at the start of a century that would bring more change than any before it. The Druce-Portland case had also coincided with the birth of the popular press. Although journalists were still showing a reverence for their social superiors that would seem laughable by the end of the century, there were already indications of the changes that were to come. The rich and powerful would not be able to conduct their lives as they wished for much longer without inviting scrutiny and comment from the media. They were going to have to become as accountable to the law and to their fellow men as everyone else. Improvements in mass education and standards of living over the following decades meant that unless the aristocracy adapted they would soon have their weaknesses exposed.

To further discomfort aristocrats who had assumed their natural superiority would last forever, there were those people who had moved to the colonies and, once away from the stifling social hierarchy of their native land, started to believe that all men truly were equal, although women might still have had some way to travel, and returned with ambitions to play the old guard at their own game. These were the precursors of the global billionaires and newspaper magnates of the late twentieth century.

The Druce-Portland case should have been a terrible warning to the upper classes of the old Empire. They might have succeeded in repelling the upstarts for a little while, but the attacks on their worlds of wealth and privilege would increase as the years went by and they would eventually be forced to change, at least a little, in order to remain among the most privileged beings ever to have walked the earth.

THE DUKES OF PORTLAND
Craignez Honte
(Fear Disgrace)

William Bentinck (b. 1645 d. 1709). The first Bentinck to come to England, accompanied William of Orange in 1677 as Page of Honour for his marriage to Mary. In 1689 he again accompanied William to England and was created Baron Cirencester, Viscount Woodstock, and earl of Portland.

his son
Henry Bentinck, the first duke of Portland (b. 1680 d. 1724). The second earl was created marquess of Titchfield and duke of Portland in 1716.

his son
William Bentinck, the second duke of Portland, (b. 1709 d. 1762).

his son
William Henry Cavendish-Bentinck, the third duke of Portland (b. 1738 d. 1809). Through his mother he inherited Welbeck Abbey, marrying the daughter of the duke of Devonshire in 1766, and later assuming the name of Cavendish in 1801. He was Prime Minister 1783–1784, Lord Lieutenant of Ireland 1782, Home Secretary 1794–1801, President of the Council 1801–1805, and again Prime Minister 1807–1809.

his son
William Henry Cavendish-Scott-Bentinck, the fourth duke of Portland (b. 1768 d. 1854). He married Henrietta, daughter of General John Scott, adding a further name. They had nine children: four sons and five daughters.

> his first son
> **Henry Cavendish-Scott-Bentinck** (b. 1796 d. 1824). He died as the marquess of Titchfield.*

his second son
William John Cavendish-Scott-Bentinck, the fifth duke of Portland (b. 1800 d. 1879). He became marquess of Titchfield upon the death of Henry and the fifth duke of Portland upon the death of his father in 1854. Never married.

his third son
George Cavendish-Scott-Bentinck (b. 1802 d. 1848). Never married.

his fourth son
Henry William Cavendish-Scott-Bentinck (b. 1804 d. 1870). Never married.

As the fifth duke of Portland died without issue, the title went to a cousin, the fifth duke's nephew...

Sir William John Arthur Charles James Cavendish-Bentinck, *Sixth Duke of Portland (b. 1857 d. 1943)*

Marquess of Titchfield in the peerage of Great Britain; became Master of the Horse; earl of Portland (Dorset); viscount Woodstock of Woodstock, Oxfordshire; Baron Cirencester of Cirencester, Gloucestershire in the peerage of England; Baron Bolsover of Bolsover, Derbyshire in the peerage of the United Kingdom. Appointed Chancellor of the Order of the Garter 1937. An heir of the donor of the Harlein Manuscripts, he was a trustee of the British Museum. He was also Provincial Grand Master of the Nottinghamshire Freemasons. In 1898 he was appointed Lord Lieutenant of Caithness-shire, and in 1898 Lord Lieutenant of Nottinghamshire. In 1889 he married Winifred Anna, only daughter of the late Mr. T. V. Hallas-Yorke of Walmsgate, Lincolnshire. They had two sons and one daughter. The elder son, the marquess of Titchfield, succeeded to the title.

Note: These citations are offered for comparison with the total absence of any form of recognition given to the fifth duke of Portland, except that of marquess of Titchfield, which was obligatory.

*Marquess of Titchfield is the mandatory title given to the first born son of a duke of Portland, and upon death is passed on to the next eldest.

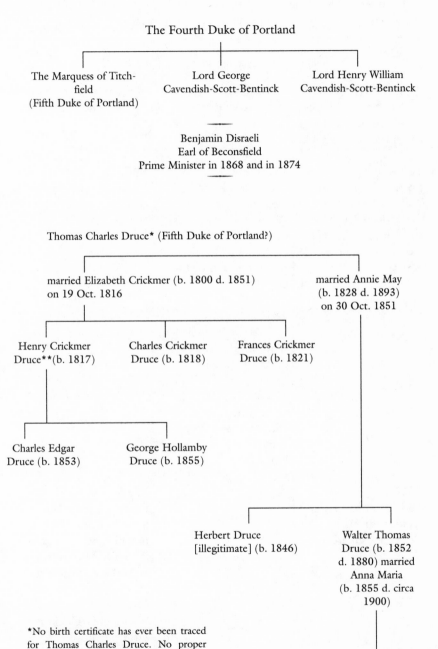

The Fourth Duke of Portland

The Marquess of Titch-field (Fifth Duke of Portland)

Lord George Cavendish-Scott-Bentinck

Lord Henry William Cavendish-Scott-Bentinck

Benjamin Disraeli
Earl of Beconsfield
Prime Minister in 1868 and in 1874

Thomas Charles Druce* (Fifth Duke of Portland?)

married Elizabeth Crickmer (b. 1800 d. 1851) on 19 Oct. 1816

married Annie May (b. 1828 d. 1893) on 30 Oct. 1851

Henry Crickmer Druce**(b. 1817)

Charles Crickmer Druce (b. 1818)

Frances Crickmer Druce (b. 1821)

Charles Edgar Druce (b. 1853)

George Hollamby Druce (b. 1855)

Herbert Druce [illegitimate] (b. 1846)

Walter Thomas Druce (b. 1852 d. 1880) married Anna Maria (b. 1855 d. circa 1900)

*No birth certificate has ever been traced for Thomas Charles Druce. No proper death certificate was ever demanded to record his death on 28 December 1864.
**relocated to Australia in 1852

Sidney George Druce (b. 1876)

Timeline of the Lives of the Fifth Duke of Portland and Thomas Charles Druce

The Fifth Duke of Portland, Firstly Lord John and Then Marquess of Titchfield	Historical Background	Thomas Charles Druce
1800 Born in London as William John Cavendish-Bentinck and baptized at St. George's, Hanover Square.	**1800** The union between England, Scotland, Wales, and Ireland is finalized. Riots all over England reflect the discontent of the populace.	**1800** No birth certificate or other records can be found.
	1812 United States President Madison declares war on Great Britain.	
	1815 Great Britain and other nations at war with Napoleon finally defeat him.	
1816 Appointed Ensign and Lieutenant in Grenadier Guards.		**1816** First appears in Bury St. Edmunds and marries Elizabeth Crickmer in St. James' Church as an eighteen-year-old.
		1817 Son, Henry Crickmer Druce, is born.

The Fifth Duke of Portland, Firstly Lord John and Then Marquess of Titchfield	Historical Background	Thomas Charles Druce
1818 Appointed Cornet in the 10th Hussars.		**1818** Son, Charles Crickmer Druce, is born.
	1820 Death of the blind and deranged King George III. He is succeeded by his son, the Prince Regent, who becomes King George.	**1820** Abandons his family, having taken part in many local affairs since marrying Elizabeth and having his name appear in numerous records.
1821 Appointed Captain in the 7th Hussars.		**1821** Elizabeth gives birth to daughter, Frances Crickmer Druce.
1823 Appointed to the 2nd Life Guards.		
1824 Eldest brother, William, marquess of Titchfield, dies, making Lord John the marquess. He is also given the Tory seat for the King's Lynn constituency.		
	1825 The world's first railway service, the stockton and Parlington Railway, opens.	
1826 The marquess conveys his seat in Parliament to brother, Lord George. This frees him to spend time in London and Welbeck.		
		1830 Recalls son, Henry, from the Navy.

THE FIFTH DUKE OF PORTLAND, Firstly Lord John and Then Marquess of Titchfield	HISTORICAL BACKGROUND	THOMAS CHARLES DRUCE
	1833 Abolition of Slavery Act passed in Great Britain along with the first English Factory Act. Dickens begins writing and exposing the conditions of the people.	
1835 The marquess hints at needing money from the syndicate for investments in London.		**1835** Druce opens the Baker Street Bazaar in London. He demands that his daughter, Frances, lives with him in London. Through 1848 Druce is seen in London from time to time but does not enter Society. He is living with a woman named Annie May.
	1837 King William IV dies. Victoria becomes queen.	
1848 The marquess agrees to join his brother, Lord George, in a loan to Disraeli.		
	1851 Opening of Great Exhibition in Hyde Park (Crystal Palace).	**1851** Druce marries Annie May upon the death of Elizabeth Crickmer at the Windsor Registry Office. Both give addresses in Windsor.

		1852 Son, Walter Thomas Druce, is born to Druce and Annie May.
	1853 The Paper Duties Bill, then described as the "Tax on Knowledge" prevents the establishment of the popular press. Disraeli attempts to stop repeal of the bill.	
1854 The marquess becomes fifth duke of Portland upon the death of his father.		**1854** Druce is seen in London and at the Baker Street Bazaar from time to time. He is also said to be seen in Windsor.
	1855 Lord Palmerston, Third Viscount, becomes Prime Minister. He is sacked by Queen Victoria at the advice of Albert, Prince Consort.	
1857 The Duke recalls the loan of £25,000 to Disraeli, and begins his vast building program and planning of his underground tunnel system. He takes his seat in the House of Lords, but is rarely seen. He is offered the Garter and twice declines.	**1857** The Second Opium War opens China to European trade. The Indian Mutiny erupts against British rule on the sub-continent.	

THE FIFTH DUKE OF PORTLAND, Firstly Lord John and Then Marquess of Titchfield	HISTORICAL BACKGROUND	THOMAS CHARLES DRUCE
	1860 Abraham Lincoln elected President of the United States of America.	
1864 Lives in his London residence, Harcourt House, but later in the year he moves to Welbeck Abbey, devoting more time to his building program.		**1864** Thomas Charles Druce dies on December 29th and is buried in a family grave in Highgate Cemetery.
		1874 A person resembling both Thomas Charles Druce and the fifth duke is seen in Dr. Winslow's asylum giving the name of Dr. Harmer.
	1875 Disraeli, with the help of Baron Lionel Rothschild, buys shares of the Suez Canal, thus paving the way for quick access to India and the creation of the Empire.	
1877 In failing health, the duke moves back to Harcourt House, 19 Cavendish Square to receive medical treatment.		

THE FIFTH DUKE OF PORTLAND, Firstly Lord John and Then Marquess of Titchfield	HISTORICAL BACKGROUND	THOMAS CHARLES DRUCE
1879 The duke dies on December 6th and is buried in Kensal Green Cemetery on December 12th.	**1879** British cut to pieces in Afghanistan.	
	1899 Beginning of the South African War (the Boer War).	
	1901 Queen Victoria dies. "Bertie," the controversial son becomes Edward VII.	

INDEX